STARS

STARS

New Edition

With a Supplementary Chapter
and Bibliography,
by Paul McDonald

RICHARD DYER

 bfi Publishing

This Edition first published in 1998 by the
British Film Institute
21 Stephen St, London W1P 2LN

The British Film Institute is the UK national agency with responsibility for encouraging
the arts of film and television and conserving them in the national interest.

First Edition published 1979
Reprinted 1982, 1986, 1990, 1992
Cover design: Swerlybird Art & Design
Cover image: Jane Fonda as Bree Daniel in *Klute*, 1971

Set in 10/12pt Minion by Fakenham Photosetting Limited, Fakenham, Norfolk NR21 8NL

British Library Cataloguing-in-Publication Data
A catalogue record for this book is available from the British Library

ISBN   978-0-85170-643-6
eISBN 978-1-83871-837-4
ePDF   978-1-83871-838-1

Contents

Acknowledgments

Stills and other illustrations used in the book are by courtesy of the following companies and individuals: the Bettman Archive; James Brough and Star Books; the British Film Institute; CIC; Cinecenta; Columbia-EMI-Warner; John Garrett and Camera Press; John Kobal; Joseph Kraft; Pictorial Parade; Rank; United Artists; World Wide Photos.

Introduction

The aim of this book is to survey and develop an area of work within film studies, namely, film stars.

Although stars form the basis of probably the larger part of everyday discussion of films, and although the majority of film books produced are fan material of one kind or another, very little in the way of sustained work has been done in the area. No work, that is, that elaborates some kind of theory of the phenomenon and uses this theory to inform empirical investigation of it.

Within film studies, reasons for studying the stars have largely come from two rather different concerns that may broadly be characterised as the sociological and the semiotic. The former centres on the stars as a remarkable, and probably influential or symptomatic, social phenomenon, as well as being an aspect of film's 'industrial' nature. In this perspective, films are only of significance in so far as they have stars in them. The semiotic concern reverses this. Here, stars are only of significance because they are in films and therefore are part of the way films signify. This division of interest is reflected in the structure of this book, in that the first part deals primarily with sociological issues and the third with semiotic, and only the second very obviously combines the two. However, one of my assumptions in writing the book has been that this distinction, while useful in helping one to handle an otherwise unmanageably large topic, is essentially one of convenience, and that both concerns are mutually interdependent. Thus, on the one hand the sociological concern can only make headway when informed by a proper engagement with the semiotics of stars, that is, their specific signification as realised in media texts (including films, but also newspaper stories, television programmes, advertisements, etc.). This is because, sociologically speaking, stars do not exist outside of such texts; therefore it is these that have to be studied; and they can only be studied with due regard to the specificities of what they are, namely, significations. Equally, on the other hand, the semiotic concern has to be informed by the sociological, partly because stars are, like all significations, also and always social facts, but also because it is only on the basis of a proper theorisation of one's object of study that one is able to pose questions of it. Semiotic analysis has to make assumptions about how texts work before proceeding to analyse them; once it is granted that all texts are social facts, then it follows that these textual assumptions must be grounded in sociological ones. You need to know what kind of thing a text is in society in order to know what kind of questions you can legitimately pose of it, what kind of knowledge you can reasonably expect it to yield. Thus although this book is structured linearly, the actual enterprise is dialectical, a constant movement between the sociological and the semiotic (and between the theoretical and the empirical).

The book is structured in three parts. In all three, it is assumed that we are dealing with the stars in terms of their signification, not with them as real people. The fact that they are also real people is an important aspect of how they signify, but we never know them directly as real people, only as they are to be found in media texts. The three parts of the book can then be seen as centring on the different questions we might pose of the stars as significations. Part One (Stars as a Social Phenomenon) – why do stars signify; i.e. what kind of social reality are stars? Why do they exist, in general and in particular? What is their relationship to other aspects of social structure and values? Part Two (Stars as Images) – what do stars signify; i.e. what meanings and affects do the image of stardom and the images of particular stars embody? Part Three (Stars as Signs) – how do stars signify; i.e. how do star images function within film texts themselves in relation to other aspects of the text, including those such as characterisation and performance which directly coincide with the star's presence?

All three sections involve the concept of ideology. As this is a widely and variously used word (and a subject of much controversy), I had better state briefly here what I understand by it.[1]

Ideology is the set of ideas and representations in which people collectively make sense of the world and the society in which they live. It is important to distinguish between ideology in general and ideologies in particular. Ideology is a characteristic of all human societies, but a given ideology is specific to a particular culture at a particular moment in its history. All ideologies are developed in relation to the concrete, material circumstances of human life – they are the means by which knowledge is made out of those circumstances. There is no guarantee that this knowledge is true in an absolute sense – indeed, all ideology is by definition partial and limited (which is not at all the same thing as saying it is 'false'). At the same time, there is no way in which we can think outside of ideology and in this sense all analysis of ideology is itself ideological.[2]

Our society is characterised by divisions of class and gender, and, secondarily but not reducible to them, by divisions between races and sexual, cultural, religious and other minorities/majorities. Within these divisions, which complexly cut across one another, sense is made out of the world, collectively but also differentially. That is to say, all ideologies are rooted in the life activity of given social groups within a given particular society, but that any group may produce several contradictory inflections of its ideology. In any society – and therefore in the ideas and representations of any society – one can always discern contradictions of two orders: *between* the ideologies of the various groups in conflict (potential or actual) and *within* each of those ideologies.

The primary concern of any attention to Hollywood must be with the dominant ideology of western society. Any dominant ideology in any society presents itself as the ideology of that society as a whole. Its work is to deny the legitimacy of alternative and oppositional ideologies and to construct out of its own contradictions a consensual ideology that will appear to be valid for all members of society. The operations of the dominant ideology are thus a ceaseless effort to mask or displace both its own contradictions and those contradictions to it that

2

arise from alternative and oppositional ideologies. The latter always enter into the account with a popular or mass medium, as the medium must engage with audiences not themselves situated within the dominant groups of society. These operations are always in process, an effort to secure a 'hegemony' that is constantly under threat from within and without. (For example, the contradiction within dominant ideology between its championing of equality and its necessary commitment to inequality, which has to be at least apparently resolved – through, for instance, universal suffrage, educational 'opportunities', access broadcasting – in the face of groups demanding that the promise of equality be realised for the working class, women, blacks, etc.) For our purposes much of the interest of Hollywood lies in this process of contradiction and its 'management' and those moments when hegemony is not, or is only uneasily, secured.

From the perspective of ideology, analyses of stars – as images existing in films and other media texts – stress their structured polysemy, that is, the finite multiplicity of meanings and affects they embody and the attempt so to structure them that some meanings and affects are foregrounded and others are masked or displaced. The concern of such textual analysis is then not to determine the correct meaning and affect, but rather to determine what meanings and affects can legitimately be read in them. How these are in fact appropriated or read by members of different classes, genders, races, etc. is beyond the scope of textual analysis (although various conceptualisations of this will be found throughout the book).

Ideological analysis of media texts does of course make the political implications of what we are studying inescapable. Since we often seek to avoid facing such implications, preferring to believe that what we do has no political consequences, this is reason enough for such an approach. It is, however, also intellectually more rigorous – as I have suggested above, all textual analysis has to be grounded in sociological conceptualisations of what texts are, and since what they are is ideology, with all its contradictory complexities, it follows that textual analysis is properly ideological analysis.

Where possible, reference to specific stars in this book has by and large been restricted to the following – Marlon Brando, Bette Davis, Marlene Dietrich, Jane Fonda, Greta Garbo, Marilyn Monroe, Robert Redford and John Wayne. In this way the same star can be seen within various perspectives. These stars were chosen to represent a cross-section according to certain considerations such as the contrast between 'classic' and modern stars and between various styles of performing in films, and an interest in stars who raise political issues directly (Fonda, Redford, Wayne) or indirectly through aspects of lifestyle (Garbo, Brando, Fonda) or sex-role typing (e.g. the notion that Davis, Monroe and Fonda 'resist' aspects of the stereotyping process).

As will be evident, this means that the examples relate to the cinema rather than television (or sport, theatre, fashion, etc.), and to the American rather than other cinemas. The specificities of these other places where stars are to be found would always have to be respected, although at the level of theorisation and methodology I believe most of what is elaborated here in relation to Hollywood film stars is broadly applicable to these other kinds of star.

As usual, my debts to others in the preparation of this book are enormous. With apologies already for omissions, I should like to thank Jack Babuscio, Ken Bartlett, Charlotte Brunsdon, Ros Brunt, Colin Cruise, Christine Geraghty, Malcolm Gibb, Ian Gilman, Stuart Hall, Gillian Hartnoll, Marion Jordan, Ann Kaplan, Angie Martin, Jean McCrindle, Stephanie McKnight, Tessa Perkins, Victor Perkins and Rachel Powell for many useful discussions and insights, Christine Gledhill and Nicky North for the same and support and encouragement throughout the project. Ed Buscombe for further editorial help, Erich Sargeant for help with the illustrations, the staff of the British Film Institute Library and Information Department and students in the American Studies and Adult Education departments at the University of Keele and in my 1977–8 London University extramural class for ideas and stimulation that I fear I never properly acknowledged or recognised at the time.

Notes

1. For a very general introduction to the notion of ideology, see Colin McArthur, *Television and History*, Chapter One. More detailed examination of the various approaches to ideology is to be found in *Working Paper in Cultural Studies* 10, 'On Ideology'. A serious gap in this last work is any consideration of the later work of Jean-Paul Sartre, notably his *The Problem of Method*. These texts are for the most part elaborated within a Marxist perspective but not a feminist one. For the latter, see *Working Papers in Cultural Studies* 11, 'Women Take Issue'.
2. For a consideration of these problems, see Janet Wolff, 'The Interpretation of Literature in Society: The Hermeneutic Approach', in Jane Routh and Janet Wolff (eds.), *The Sociology of Literature: Theoretical Approaches*.

(N.B. Publication details of all texts cited can be found in the bibliography.)

PART ONE

Stars as a Social Phenomenon

The stars are a reflection in which the public studies and adjusts its own image of it-self . . . The social history of a nation can be written in terms of its film stars.
(Raymond Durgnat, *Films and Feelings*, pp. 137–8)

Far more than men, women [stars] were the vessels of men's and women's fantasies and the barometers of changing fashion. Like two-way mirrors linking the immediate past with the immediate future, women in the movies reflected, perpetuated, and in some respects offered innovations on the roles of women in society.
(Molly Haskell, *From Reverence to Rape*, p. 12)

Take Robert Taylor, M. Boyer, Mr Laurence Olivier, and take Miss Durbin, Miss Garson and Miss Davis and a few more film actors and actresses, and you may be able to arrive at a complete anthropological typology of which no La Rochefoucauld, Pascal or Jung could ever dream.
(J. P. Mayer, *Sociology of the Film*, p. 262)

Stars . . . are the direct or indirect reflection of the needs, drives and dreams of Ameri-can society.
(Alexander Walker, *Stardom*, p. xi)

Part One is concerned with the question – why do we get the phenomenon of star-dom and, given that we do, why do we get the particular stars we do? How are we to account for the phenomenon in both general and specific terms?

It is organised as follows:
— discussion of the general social *conditions* favouring stardom
— the role of forces of *production* and *consumption* in shaping stardom and stars
— the *ideological* functioning of the star phenomenon.

1 Conditions for Stardom

Francesco Alberoni and Barry King have both suggested various social structures that must obtain for the phenomenon of stardom to exist. These conditions are necessary rather than sufficient – that is, they do not automatically produce stars but are the grounds on which stardom may be produced.

Alberoni is concerned with stardom as a general social phenomenon and not just with film stardom. His definition of stardom, already indicated in the title of his article ('The Powerless Elite'), centres on the fact that stars are a group of people 'whose institutional power is very limited or non-existent, but whose doings and way of life arouse a considerable and sometimes even a maximum degree of interest' (Alberoni, p. 75).

The basic conditions for this phenomenon, Alberoni suggests, are:

— a state of law
— an efficient bureaucracy
— a structured social system.

(These three factors ensure that social roles are delimited and judged according to 'objective' criteria (e.g. efficiency). In this situation, stars operate only in their own sphere and there is no 'danger' of their 'charisma' becoming important 'from a political point of view'.)

— a large-scale society (stars cannot know everyone, but everyone can know stars)
— economic development above subsistence (though this need not be very great development – cf. film stars in India)
— social mobility (anyone, in principle, may become a star).

Thus, argues Alberoni, stars are a remarkable social phenomenon – an elite, privileged group who yet on the one hand do not excite envy or resentment (because anyone may become one) and on the other hand have no access to real political power.

Alberoni's discussion is useful for suggesting explanations for such features of the star phenomenon as: why during the Depression starving people could hear and read of the high life of the stars without apparent resentment; why only minor stars have become politicians; why the socialist press has had far more pity than scorn for stars, stressing them more as victims than beneficiaries of capitalism.

However, because a star cannot become a crucial decision-maker (and remain a star), this does not mean that s/he is without political significance. Alberoni ignores the ideological significance of the stars. In his terms, the overt political

7

stands of a John Wayne or a Jane Fonda, or the implicit political meanings of a Bette Davis or a Marlon Brando, are irrelevant or insignificant. Whilst no one would claim that they have a direct political 'effect', surely these form part of the way by which values and attitudes are shaped? However, it is probably true to say that Wayne, Fonda et al. are widely believed to be politically insignificant and unimportant, and that the only 'real' politics is decision-making within the institutions of society. Because of this belief, the ideological significance of stars is masked or discounted. One might then suggest that just because it is so masked its real political power is all the greater for being less easily resisted.

King[1] takes up the argument with Alberoni by pointing out that stars have a major control over the representation of people in society – and how people are represented as being in the mass media is going to have some kind of influence (even if only of reinforcement) on how people are in society. Stars have a privileged position in the definition of social roles and types, and this must have real consequences in terms of how people believe they can and should behave.

King also suggests his own set of preconditions for stardom:

— production of surplus (i.e. commodities in excess of basic material needs)
— development of a technology of mass communication
— extensive penetration of the cultural sphere by industrialisation which leads to a separation between a system of action committed to instrumental goals (utilitarian and predominant) and a system of action committed to expressive goals (moralistic and subordinant)
— rigid separation of work and leisure: division of role structure between expressive and instrumental roles
— decline of local cultures and the development of a mass level of culture, transformation from specific to universalistic modes of evaluation
— organisation of the motion picture industry around commodity production and the progressive centralisation of control over production
— a relative increase of social mobility into expressive role positions unconnected with sacred institutions (which in feudal society constituted centres of power).

To some extent, King's preconditions cover the same ground as Alberoni's. King's instrumental–expressive distinction reworks Alberoni's distinction between effective (i.e. in his terms politically significant) roles and non-effective ones. The advantage of King's terms is that they allow one to see the political or ideological significance of expressive roles as well as of instrumental ones. Alberoni's terminology on the other hand does remind us, as suggested above, that expressive roles are not *believed* to be politically significant.

2 Production: Consumption

Both Alberoni, by default, and King, expressly, point to the need to examine stars in terms of ideology. However, in supplying a list of preconditions, neither explain why stars arise on the basis of those preconditions. This question can be approached first in terms of what Edgar Morin (in *New Trends in the Study of Mass Communications*) calls the 'production–consumption dialectic of mass communications'. That is, are stars a phenomenon of production (arising from what the makers of films provide) or of consumption (arising from what the audience for films demands)?

Origins of stardom

The problem of what determines what – production or consumption – is endemic to all discussions of the mass media, and emerges clearly from accounts of the origins of stardom in Hollywood. Looking at this is a good way of highlighting the issues and problems involved.

'The history of movie stardom as an institution is a familiar one', states Richard Schickel in *His Picture in the Papers*, and proceeds to provide a very useful summary of it:

> how the producers had resisted giving billing to the actors who played in their little films; how the actors themselves, regarding appearance in a medium that robbed them of what they regarded as their prime artistic resource, their voice, had been glad to hide their shame in anonymity; how the public had begun singling them out of the crowds on the screen, demanding to know more about them, and, more important, demanding to know, in advance, which pictures featured their favourites; how a few independent producers, grasping at any weapon to fight the motion picture trust (composed of the major studios), had acceded to public opinion and had been rewarded by the most deliciously rising sales curves; how the demand for stars was quickly perceived as a factor that could stabilize the industry, since this demand was predictable in a way that the demand for stories or even genres was not; how, as feature-length films established their popularity and the cost of producing these longer films required bank loans, star names came to lead the list of collateral that bankers looked upon with favor when their assistance was sought; how certain actors achieved unprecedented heights of popularity and prosperity almost overnight in the period 1915–1920; and how this phenomenon, this beginning of a new celebrity system, destroyed or crippled almost everyone caught up in it ... (p. 27)

The key event in this history is usually taken to be Carl Laemmle's action of planting a story in the St Louis Post-Despatch to the effect that Florence Lawrence, up to then known as the 'Biograph Girl', had been killed by a trolley car in St Louis, and following it a day later with an advertisement in the trade press denouncing the story as a vicious lie. This event was the first occasion that a film actor's* name be-

---

* I have throughout used the term 'actor' to refer to both female and male performers, as the term 'actress' seems to me to have strong connotations that both belittle and trivialise women actors.

came known to the public. It is the first example of the deliberate manufacture of a star's image. Equally, runs the argument, it is the first example of the producers of films responding to public demand, giving the public what it wanted. It is thus at the point of intersection of public demand (the star as a phenomenon of consumption) and the producer initiative (the star as a phenomenon of production).

Left at that, within the confines of the film industry and market, there can be little argument that films stars were a phenomenon of consumption that had even been strenuously resisted by the producers in the first instance, although they mightily capitalised upon it once it was under way. There are, however, a couple of problems with the history as it stands. First, the notion of 'demand'. Stars have not existed in all societies at all times. Where does the demand for them stem from? Who defines it? Second, the star system was already a well-developed feature of the popular theatre (especially vaudeville, from which the cinema took its first audiences). Stars were part of the business of show business. If the public demanded it of the cinema, then this was because the public had come to expect it of the entertainment industry as a whole. This then forces us back to the question of why it was part of all entertainment.

A look at how the origins of stardom have been discussed is useful because it orchestrates and concretises the more general issues involved in this section. Let me now turn to some of the explanations of the star system, all of which could be considered in relation to the early period, although they are discussed below in general terms.

Stars as a phenomenon of production

Stars are images in media texts, and as such are products of Hollywood (or wherever). Discussion of Hollywood production generally takes place between two polar views. The first considers Hollywood production as a capitalist production like any other, and in this perspective stars are to be seen in terms of their function in the economy of Hollywood, including, crucially, their role in the manipulation of Hollywood's market, the audience. At the other extreme come views that seem innocent of any consideration of Hollywood in terms of profit, and account for the star phenomenon in terms either of some intrinsic property of the film medium or else the special magic of the stars themselves. (For discussion of stars as the producers of their own images, see Chapter 9.)

Economics

Stars are widely regarded as a vital element in the economics of Hollywood in terms of:

— *capital.* Stars represented a form of capital possessed by the studios. Robert A. Brady sees this as part of the 'monopolistic' character of the Hollywood industry: 'each star is to some extent a holder of a monopoly, and the owner of contracts for the services of a star is the owner of a monopoly product. The majors dominate the employment of this individual monopoly talent' ('The Problem of Monopoly', pp. 131–2).

— *investment*. Stars were a guarantee, or a promise, against loss on investment and even of profit on it.
— *outlay*. Stars were a major portion of a film's budget – hence their handling, in filmic terms, had to be careful and correct.
— *the market*. Stars were used to sell films, to organise the market. Alexander Walker talks of 'the use of a star to stabilise audience response' (*Stardom*, 1974, p. 15). Alice Evans Field writes: 'Star names on the theatre marquee, above the title of the picture, draw great audiences not only because of their personal magnetism but also because they are symbols of certain types of entertainment and because they assure production efforts far above average' (*Hollywood USA*, p. 74.) This suggests how stars both organise the market and act back upon the 'quality' of the films they are in.

Hortense Powdermaker in her 'anthropological investigation' of Hollywood, the Dream Factory, sums this up:

> From a business point of view, there are many advantages in the star system. The star has tangible features which can be advertised and marketed – a face, a body, a pair of legs, a voice, a certain kind of personality, real or synthetic – and can be typed as the wicked villain, the honest hero, the fatal siren, the sweet young girl, the neurotic woman. The system provides a formula easy to understand and has made the production of movies seem more like just another business. The use of this formula may serve also to protect executives from talent and having to pay too much attention to such intangibles as the quality of a story or of acting. Here is a standardised product which they can understand, which can be advertised and sold, and which not only they, but also banks and exhibitors, regard as insurance for large profits ... (pp. 228–9)

The economic importance of stars can be highlighted by certain moments in film history: for example, it was the development of the star system by the independent producers (especially Adolph Zukor, but also Laemmle, Fox, Loew, Schenck, Warner) which broke up the monopolistic hold the MPPC (Motion Pictures Patents Company) had on the industry. Also, in 1933 'Paramount ... went into unexpected receivership in January ... Only a break in the European market and the unexpected success of Mae West's films at home enabled Paramount to refloat itself with its own resources at the end of the year' (Walker, *Stardom*, p. 235). Similarly Deanna Durbin 'saved' Universal in 1937, and Edgar Morin argues that Marilyn Monroe (and wide screen) were the industry's answer to the threat of television in the 50s.

Against this, however, it must be pointed out that, even in Hollywood's heyday, stars did not absolutely guarantee the success of a film. Stars move in and out of favour, and even at the height of their popularity may make a film that nobody much goes to see. If some of the careers charted by David Shipman in his two books[2] are brought down by ill-health or sheer lousy pictures, the majority rise and fall for reasons unconnected with either of these (e.g. Joan Crawford, Bette Davis, John Wayne). For this reason, stars were a very problematic necessity from an economic point of view.

I. C. Jarvie suggests in *Towards a Sociology of the Cinema* that 'stars are neither necessary nor sufficient for success' (p. 188), basing this on a comparison of the failure of the star-studded *Cleopatra* and the success of *Dr No*, *The Sound of Music* and

The Graduate, whose stars were at the time little known. This is fair enough, but it does not demonstrate that stars do not sell films, simply that films do not have to have them for success. (The recent-ness of the examples may also be worth bearing in mind; stars may be less crucial than they were twenty, thirty or forty years ago.)

The economic importance of the stars is of aesthetic consequence in such things as the centring of spectacle on the presentation of the star, and the construction of narratives which display the star's image, and so on. However, the rise and fall of the stars indicates that economics alone cannot explain the phenomenon of stardom.

Manipulation

The success of stardom and stars has been attributed to the manipulation of the market, an analogy with the 'manipulations' of advertising. This is an extension of the economic argument about the stars, although it need not be developed in a Marxist direction (i.e. one can be against manipulation, without being against profits; the question of manipulation can be treated as a question of ethics, unless, following Paul Baran and Paul Sweezy in *Monopoly Capitalism,* for instance, you argue that manipulation of the market is the inevitable consequence of the development of monopoly capitalism). Manipulation arguments in relation to the stars have in fact tended to stress the social-ethical aspect of the question rather than the economic.

The star system lends itself particularly well to the manipulation thesis because of the enormous amount of money, time and energy spent by the industry in building up star images through publicity, promotion, fan clubs, etc. Thomas Harris has described this process in relation to Grace Kelly and Marilyn Monroe. The basic mechanisms for promoting the stars include:

> a preliminary publicity buildup starting months or even years before the star is seen on the screen. Frequent devices used in such a buildup are a 'discovery' usually concocted by studio publicists, a series of glamour pictures sent to all the print media, a rumoured romance with another star already well known to the public, or a rumoured starring role in a major film. This publicity finds a primary outlet in syndicated Hollywood gossip columns and movie fan magazines. When the actor or actress is actually cast in a film, the studio assigns a 'unit man' to 'plant' items about the personality in these places as well as national magazines and Sunday newspaper supplements. A network television appearance is also a highly coveted plum in the studio 'pre-sale' campaign for both the picture and the personality. Prior to and during the filming of a picture all publicity emanates from Hollywood. The New York publicity office of the studio then take over the film and continue to handle publicity through the distribution-exhibition phase. New York is also charged with the development of national advertising and the creation of stunts and merchandise tie-ins to exploit the picture. Especially important in this total process is the perpetuation of the star stereotype. It is the publicist's job to interpret the new film role in terms of the pre-established stereotypes and to communicate through the variety of means at his [sic] disposal. ('The Building of Popular Images', p. 46)

Given the sheer elaboration of this apparatus, it is not surprising that the notion of stars as manufactured has developed. Edgar Morin observes:

> The internal characteristics [of the star system] are the very ones of grand-scale industrial, mercantile and financial capitalism. The star system is first of all fabrication. This

is the word chosen instinctively by Carl Laemmle, the inventor of the stars: 'The fabrication of stars is the fundamental thing in the film industry'. (*The Stars*, 1960, p. 134)

[this merchandise] is the very type of grand scale capitalism: enormous investment, industrial techniques of rationalisation and standardisation of the system have effectively made the star a merchandise destined for mass consumption. (p. 135)

Out of this emphasis on manufacture, there develops an account of the star system as 'pure' manipulation. That is, both stardom and particular stars are seen as owing their existence solely to the machinery of their production. Not only are they not a phenomenon of consumption (in the sense of demand); they do not even have substance or meaning. This is the essence of Daniel Boorstin's argument in his book *The Image*. According to Boorstin, stars, like so much of contemporary culture, are pseudo-events. That is, they appear to be meaningful but are in fact empty of meaning. Thus a star is well-known for her/his well-knownness, and not for any talent or specific quality. They are an example of the 'celebrity', marketed on the strength of trivial differences of appearance. Stars do not have a 'strong character, but a definable, publicizable personality: a figure which can become a nationally-advertised trademark' (p. 162). 'The qualities which now commonly make a man or woman into a "nationally advertised" brand are in fact a new category of human emptiness' (p. 58).

Boorstin's argument is close to that of Herbert Marcuse in *One-Dimensional Man*, where the culture of late capitalist society is characterised by just such thin, pseudo, fabricated elements as Boorstin describes in *The Image*. Marcuse gives this a more intellectually tough argument than Boorstin. He maintains that in previous periods culture (including technology and the sciences as well as the arts and philosophy) acted as a 'negation' of the existing society, pointing to an Other or an Absolute to set over against the *status quo*. (Art he calls a *promesse de bonheur*.) In contemporary society, however, culture has become 'positive', that is, it merely reproduces the *status quo*. This does not mean that art is affirmative of bourgeois values, for to affirm those values, however limited they are, is still to affirm a value, a positive quality, to set against the tawdriness of the achievements of bourgeois society. Rather, art has been drained of meaning, of values, is simply a sideshow. It does not affirm values, merely that which is. The typical becomes the ideal, the average the best. The 'cultural predecessors' of stars can be seen as 'disruptive-characters [such] as the artist, the prostitute, the adultress, the great criminal and outcast, the warrior, the rebel-poet, the devil, the fool', but the tradition has been 'essentially transformed'. 'The vamp, the national hero, the beatnik, the neurotic housewife, the gangster, the star, the charismatic tycoon perform a function very different ... They are no longer images of another way of life but rather freaks or types of the same life, serving as an affirmation rather than negation of the established order' (p. 60).

This is not the place to discuss all the problems of Marcuse's work (see Paul Mattick's *Critique of Marcuse*). One can see the stars as a manifestation of the one-dimensionality of advanced capitalist society, although I would prefer to see it as a *tendency* of the society rather than a fully worked-through process.

The following objections can be raised against the view of the star phenomenon as sheer manipulation:

— Not all manipulation works. There are many cases of stars who are given the full promotion treatment, but do not make it. (See, for instance, David Shipman's account of Anna Sten in *The Great Stars – the Golden Years*, pp. 505–6.) The fluctuating careers of stars also indicate that audience control was a problem for the studios. This does not mean that the analogy with advertising does not hold, but, equally, not all advertising works – one needs to conceptualise why some advertisements/stars catch on and some do not.

— Boorstin and Marcuse do not examine the content of star images. Indeed, their argument rests upon the idea that there is no content to star images, only surface differences of appearance. But differences of appearances are not, in a visual medium, necessarily superficial, and stars need also to be seen in the context of their roles and their filmic presentation. Examination of stars' images reveals complexity, contradiction and difference. (It might still be legitimately argued that the complexity, etc. is all part of the beguiling, empty spectacle of capitalism. In the end it all depends on how closed (and hopeless) you see society and people as being.)

— In a sense, both Boorstin and Marcuse treat society as a vast mechanism in which human consciousness plays no part except to be used. Manipulation arguments (although it is unfair in the final analysis to lump Marcuse with Boorstin here) depend upon a behavioural concept of human beings. That is, media 'input' has a given 'effect' (in this case, passive acceptance) on the human subject without the intervention of that subject's mind or consciousness. Where the semiotic model of communication stresses the human practices of encoding and decoding, behavioural/manipulation models stress the mechanics of human 'response'. One's position on the stars-as-manipulation will then depend upon one's position on behavioural models of the media and indeed of communication in general.

Fashion

Fashion can be seen as a variation on the manipulation thesis, which takes one of the objections to that thesis, namely the rise and fall in a star's popularity, as a question of the star coming in as a novelty and going out as a has-been. This can be seen as a pure phenomenon of manipulation, and as such is open to the same objections detailed in the previous paragraphs. A further point may be made. Fashion is often assumed to be the ultimate in manipulation because it is so superficial. However, as Jarvie suggests: 'One function a star serves is to fix a type of beauty, to help a physical type identify itself.' Clearly types of beauty define *norms* of attractiveness. Fashion in this sense is a much less superficial or trivial phenomenon than it appears. Seen in this perspective, a change in physical style is also always a change in social meaning. (For further considerations on fashion and social meaning, see Mary Ellen Roach and Joanne Bubolz Eicher (eds.), *Dress, Adornment and The Social Order*.)

The nature of the medium

The economic and manipulation arguments outlined above all tend to come from a perspective hostile to the cinema. From a more friendly perspective comes the argument that there is something inherent in the film medium that creates stars. Some writers stress the role of the close-up in the creation of stardom. Says Alexander Walker:

> until the camera got close enough to record the player's own personality, the film star could not emerge from the stage group. The close-up was the first step to this ... by isolating and concentrating the player's looks and personality, sometimes unconnected with his or her abilities, it was to be the decisive break with stage convention, the most potent means of establishing an artist's uniqueness and the beginning of the dynamic psychological interplay of the filmgoers' and the film actors' emotions. (*Stardom, the Hollywood Phenomenon*, p. 5)

Similarly Richard Schickel compares film and theatre:

> the stage is a less intimate medium (even though the audience is physically in the presence of the actors) because the proscenium has a profoundly distancing effect – no close-ups here. (*His Picture in the Papers*, p. 6)

In this way, the star process already under way in the theatre could be intensified by film's supposed inherent intimacy.

This view of the importance of the close-up has been more philosophically considered by Bela Balazs.[3] He sees the close-up as a fundamental aspect of the film medium which reveals 'the hidden mainsprings of a life which we had thought we already knew so well', for instance, 'the quality in a gesture of the hand we never noticed before when we saw that hand stroke or strike something' (p. 185). The close-up led to 'the discovery of the human face':

> Facial expression is the most subjective manifestation of man [sic], more subjective even than speech, for vocabulary and grammar are subject to more or less universally valid rules and conventions, while the play of features, as has already been said, is a manifestation not governed by objective canons, even though it is largely a matter of imitation. This most subjective and individual of human manifestations is rendered objective in the close-up. (p. 188)

Close-ups are a kind of 'silent monologue' in which:

> the solitary human soul can find a tongue more candid and uninhibited than in any spoken soliloquy, for it speaks instinctively, sub-consciously. The languages of the face cannot be suppressed or controlled. (p. 190)

Quite apart from notions of the soul, and Balazs' emphasis on the 'solitariness' of human individuals, this account of the role of the close-up does raise problems. Balazs is essentially treating film as transparent, just 'capturing' the face and the soul it reveals. However, we know that how we read (and produce) facial expressions is deeply dependent on conventions of various kinds: filmic (e.g. Kuleshov's experiments with editing; the role of lighting in highlighting different facial features and so changing expressions), artistic (i.e. the iconography of expressions developed in painting, etc.), and cultural (i.e. facial expressions are coded; cf. Polhemus, Social Aspects of the Human Body). However, Balazs is important because he gives expression to a widely held view, namely that the close-up reveals the unmediated personality of the individual, and this belief in the 'capturing' of the 'unique' 'person' of a performer is probably central to the star phenomenon.

15

Further differences between film and theatre that relate to the star phenomenon are the fact that 'stars of the popular melodramatic and spectacular stage tended to submerge themselves in one or two or three roles' and that the popular press before the arrival of the movies was less interested in entertainers than in 'political and business leaders and inventors' (Schickel op. cit., p. 6). However, all these aspects of film, though they have come to be virtually inseparable from the medium, are not intrinsic to it. As Edgar Morin puts it, 'The stars are typically cinematic and yet there is nothing specifically cinematic about them' (*The Stars*, p. 6). Another way of putting this is to say that stars are not inherent in film as a medium but they are inherent in the cinema as a specific social institution. The change of interest on the part of the popular press related to a wider phenomenon, discussed by Leo Lowenthal in 'The Triumph of Mass Idols', in which hero figures that make the world ('heroes of production') have been displaced by figures who simply enjoy the fruits of the world ('heroes of consumption'). (For further discussion of this see Part Two of this book.) The notions of the importance of the close-up, and of the role being less important than the performer in the cinema, can be related to the aesthetic of realism with which the cinema has predominantly been burdened, the belief that film, like photography, 'captures' or 'reflects' reality. That is, despite their extravagances and extraordinariness, the stars are an aspect of realism because what is foregrounded is their person as much as the characters they play. (See Part Three.)

Magic and talent

The examinations of the star phenomenon so far discussed tend to explain it away, accounting for it by reference to something else (economics, the medium). A very common view, however, though not intellectually very respectable, is that stars are stars because they are exceptional, gifted, wonderful. An extreme version of this view was expressed by Samuel Goldwyn: 'God makes the stars. It's up to the producers to find them' (quoted in Richard Griffith, *The Movie Stars*, p. 25). But even a sociologist, I. C. Jarvie, ultimately comes up with the same sort of notion, maintaining that stars are stars because of 'talent', which includes, according to him, 'striking photogenic looks, acting ability, presence on camera, charm and personality, sex-appeal, attractive voice and bearing' (*Towards a Sociology of the Cinema*, p. 149). Again, Molly Haskell, in discussing the way some women stars counteracted the demeaning roles they had to play, points to their 'special' qualities: 'in the midst of mediocre material, they rose to the surface and projected, through sheer will and talent and charisma, images of emotional and intellectual power' (*From Reverence to Rape*, p. 8).

How much credence you give to such ideas will in the end depend on how much you believe in 'great unique individuals' as opposed to famous people being 'the right type in the right place at the right time' (always remembering that type, place and time are shaped by the same society). However, there are also more immediate, less 'heady' objections to the 'magic' explanation of stars. First, there is the empirical observation that not all highly talented performers becomes stars, nor are all stars highly talented. I imagine anyone can supply their own examples of both these categories. Second, the notion of 'talent', especially as defined by Jarvie, is historically and culturally specific. Even if one simply meant talent as skill, one would have to ask, skill at what? Not 'acting' in the classic sense, as innumerable examples show. Skill then at being a certain sort of person or image. This may be right, but then the key question is, why does that sort of person become a star? A question once again of culture and ideology. Third, Haskell's positing of a gap between role and performance in the case of certain stars need not be discussed in terms of those stars' magic powers. One can see it either as a contradiction in the film text between the role-as-written and the star image (see p. 129), or else as a question of authorship (i.e. the star's authorial concerns being in conflict with those of a film's other authors; see p. 155).

The enormous economic importance of the stars, the elaborate machinery of image-building and film's importance in establishing character-types all suggest the potential power of the forces of cinematic production for creating the star phenomenon. However, these explanations of the star phenomenon are not sufficient in themselves, and we need to see the phenomenon in its cultural, historical and ideological context to understand where the producers' ideas and images of stardom and of specific stars themselves come from. This will be returned to after a consideration of the stars in terms of consumption.

Stars as a phenomenon of consumption

Looking at the stars from the point of view of production puts the emphasis on the film-makers (including the economic structures within which they work and the medium they use) who make stars, or cause them to exist. However, it has been argued that a more determining force in the creation of stars is the audience – that is, the consumers – rather than the producers of media texts.

Andrew Tudor has suggested a typology of audience/star relationships, drawing on Leo Handel's work and reinforced by the latter's finding that people's favourite stars tend to be of the same sex as themselves, which Handel and Tudor take to indicate that star/audience relationships cannot be based on sexual attraction. (One could of course argue that attraction to one's own sex is also sexual, and that, as homosexuality is taboo in this society, the cinema has provided through the star phenomenon the vicarious and disguised experience of gay feeling for non-gay audiences.) Tudor's model (as given in *Image and Influence*, p. 80) is as follows:

		Range of consequences	
		Context specific	Diffuse
	High	Self-identification	Projection
Range of star/individual identification	Low	Emotional affinity	Imitation (of physical and simple behavioural characteristics)

TYPES OF AUDIENCE/STAR RELATION

The distinction between specific and diffuse consequences is not hard and fast, but is intended to catch the difference between a response that is limited to the 'watching-the-movie situation' and one that has 'consequences for a diffuse range of aspects of the fan's life'.

The four categories of star/audience relationship that emerge in this classification are thus:

— *emotional affinity.* This is the weakest category and 'probably' the most common. 'The audience feels a loose attachment to a particular protagonist deriving jointly from star, narrative and the individual personality of the audience member: a standard sense of involvement' (*Image and Influence*, p. 80).
— *self-identification.* This happens when 'involvement has reached the point at which the audience-member places himself [sic] in the same situation and persona of the star' (p. 81). He quotes one of the women interviewed by Handel as an example of this: 'These actresses I mentioned are great. They make me feel every emotion of their parts. I feel as if it were myself on the screen experiencing what they do' (p. 81).
— *imitation.* This is apparently commonest among the young and takes the star/audience relationship beyond cinema-going, with 'the star acting as some sort of model for the audience' (p. 81).
— *projection.* Imitation merges into projection 'at the point at which the process becomes more than a simple mimicking of clothing, hairstyle, kissing and the like' (pp. 81–2):

> The more extreme the projection, the more the person lives his or her life in terms bound up with the favoured star . . . In asking themselves what the star might have done in this situation the star-struck are using the star as a way of dealing with their realities. At the extreme the whole range of life experiences are mediated in this way. The 'real world' becomes constituted in terms derived from the 'star-world'. (pp. 82–3)

(Tudor warns against our taking examples of extreme projection as being widespread.)

What is clear from this account of the star/audience relationship is that the audience's role in shaping the star phenomenon is very limited. That is, the account tells us what audiences do with the star images that they are offered and hence indicates the sources of the success of stardom, but it does not tell us why the offered images take the form they do.

Needs, dreams and the collective unconscious

Many writers see the stars, in general and in specific instances, as giving expression to variously conceptualised inner wants on the part of the mass of the people. Richard Griffith states: 'no machinery ever of itself and by itself made a star. That takes place in the depths of the collective unconscious' (*The Movie Stars*, p. 23). The notion of the collective unconscious is suspect on several counts. It tends to suggest a supra-individual, quasi-metaphysical human consciousness (rather than people having in common the codes of the culture they live in); it is presented as being beyond determination, an essence that precedes existence.

Edgar Morin and Robert K. Merton in their use of 'dreams' and 'needs' do not perpetuate the problems just outlined, but their formulations have their own drawbacks. Morin quotes from some of J. P. Mayer's correspondents who speak of their dreaming about stars, and concludes:

> The star thus becomes the food of dreams; the dream, unlike the ideal tragedy of Aristotle, does not purify us truly from our fantasies but betrays their obsessive presence; similarly the stars only partially provoke catharsis and encourage fantasies which would like to but cannot liberate themselves in action. Here the role of the star becomes 'psychotic': it polarises and fixes obsessions. (*The Stars*, p. 164)

It is not clear where Morin gets these ideas of how dreams work from, nor whether they have any theoretical support or validity. Why should one assert that dreams are necessarily more obsessive than cathartic? The way Morin writes does suggest that he sees this 'polarising' effect as in some sense an ideological – or simply 'bad'! – function of the star system, but he does not question where the imagery of dreaming comes from. Finally, he does not examine the problems of the analogy between the dream as a sub- or unconscious individual mental process and films as an at any rate part conscious, rule-governed (the codes of art, etc.), collective/corporate form of cultural production. (This could be said, of course, of other celebrated uses of the film/dream analogy, including Kracauer and Wolfenstein and Leites.)

Robert K. Merton, in his study of the success of Kate Smith's war-bond drive (*Mass Persuasion*, described below, p. 29), stresses her embodiment of 'sincerity' and links this to the experience in the audience of feeling that they are endlessly being 'manipulated' by contemporary society. Smith then responds to a need. This seems to me to be acceptable enough, provided that one puts it (as Merton only partially does) in the context of ideological questions. That is – where does that need itself, and the response to it, come from? What shapes them? Every society (and each class/group at each period of that society) foregrounds certain needs (which may or may not be innate – see Abraham Maslow, *Motivation and Personality*), by virtue of both what it promises and what it fails to deliver. Likewise agencies in those societies (e.g. the cinema) provide and/or define answers to those needs. For this reason then I discuss the detail of analyses such as Merton's in the next chapter, under the rubric of ideology.

Alberoni, in arguing against the manipulation thesis of the mass media, comes up with this formula for understanding the production/consumption dialectic: 'the star system ... never creates the star, but it proposes the candidate for "election", and helps to retain the favour of the "electors"' ('The Powerless Elite' p. 93). This seems to me to be a very useful statement provided one remembers that organising an election is a way of defining and delimiting choice, and that both those who propose candidates and those who elect them are shaped by the particular ideological formations of their situation in society.

3   Ideology

Production and consumption are differentially determining forces in the creation of stars (producers always having more power over commodities than consumers), but both are always mediated by and in ideology. This chapter is not concerned with the ideological content of the star phenomenon (see Part Two), but with what specific kind(s) of ideological work it does, or tries to do, the nature of its 'ideological effect'.[4]

Star versus character *(see also Part Three)*

Stars are, like characters in stories, representations of people. Thus they relate to ideas about what people are (or are supposed to be) like. However, unlike characters in stories, stars are also real people. This point is suggested time and again in writing about stars: 'The people of the movies [come] before us first of all as people, and only secondarily as actors – artists – if at all' (Griffith, *The Movie Stars,* p. xiii). Because stars have an existence in the world independent of their screen/'fiction' appearances, it is possible to believe (with for instance ideas about the close-up revealing the soul, etc.) that as people they are more real than characters in stories. This means that they serve to disguise the fact that they are just as much produced images, constructed personalities as 'characters' are. Thus the value embodied by a star is as it were harder to reject as 'impossible' or 'false', because the star's existence guarantees the existence of the value s/he embodies.

This is to position it at its extreme, and put like this it implies an extreme gullibility on the part of the audience. I do not mean to imply that audiences did not realise that stars had different lives from those of the characters they played. It would be a sign of mental disorder to believe that Greta Garbo actually was Queen Christina. What I think is the case, however, is that the roles and/or the performance of a star in a film were taken as revealing the personality of the star (which then was corroborated by the stories in the magazines, etc.). What was only sometimes glimpsed and seldom brought out by Hollywood or the stars was that that personality was itself a construction known and expressed only through films, stories, publicity, etc. (It is not clear to what extent this elision of star as person and star as image is current today.)

Life-as-theatre

This process was perhaps aided by the growth of notions of life-as-theatre. As Elizabeth Burns points out in her book *Theatricality*, the analogy between life and drama or theatre has been in use from Plato onwards. However, where in earlier

20

times the analogy derived from 'a view of life directed by God, Providence or some less anthropomorphic spiritual force', current usage derives from 'a growing awareness of the way in which people compose their own characters, contribute to situations and design settings': 'the commonplace analogy is of the world itself as a place where people, like actors, play parts, in an action which is felt obscurely to be designed by "social forces" or the natural drives of individual men' (p. 11). One of the consequences of the growth of this notion is that we have two distinct conceptions of what we are, of our 'selves'. On the one hand, we can believe in the 'existence of a knowable and constant self', which is theoretically distinct from the social roles we have to play and the ways we have of presenting our 'personality' to others. On the other hand, as Burns stresses, there is increasing anxiety about the validity of this autonomous, separate identity – we may only be our 'perform-ance', the way in which we take on the various socially defined modes of behav-iour that our culture makes available. Clearly this is not the place to tease out all the philosophical consequences of this, but if we accept for the moment the fact of uncertainty with regard to notions of a separate self and public self-presen-tation, performance, role-playing, etc., we can I think see a connection with the star phenomenon.

Burns stresses the shared conventions of performance in the theatre, whereby the actor performs and interprets a role and thereby constructs a character. The actor 'intervenes . . . between the *authenticity* of his own life, of his own self and its past as known to himself (and as known or assumed at least in part to the audi-ence) and the *authenticated* life of the character he is playing' (pp. 146–7). ('Au-thenticated' refers to the way an actor establishes a correspondence between the character as played and the social norms of the time – or the way s/he embodies a social type; see Part Two.) Stars, as I've already suggested, collapse this distinc-tion between the actor's authenticity and the authentication of the character s/he is playing. While in some cases (John Wayne, Shirley Temple) this collapse may root the character in a 'real', 'authentic', 'true' self (the star's), in others (Bette Davis, Lana Turner) the gap between the 'self' and the performance, appearance, constructed persona may be part of the meaning of those stars. That is to say, whereas Wayne and Temple point to a belief in a separate identity, Davis and Turner point to the anxieties surrounding the validity of that notion of individual identity. (Wayne and Davis are discussed below; on Temple see Charles Eckert's article in *Jump Cut*, 2; on Turner refer to my article in *Movie*, no. 25.) The star phenomenon orchestrates the whole set of problems inherent in the common-place metaphor of life-as-theatre, role-playing, etc., and stars do this because they are known as performers, since what is interesting about them is not the charac-ter they have constructed (the traditional role of the actor) but rather the business of constructing/performing/being (depending on the particular star involved) a 'character'.

A historical paradigm – from gods to mortals

A third aspect of the question of how the star phenomenon works ideologically emerges from the historical paradigm of the development of stardom, found in Morin, Walker, Schickel, Griffith and others. This is that in the early period, stars were gods and goddesses, heroes, models – embodiments of *ideal* ways of behaving. In the later period, however, stars are identification figures, people like you and me – embodiments of *typical* ways of behaving.

Some take the transition point as being the coming of sound. Walker writes:

> A 'loss of illusion' was certainly one of the first effects that the talkies had on audiences. Richard Schickel defined 'silence' as the most valuable attribute of the pre-talkie stars. 'A godhead is supposed to be inscrutable. It is not expected that he speaks directly to us. It is enough that his image be present so that we may conveniently worship it.' (Schickel and Hurlburt, p. 13) Once they had dialogue on their lips, the once-silent idols suffered a serious loss of divinity. They ceased to be images in a human shape personifying the emotions through the delicately graded art of pantomime. Their voices made them as real as the audience watching them. (*Stardom*, p. 223)

Alexander Walker sees sound itself as creating de-divinisation of the stars, partly because it enhanced the naturalism of the medium. Edgar Morin on the other hand sees the progress from gods to identification figures as part of the 'embourgeoisement' of the medium. He suggests 1930 as the turning point, but maintains that sound is only one of the elements in the process. Sound brought a certain realism ('the concrete truth of noises, the precision and nuances of words', *The Stars*, p. 15), but the search for 'realism' was also marked by the growth of 'social themes' in Hollywood cinema (Vidor, *Fury*, *Mr Deeds Goes to Town*, etc.). Concurrently, the Depression caused Hollywood to commit itself to the 'dogma' of the happy end: 'The new optimistic structures favoured the "escapism" of the audience and in this sense departed from realism. But in another sense, the mythic content of films were "profaned", brought down to earth' (p. 16). This, Morin argues, constitutes the embourgeoisement of the cinematic imagination. The cinema was a 'plebeian spectacle' at first, drawing on the melodrama and penny-dreadful, characterised by magic, extraordinary adventures, sudden reversals, the sacrificial death of the hero, violent emotions, etc. 'Realism, psychologism, the "happy end" and humour reveal precisely the bourgeois transformation of this imagination' (p. 16). Chance and occult possession are replaced by psychological motivation. Bourgeois individualism cannot take the death of the hero, hence the insistence on the happy end. So stars become more usual in appearance, more 'psychologically' credible in personality, more individuated in image (and hence less obviously standing for a given virtue or, as Janet Gaynor said of herself, 'essence'[5]). The star does not cease to be special, but now combines 'the exceptional with the ordinary, the ideal with the everyday' (p. 19).

In Morin's formulation, this combination of the ideal and the typical is a product of the mingling of the proletarian and the bourgeois imagination. (There are, it needs to be said, considerable problems with identifying early cinema with proletarian culture/consciousness – since it can hardly be said to have been a *product* of the proletariat – and with the apparent valuation, simply because 'proletarian', of notions of chance, the occult and violent emotion.) The same combination could be seen as another aspect of the wider process (affecting all levels of art and culture) of one-dimensionality described by Marcuse. Thus the early stars maintained the distinction between the ideal (what should be) and the *status quo* (what is) – they were a 'negation'. However, the later, demystified stars closed the gap between the ideal and the *status quo*, and can be seen as part of the process whereby the type, the average, has become the ideal.

Another way of looking at this process is suggested in the discussion by Orrin E. Klapp and Leo Lowenthal of the 'deterioration of the hero'. Morin and Marcuse both work within forms of Marxist thought; Klapp and Lowenthal on the other hand work within a context of liberal thought, seeing the deterioration of the hero as the corruption of bourgeois ideals.

Klapp's account of the deterioration of the hero, in *Heroes, Villains and Fools*, focuses on the following points in contemporary images: the fact that the hero as a model is not much (if any) better than the average; that high 'character' is not stressed; that the 'goodfellow' quality so currently valued is easily simulated; that models are diverse and contradictory. Klapp does not suggest what should have caused this change, nor does he link this account to specific earlier ideals, just to 'ideal' in general.

Lowenthal's account is based on an analysis ('The Triumph of Mass Idols', described below, in Part Two) of biographies of heroes/celebrities in popular magazines, in which he sees a shift away from heroes who embody the ideals of what he calls an 'open-minded liberal society' (p. 113) to those who are 'adjusted to a closed society'. Thus success is shown as based not on work but on luck: 'There is no longer a pattern for the way up. Success has become an accidental and irrational event' (p. 126). Everything in the biographies points towards a conception of the hero as 'passive': s/he is a 'product' of her/his background (by virtue of 'a kind of primitive Darwinian concept of social facts', p. 119); there is no 'development', i.e. progress from childhood to adulthood, for the child is just seen as 'a midget edition' (p. 124) of the adult: 'people are not conceived as the responsible agents of their fate in all phases of their lives, but as the bearers of certain useful or not so useful character traits which are pasted on them like decorations or stigmas of shame' (p. 125). There is an emphasis on co-operation, sociability, good sportsmanship as against unrestrained 'emotional' behaviour, hence 'it is a world of dependency' (p. 129).

Lowenthal, like Klapp, writes within the context of liberal discontent. This view is concerned with the erosion of liberal values such as individualism and freedom by the large-scale development of industrial, urban society, and in particular by such pressures towards conformism as production-line goods, the mass media, the centralised organisation of education and government, etc. The key concept of this view is the 'mass', as in 'mass society', 'mass communications', 'mass culture', etc. Social issues are then posed in terms of the individual versus society/the mass, rather than class struggle, and inevitably, as with Lowenthal, notions like sociability and dependence are devalued. Nevertheless, Lowenthal's analysis does suggest a further possible way of conceptualising the work the star phenomenon performs for ideology, namely the suppression of notions of human practice, achievement, making the world.

Stars and the status quo

Discussion of Marcuse and Lowenthal has already pointed to possible ways of conceptualising the ideological function of the star phenomenon – as negation of

23

negation (Marcuse), as concealer of the humanity which makes history (Lowenthal): functions which serve to preserve the *status quo*. The majority of accounts of the star phenomenon are concerned with this 'conservative' function, but conceptualised in different ways.

In his *Collective Search for Identity* Klapp suggests that stars (and other celebrities) can have one of three different relationships to prevalent norms – *reinforcement, seduction* and *transcendence*.

'To reinforce a person in social roles – encourage him [sic] to play those which are highly valued – and to maintain the image of the group superself are presumably the classic functions of heroes in all societies' (p. 219). Given Klapp's alternative, but necessarily exceptional, categories of seduction and transcendence (see below), this is acceptable. His elaboration of the concept is more problematic:

> The beauty of heroes as a character-building force is that the individual, daydreaming, *chooses for himself* [sic], within the opportunities the available models provide – which, fortunately for the social order, usually 'just happen to be' more supporting than erosive or subversive. (p. 220)

We might want to question here the extent to which the individual is not so shaped by the ideologies of her/his culture, or so structurally placed within her/his society, that choice becomes very delimited and predefined indeed. Equally, Klapp does not explore the implications of his view that models 'just happen to be' supportive of the *status quo* – his inverted commas show he is aware of the problem, but his liberalism does not allow him to ask who fashions the *status quo* or who controls the provision of models.

In the seduction scenario the hero breaks the rules or norms, but in a charming way. Klapp's examples are Mickey Spillane or James Bond, who demonstrate that 'it is possible, permissible, even admirable, to romp in the forbidden pasture' (p. 227). Klapp points out that:

> the main shortcoming of the seductive hero as teacher is that he [sic] leads a person into experience felt traditionally to be wrong, but does not redefine and recreate standards by which experience is to be judged. He [sic] eludes and confuses morality, but makes little contribution to it in terms of insight. (p. 228)

In the case of transcendence, the hero 'produces a fresh point of view, a feeling of integrity, and makes a new man [sic]' (p. 229). This is more than just getting away with something, as in the previous category, since it does 'redefine and recreate standards by which experience is to be judged'. One of Klapp's examples in this category is Jean-Paul Belmondo, whose popularity with college students he sees as epitomising their discovery of a radical new lifestyle. Another example is I think more interesting, since it suggests the possibility of transcendence in a much less intellectually respectable instance. He quotes an account by a woman student recalling her enjoyment of Sandra Dee in *Gidget*, particularly her perseverance in learning to be a surfer, despite mockery, setbacks, etc. Here is an example, Klapp suggests, of a star offering 'a springboard by which a girl can vicariously leap from femininity into a role usually reserved for boys' (p. 234). There are problems with Klapp's categories of seduction and transcendence. How, for instance, can one actually distinguish with any rigour between the two? Can one not see both, and especially transcendence, as simply providing a 'safety-valve' for discontent, and by providing expression of it siphoning it off as a substantial subversive force? The answer to that depends on how hermetic your conception of the mass media, and of ideology, is. My own belief is that the system is a good deal more 'leaky' than many people would currently maintain. In my view, to assert the total closure of the system is essentially to deny the validity of class/sex/race struggles and their re-production at all levels of society and in all human practices. I find the Sandra Dee/*Gidget* example particularly suggestive because it stresses both the possibility of a leak at a very unprestigious, ordinary, exploitative part of the system, and the role of the spectator in making the image subversive *for her.*

The notion of subversion is discussed elsewhere in this book (see p. 52), but most examinations, of the star phenomenon, other than this brief section in Klapp, discuss stars as in some sense or other reinforcing of dominant values.

Reinforcement of values under threat

Klapp's category of reinforcement suggests only that heroes reinforce by embody-ing dominant values. Two studies of individual stars, William R. Brown on Will Rogers and Charles Eckert on Shirley Temple, suggest that stars embody social values that are to some degree in crisis.

In *Imagemaker: Will Rogers and the American Dream* Brown shows how Rogers embodied the four strands of the American Dream (the dignity of the common individual, democracy as the guarantee of freedom and quality, the gospel of hard work and the belief in material progress) at a point in time when the dream was becoming increasingly hard to believe in. Thus the 'dignity of the common indi-vidual' strand of the dream was linked in Rogers's image with that of the 'sturdy yeoman' at a time when farmers were suffering from a decline in their purchasing power as compared to other groups in the economy and from their gradual in-corporation into a vast market economy. There was concurrently 'governmental corruption, financial greed, crime and a revolution in morals' (p. 60) and the emergence of anti-heroes, notably Al Capone:

> Thus, during the twenties, the times called for an embodiment of the dream of the worth and dignity of the individual. During the thirties, when the great famine came, citizens cried out for such affirmation. Where were the dignity and worth as the hungry in the cities stood in line for bread or soup; as lonely men left families and walked or rode forth on the quest not for the holy grail but for gainful employment – only to be lost or followed later by wives and children with nowhere to go except to look for the father ... as there seemed no end to the suffering in the winters and no way of coun-tering human misery? (p. 61)

In the face of this experience, Brown argues, Rogers reaffirmed the reality and val-idity of the 'sturdy yeoman', and similarly with the other values of the American Dream. One could say that at a time when the American value system might have been redirected, the old goals appearing inadequate, Rogers was there to demon-strate that there was life still in the traditional values and attitudes.

Eckert's article, 'Shirley Temple and the House of Rockefeller', uses a similar model, but with greater attention to the specificities of ideology. This leads him to stress the function of Temple for dominant ideology and interests, rather than for the reassurance of the audience as in Brown's approach. Eckert links Temple to the political solutions offered by the Republicans and Democrats to the poverty born of the Depression – the former stressed the role of individual charity (giving to the poor), seeing the federal relief programme proposed by the Democrats as an attack on the American ideals of initiative and individualism. By 1934, says Eckert, there was a deadlock – federal relief was not really working, yet its introduction had 'utterly demoralised charity efforts'. Into this situation comes Temple. The emphasis in her films is on love as a natural, spontaneous opening of one's heart so that 'the most implacable realities alter and disperse'; it is a love that is not universal but rather elicited by need:

> Shirley turns like a lodestone toward the flintiest characters in her films – the wizened wealthy, the defensive unloved, figures of cold authority like Army officers, and tough criminals. She assaults, penetrates and opens them, making it possible for them to *give* of themselves. All of this returns upon her at times, forcing her into situations where she must decide who *needs* her most. It is her *agon*, her calvary, and it brings her to her most despairing moments. This confluence of needing, giving, of deciding whose need is greatest, also obviously suggests the relief experience. (p. 19)

Eckert stresses that one has to take other elements into account to understand fully Temple's star status – e.g. 'the mitigation of reality through fantasy, the exacerbated emotions relating to insufficiently cared for children, the commonly stated philosophy of pulling together to whip the Depression', but none the less insists that 'Shirley and her burden of love appeared at a moment when the official ideology of charity had reached a final and unyielding form and when the public sources of charitable support were drying up' (ibid.). I would generalise from this the notion of the star's image being related to contradictions in ideology – whether within the dominant ideology, or between it and other subordinated/revolutionary ideologies. The relation may be one of displacement (see next section, 'Displacement of values'), or of the suppression of one half of the contradiction and the foregrounding of the other (see Merton on Kate Smith, p. 29 below), or else it may be that the star effects a 'magic' reconciliation of the apparently incompatible terms. Thus if it is true to say that American society has seen sexuality, especially for women, as wrong and, in effect, 'extraordinary', and yet has required women to be both sexy and pure and ordinary, then one can see Lana Turner's combination of sexuality and ordinariness, or Marilyn Monroe's blend of sexiness and innocence, as effecting a magical synthesis of these opposites. This was possible partly through the specific chains of meaning in the images of those two stars, and partly through, once again, the fact of their real existence as individuals in the world, so that the disunity created by attaching opposing qualities to their images was none the less rendered a unity simply by virtue of the fact that each was only one person. (One can see this process in *The Postman Always Rings Twice*, where the character of Cora is totally contradictory, endlessly given 'inconsistent' motivation by the script; so a discussion of Cora as a constructed character would reveal nothing but fragmentation, yet, because it is played by Lana Turner, a unity imposes itself. See Dyer, 'Four Films of Lana Turner'.)

Displacement of values

So far I have been discussing the way stars may reinforce aspects of ideology simply by repeating, reproducing or reconciling them. However, both Barry King and Eckert (in his article on Shirley Temple) suggest that reinforcement may be achieved not so much by reiterating dominant values as by concealing prevalent contradictions or problems.

King discusses this in general terms. What he calls 'Hollywood studio realism' is built around 'the centrifuge of the hero', and is, he claims, 'inescapably social commentary' – yet it must not offend the audience (for else it would not sell). The star solves this problem 'because he or she converts the opinion expressed in the film to an expression of his being ... he converts the question "why do people feel this way?" to "how does it feel to have such feelings?" ' This works in terms of the producers: 'The stars ... ease the problem of judgement (which would politicise media) off the shoulders of those controlling the media by throwing it onto the realm of personal experience and feelings.' Equally it works for the audience, depoliticising their consciousness by individualising it, rendering the social personal:

> By embodying and dramatising the flow of information, the stars promote depoliticised modes of attachment (i.e. acceptance of the *status quo*) in its audience. The stars promote a privatisation or personalisation of structural determinants, they promote a mass consciousness in the audience. Individuals who perceive their world in terms of personal relevance alone are individuals in a privatised mass. Their personal troubles tend to remain personal troubles.

The stars serve to mask people's awareness of themselves as class members by reconstituting social differences in the audience 'into a new polarity pro-star/anti-star ... collective experience is individualised and loses its collective insignificance'. In all these ways then stars, by virtue of being experienced (that is they are a phenomenon of experience not cognition) and individuated (embodying a general social value/norm in a 'unique' image), and having an existence in the real world, serve to defuse the political meanings that form the inescapable but potentially offensive or explosive point of departure of all media messages. King has not argued this through in the case of a specific star, but the argument might run that John Wayne or Jane Fonda, both stars with obvious political associations, act unavoidably to obscure the political issues they embody simply by demonstrating the lifestyle of their politics and displaying those political beliefs as an aspect of their personality. This means that films and stars are ideologically significant in the most general sense of cutting audiences off from politics, rendering them passive (cf. Lowenthal), but not ideologically significant in the narrower sense of reinforcing a given political standpoint. The specific politics of Wayne and Fonda would thus be irrelevant in discussing their ideological function, which is identical with that of all stars.

Whilst I would certainly share King's view as a description of a *tendency* of the star phenomenon, nevertheless I find it hard to discount the specific ideological meaning/function of given stars. King's view depends upon dismissing as politically irrelevant such things as lifestyles, feelings and 'the personal'. Obviously whether or not one regards these things as political depends upon one's politics.

My own feeling is that we are so shaped and penetrated by our society that the personal is always political. In this perspective it may be true to say that Wayne or Fonda are politically irrelevant in terms of converting the 'issues' of conventionally conceived right or left politics respectively, but precisely because they are experiential, individual living embodiments of those politics they may convey the implications of those politics in terms of, for example, sex roles, everyday life, etc. Under what circumstances this can happen is discussed below, pp. 77–83.

Charles Eckert's discussion of Shirley Temple stresses the way in which Temple's image both 'asserts and denies' problem aspects of Depression-capitalist society. Money, in the Republican ideological complex to which Temple's films belong, was a problematic issue: 'as a charitable gift [it] was benevolent, whereas [money] in the form of dole was destructive'. Charity and initiative were the values to be foregrounded, while money was 'ambivalent and repressed':

> In Shirley Temple's films and biographies, through a slight but very important displacement, charity appears as love and initiative as work. Both love and work are abstracted from all social and psychological realities. They have no causes; they are unmotivated. (...) Money is subjected, in keeping with its ambivalent nature, to two opposing operations. In Shirley's films and the depictions of real life attitudes toward money, it is censored out of existence. It is less than destructive. It is nothing. But in an opposing movement, found largely in Shirley's biographies, money breaks free and induces an inebriated fantasy that a Caliban would embrace, a vision of gold descending from the heavens, a treasure produced from a little girl's joy and curls and laughter. (p. 20)

Eckert's analysis seems to me to be in many respects exemplary for its linking of the produced image to the specific ideological realities of its time. Of course, not all stars will require the concept of displacement to account for their ideological functioning, but many will and Temple is a good example of the usefulness of the concept, since she is the kind of star so apparently without ideological significance. (It is a pity all the same that Eckert does not discuss her more direct, obvious embodiment of ideological conceptions of the family, childhood and feminity, and her relationships with black characters in the films.)

Compensation

The notion of stars compensating people for qualities lacking in their lives is obviously close to the concept of stars embodying values that are under threat. The latter are presumably qualities which people have an idea of, but which they do not experience in their day-to-day lives. However, compensation implies not that an image makes one believe all over again in the threatened value, but that it shifts your attention from that value to some other, lesser, 'compensatory' one.

Leo Lowenthal sees the shift as one from active involvement in business, politics, the productive sphere, to active involvement in leisure and consumption:

> It is some comfort for the little man [sic] who has become expelled from the Horatio Alger dream, who despairs of penetrating the thicket of grand strategy in politics and business, to see his heroes as a lot of guys who like or dislike highballs, cigarettes, tomato juice, golf, and social gatherings – just like himself. ('The Triumph of Mass Idols', p. 135)

Lowenthal sees that this is a problem of real structural failures in society, not just a crisis of belief in an ideology. This perspective also informs Robert K. Merton's study of Kate Smith in his book *Mass Persuasion*. This is a study of the enormously successful war-bond drive conducted by Kate Smith on 21 September 1943. Many factors contributed to this success (length of broadcast, its special build-up, the content of what Smith said, etc.), but none more so than the image of Smith herself. Merton suggests that there was a congruence between Smith's image and the themes used to sell the bonds (e.g. partriotism, self-sacrifice, etc.), but above all notes that interviewees for his study stressed time and again Smith's sincerity. The radio broadcast itself 'corroborated' Smith's image of sincerity by the fact that she was doing it for nothing and that it went on for so long and yet she never flagged. Equally her image had been built up by the convergence of a variety of factors:

> published accounts of her charities; inadvertent and casual radio references to her contributions; expressions of her identification with other plain people; the halo transferred from the kind of people she talks about to herself – all these contribute to her established reputation as a doer of good. (p. 100)

Smith's image is then a condensation of various traditional values, 'guaranteed' by the actual existence of Smith as a person, producing her as an incarnation of sincerity.

Merton's interviewees contrasted Smith's sincerity with 'the pretenses, deceptions and dissembling which they observe in their daily experience' (p. 142). Merton suggests that the experience of being manipulated characterises contemporary society, it is one of 'the psychological effects of a society which, focused on capital and the market, tends to instrumentalise human relationships' (p. 143):

> The emotional emphasis placed on Smith's 'really meaning what she says' derives from the assumption that advertisers, public relations counsels, salesmen, promoters, script writers, politicians and, in extreme cases, ministers, doctors and teachers are systematically manipulating symbols in order to gain power or prestige or income. It is the expression of a wish to be considered as a person rather than a potential client or customer. It is a reaction against the feelings of insecurity that stem from the conviction that others are dissembling and pretending to good-fellowship to gain one's confidence and make one more susceptible to manipulation. (p. 144)

> The Smith following . . . is no mere aggregate of persons who are entertained by a popular singer. For many, she has become the symbol of a moral leader who 'demonstrates' by her own behaviours that there need be no discrepancy between appearance and reality in the sphere of human relationships. That an entertainer should have captured the moral loyalties of so large a following is itself an incisive commentary on prevailing social and political orientations. (p. 145)

Although one could quarrel with aspects of Merton's formulation (the notion of 'a person' should not be taken as a given or an absolute, since notions of what it is to be human are culturally and historically specific; it may be that the discrepancy between appearance and reality in human relationships is necessary and inescapable, Smith's appeal therefore being unrealisably utopian), at the level of description it seems very persuasive.

Merton also explores other aspects of Smith's image, unfortunately in less detail. Thus he suggests that Smith embodies the first of the 'three prevailing models for the feminine sex role: the domesticity pattern, the career pattern, and the glamour pattern' at the expense of the other two. By reinforcing and therefore legitimating the domesticity pattern, she 'serves to mitigate the strain and conflict' these contradictory roles impose on women. 'Smith is taken as a living testimonial that the cultural accent on feminine attractiveness may be safely abandoned' (p. 147). 'She ... provides emotional support for those who are shut off from occupational achievement.' Merton discusses her mother image, her success (though remaining 'just one of us') and her 'unspoiledness' in similar terms, always relating it to specific senses of lack of anxiety in sectors of the audience. (The sincerity emphasis, unlike the others, Merton found in all classes and both sexes.)

Charisma

Merton's ideas, as well as those of Eckert and Brown, all relate to the notion of 'charisma' as developed by Max Weber in the field of political theory. I'd like to end Part One by discussing Weber's theories and their relevance to the star phenomenon, as, in a suitably modified form, the notion of charisma (in the Weberian sense, not just meaning 'magic', etc.) does combine concepts of social function with an understanding of ideology.

Weber was interested in accounting for how political order is legitimated (other than by sheer force), and suggested three alternatives: tradition (doing what we've always done), bureaucracy (doing things according to agreed but alterable, supposedly rational rules) and charisma (doing things because the leader suggests it). Charisma is defined as 'a certain quality of an individual personality by virtue of which he [sic] is set apart from ordinary men and treated as endowed with supernatural, superhuman or at least superficially exceptional qualities' (*On Charisma and Institution Building*, p. 329).

There are certain problems about transferring the notion of charisma from political to film theory. As Alberoni has pointed out, the star's status depends upon her/his not having any institutional political power. Yet there is clearly some correspondence between political and star charisma, in particular the question of how or why a given person comes to have 'charisma' attributed to him/her. E. A. Shils in 'Charisma, Order and Status' suggests that

> The charismatic quality of an individual as perceived by others, or himself [sic] lies in what is thought to be his connection with (including possession by or embedment in) some *very central* feature of man's existence and the cosmos in which he lives. The centrality, coupled with intensity, makes it extraordinary.

One does not have to think in terms of 'man's existence' and 'the cosmos', somewhat suspect eternal universals, to accept the general validity of this statement, especially as it is probably very often the case that what is culturally and historically specific about the charismatic person's relationship to her/his society may none the less present itself, or be read, as being an eternal universal relationship.

S. N. Eisenstadt in his introduction to Weber's *Charisma and Institution Building* has taken this one stage further by suggesting, on the basis of a survey of communications research, that charismatic appeal is effective especially when the social order is uncertain, unstable and ambiguous and when the charismatic figure or group offers a value, order or stability to counterpoise this. Linking a star with the whole of a society may not get us very far in these terms, unless one takes twentieth-century western society to have been in constant instability. Rather, one needs to think in terms of the relationships (of the various kinds outlined above) between stars and specific instabilities, ambiguities and contradictions in the culture (which are reproduced in the actual practice of making films, and film stars).

This model underlines one of the earliest attempts to analyse a star image, Alistair Cooke's *Douglas Fairbanks: The Making of a Screen Character*, published in 1940. Cooke accounts for Fairbanks's stardom in terms of the appropriateness of his 'Americanness' to the contemporary situation of America:

> At a difficult time in American history, when the United States was keeping a precarious neutrality in the European war, Douglas Fairbanks appeared to know all the answers and knew them without pretending to be anything more than 'an all-round chap, just a regular American' (*The American*). The attraction of this flattering transfer of identity to the audience did not have to be obvious to be enjoyed. The movie fan's pleasure in Fairbanks might have been expressed in the simple sentence of a later French critic: 'Douglas Fairbanks is a tonic. He laughs and you feel relieved.' In this period of his earliest films it was no accident that his best-liked films should have been *His Picture in the Papers*, *Reggie Mixes In*, *Manhattan Madness*, and *American Aristocracy*. These were respectively about the American mania for publicity; about a society playboy who was not above finding his girl in a downtown cabaret and fighting a gangster or two to keep her; about a Westerner appalled at the effete manners of the East, and about a Southerner of good family who married into 'bean-can' nobility, and was healthily oblivious of any implied snobbery. Here already was the kernel of a public hero close enough, in manner and get-up, to contemporary America to leave his admirers with the feeling that they were manfully facing the times rather than escaping from them. (pp. 16–17)

Marilyn Monroe provides another example. Her image has to be situated in the flux of ideas about morality and sexuality that characterised the 50s in America and can here be indicated by such instances as the spread of Freudian ideas in post-war America (registered particularly in the Hollywood melodrama), the Kinsey report, Betty Friedan's *The Feminine Mystique*, rebel stars such as Marlon Brando, James Dean and Elvis Presley, the relaxation of cinema censorship in the face of competition from television, etc. (In turn, these instances need to be situated in relation to other levels of the social formation, e.g. actual social and sexual relations, the relative economic situations of men and women, etc.) Monroe's combination of sexuality and innocence is part of that flux, but one can also see her 'charisma' as being the apparent condensation of all that within her. Thus she seemed to 'be' the very tensions that ran through the ideological life of 50s America. You could see this as heroically living out the tensions or painfully exposing them.

Just as star charisma needs to be situated in the specificities of the ideological configurations to which it belongs (a process discussed in Part Two), so also virtually all sociological theories of stars ignore the *specificities* of another aspect of the phenomenon – the audience. (Assumptions about the audience as a generalised, homogenous collectivity abound in the material surveyed above.) The

importance of contradictions as they are lived by audience members in considering the star phenomenon is suggested by asides in J. P. Mayer, Andrew Tudor and
Edgar Morin to the effect that particularly intense star/audience relationships
occur among adolescents and women. They point to some empirical evidence for
this. I would also point out the absolutely central importance of stars in gay ghetto
culture. These groups all share a peculiarly intense degree of role/identity conflict
and pressure, and an (albeit partial) exclusion from the dominant articulacy of,
respectively, adult, male, heterosexual culture. If these star/audience relationships
are only an intensification of the conflicts and exclusions experienced by everyone,[6] it is also significant that, in the discussion of 'subversive' star images in the
next part, stars embodying adolescent, female and gay images play a crucial role.

Notes

1. All reference to King's work is based on an unpublished manuscript, 'The Social Significance of Stardom', which is part of King's ongoing research into the subject.
2. David Shipman, *The Great Stars – the Golden Years* and *The Great Stars – the International Years*.
3. Quotations from Balazs are taken from the extracts of his work in Gerald Mast and Marshall Cohen (eds.), *Film Theory and Criticism*.
4. The term 'ideological effect' is taken from the article by Stuart Hall, 'Culture, the media
   and the "Ideological Effect" '.
5. 'We were essences, you see ... Garbo was the essence of glamor and tragedy ... I was the
   essence of first love.' Janet Gaynor in an interview with Roy Newquist in *Showcase*.
6. I do not know of any research which looks at the differences in star/audience relationships according to class and race.

PART TWO

Stars as Images

Looking at stars as a social phenomenon indicates that, no matter where one chooses to put the emphasis in terms of the stars' place in the production/consumption dialectic of the cinema, that place can still only be fully understood ideologically. The questions, 'Why stardom?' and 'Why such-and-such a star?', have to be answered in terms of ideology – ideology being, as it were, the terms in which the production/consumption dialectic is articulated.

With stars, the 'terms' involved are essentially images. By 'image' here I do not understand an exclusively visual sign, but rather a complex configuration of visual, verbal and aural signs. This configuration may constitute the general image of stardom or of a particular star. It is manifest not only in films but in all kinds of media text.

As suggested in the final pages of Part One, star images function crucially in relation to contradictions within and between ideologies, which they seek variously to 'manage' or resolve. In exceptional cases, it has been argued that certain stars, far from managing contradictions, either expose them or embody an alternative or oppositional ideological position (itself usually contradictory) to dominant ideology. The 'subversiveness' of these stars can be seen in terms of 'radical intervention' (not necessarily conscious) on the part of themselves or others who have used the potential meanings of their image – the struggles of Mae West, Greta Garbo, Bette Davis and Barbra Streisand over representation (expressed as a demand for 'decent parts for women') would clearly suggest them as interventionists. However, the question of subversion need not be conceptualised in this way. One can think of it simply as a clash of codes, quite possibly fortuitous, in which the very clash or else the intensity with which the alternative/oppositional code is realised result in 'subversion' (or, at any rate, make reading them 'subversively' possible or legitimate). The discussion of images in this part looks at examples of stars and ideological contradiction, both in terms of how they are grounded in such contradictions and how they 'manage' or 'subvert' them.

4 Stars as Stars

In this chapter I want to look briefly at some of the characteristics of the overall image of stardom. This general image forms a background to the more specific analyses of particular stars in chapters 5 and 6.

Stardom is an image of the way stars live. For the most part, this generalised lifestyle is the assumed backdrop for the specific personality of the star and the details and events of her/his life. As it combines the spectacular with the everyday, the special with the ordinary, and is seen as an articulation of basic American/western values, there is no conflict here between the general lifestyle and the particularities of the star. In certain cases, however, the relationship between the two may be ambivalent or problematic. Marilyn Monroe's aspiration to the condition of stardom and her unhappiness on attaining it are part of the pathetic/tragic side of her image. Much of the early publicity surrounding Marlon Brando concerns his unshaven, unkempt appearance and his unruly behaviour at parties, matters that signified a rejection of the general lifestyle of stardom. Jane Fonda has sought in recent years to negotiate stardom politically – that is, to maintain a certain level of star glamour in order to connect with the predominant culture of working people while at the same time gaining credibility for her progressive views by living in an ordinary house in an ordinary working-class neighbourhood.

I have illustrated this section chiefly from *The Talkies, Hollywood and the Great Fan Magazines* and *Photoplay Treasury.*[1] As these all cover much the same period (the 20s to the 40s), the image that emerges is essentially that of Hollywood's classic period. It might be useful to compare this with contemporary film magazines (e.g. *Photoplay, ABC Film Review, Modern Screen, Films and Filming*) to see where the different emphases lie – e.g. fashion seems less important now than sex, there is perhaps more interest in films as such, the 'dream' of stardom is more jaded and sour. (The emphases also differ, of course, from one publication to another.)

The general image of stardom can be seen as a version of the American Dream, organised around the themes of consumption, success and ordinariness. Throughout, however, there is an undertow that, as it were, 'sours' the dream. In addition, love, marriage and sex are constants of the image.

Consumption

The way stars lived is one element in the 'fabulousness' of Hollywood. One can approach this in different ways.

See These Latest Chanel

Look at those wing-like draperies! Who but Chanel would add them to a black velvet evening gown? Who but Gloria could wear them so smartly? Both front and back decolletages are tricky. Those are jeweled clips on the shoulder. Note the straighter line, too

Chanel goes in for sleeves in a big way, it seems. Huge muffs of fur match a face-framing collar on the short satin jacket which accompanies this regal white satin evening gown. That train is dramatic, isn't it?

February 1932

1 *From* Photoplay, *January 1932.*

Styles in Gloria's Picture

Chanel has caught all the glamour that surrounds an opera singer in these clothes she has designed for Gloria's operatic screen rôle. Look at this afternoon ensemble in black satin and ermine. Every line of it is distinctive. The coat is long and slightly fitted. Barrel cuffs of ermine trim the sleeves, while a double collar of the fur rises about the face. The dress depends upon intricate seaming for its chic. Bands of ermine trim the surplice neckline. A barrel muff echoes the sleeve detail and a pert turban tops the unusual costume.

Longer and more elegant goes the trend of evening wraps as by Chanel. This gorgeous satin one is invisibly trimmed with that precious fur, chinchilla. Again the unusual cuff detail that marks all these "Tonight or Never" costumes.

An anatomy of the lifestyle

A list of the recurrent features of that lifestyle would include, to begin with, swimming pools, large houses, sumptuous costumes, limousines, parties, etc. Let us look at the connotations of one of those features, fashion.

For instance what meanings are packed into the recurrent image of women stars as leaders of fashion? If we look at the feature 'See These Latest Chanel Styles in Gloria's Picture' (Fig. 1), the fact that the designer is Chanel links Gloria Swanson to the world of *haute couture*, with its connotations of high society, European 'taste' and exclusiveness. A certain awareness of the idiosyncrasies of couturiers is assumed on the part of the reader by a remark like 'Who but Chanel would add [wing-like draperies] to a black velvet evening gown?' Equally, the expensiveness of the materials used is stressed (satin, fur, jewels), while the designs themselves are examples of 'conspicuous consumption' (see below), with their yards of material and awkward hanging pieces that would make any form of industry (including, be it noted in passing, the activity of acting) impossible. Finally, all of this promotes the notion of woman as spectacle, a theme that is even more insistent in other articles such as 'Motoring Beauty Hints' and 'How I Keep My Figure' (by Betty Grable) (Gelman, *Photoplay Treasury*, pp. 132–4, 286–7), and 'Beauty "Tips" from the Beautiful – Little Things That Add to the Good Looks of the Stars Could Add, Also, to Your Own Attractions'.[2] As these last examples show, however, fashion and notions of beauty (charm/glamour/sex appeal, etc.) were also to be shared by star and fan. In this context, the 'exclusiveness' of the *haute couture* connection was problematic, and in fact there is increasing emphasis over the years in the fan magazines on the idea of Hollywood itself as the arbiter of fashion. (The ascendancy was finally achieved when America was effectively cut off from Paris styles during World War II.) This is indicated by the article 'Hollywood Snubs Paris. Movie Capital is Self-Reliant as a Style Center. Designer [Travis Banton] No Longer Looks to "Shabby" Paris for Ideas' (*The Talkies*, pp. 192–3, 347). In this article, the fact of Paris as a leader of fashion is rejected with the implication that America and/or democracy can do just as well. At the same time, the notion of 'taste' as an absolute value is still asserted, without any recognition of the relativity of the term or its provenance, in the discourse of fashion; namely, Paris . . .

One could similarly explore the associations and contradictions of other image clusters – sport, dances, architecture (of the stars' homes), and so on.

Conspicuous consumption

Thorstein Veblen made the notion of conspicuous consumption central to his *Theory of the Leisure Class*. Conspicuous consumption is the way by which the wealthy display the fact that they are wealthy. It displays not only the fact that they have wealth in the scale on which they consume and their access to the canons of taste and fashion but also the fact that they do not have to work. Women are crucial in this process – a man may have to work, but his wife must not. It is she who carries in her consumption patterns the signs of his wealth. Fashion is one example of this – access to the canons of taste, wearing clothes made of expensive materials in exclusive designs, designs that clearly make work impossible and are even, in the pursuit of this aim, debilitating for the wearer, as they squeeze, shape, misshape and constrict her body. Equally, activities such as sport or the arts are not pursued for health or enlightenment but for the sake of displaying the leisure time and money at one's disposal. Thus a man's athletic body may be much admired, but only on condition that it has been acquired through sports not labour.

These themes emerge very clearly in an analysis of the fan magazines: 'Hollywood at Play' and 'Stars off the Set',[3] for instance, the latter showing how a star's non-working life is presented as consisting in sports and hobbies. What is suppressed, or only fleetingly acknowledged, in these articles is that making films is work, that films are produced. An interestingly self-conscious play on this occurs in the article 'Those Awful Factories' with a spread of pictures of stars 'at work' in their sumptuous studio dressing rooms (see overleaf). Even on the shop-floor, stars are not shown working, that is, making films. (Note also the delineation of sex roles by decor.)

Idols of consumption

Leo Lowenthal in his study of biographies in popular magazines noted a marked shift in emphasis between 1901 and 1941. In the earlier period the biographies' subjects were 'idols of production' – people who were interesting because they had achieved something in the world, made their own way, worked their way to the top, were useful to society: bankers, politicians, artists, inventors, businessmen. In the intervening years, however, there is a shift to 'idols of consumption'. Lowenthal had this to say of 'present-day magazine heroes':

> almost every one . . . is directly, or indirectly, related to the sphere of leisure time: either he does not belong to vocations which serve society's basic needs (e.g. the heroes of the world of entertainment and sport), or he amounts, more or less, to a caricature of a socially productive agent. (p. 115)

Contemporary heroes 'stem predominantly from the sphere of consumption and organised leisure time' (p. 121) (i.e. they are entertainers or sportspeople), and equally their 'private' lives are lives of consumption. So 'in the course of the presentation the producers and agents of consumer goods change into their own customers' (ibid.).

Although Veblen's account of the way in which leisure, dress, consumption patterns, etc. bespeak wealth is useful in the analysis of the image of stardom, Lowenthal's model perhaps comes closer to the social significance of all this consumption. For whereas with Veblen conspicuous consumption preserves the leisure class as a distinctive class, with Lowenthal the stars become models of consumption for everyone in a consumer society. They may spend more than the average person, but none the less they can be, on a smaller scale, imitated. Their fashions are to be copied, their fads followed, their sports pursued, their hobbies taken up. Heroes, in Lowenthal's words, are 'a lot of guys [sic] who like or dislike highballs, cigarettes, tomato juice, golf and social gatherings . . .' (p. 135). We may note that many economists (e.g. Galbraith, Baran and Sweezy) consider that during the 20th century capitalism has shifted decisively from an economy based on production to one based on consumption – that the 'problem' for capitalism is not

THOSE AWFUL

There's where the Stars have to slave!

2 *From* Photoplay, *November 1937. Stars' rooms:* (clockwise from top right) *Ginger Rogers, Ann Sothern, Joan Crawford, Jeanette MacDonald, Nelson Eddy, Lionel Barrymore.*

FACTORIES

Presenting that glorified institution of the Hollywood proletariat—the star's dressing room. Nelson Eddy, in a knotty-pine atmosphere, relaxes on a soft chaise lounge; Lionel Barrymore, at ease with his newspaper, is proud of his ship model (hobby hangover from "Captain Courageous"). The feminine contingent has other ideas of soul-soothing decoration. Jeanette MacDonald chooses an all-white piano to match her all-white room; Ginger Rogers likes old ivory work and peach satin; Ann Sothern goes for blue dots and taffeta upholstery; but Joan Crawford's forte is that big picture of Franchot Tone enthroned on her piano.

41

how to produce enough for the market but how to sell the amount produced in excess of immediate market demand.[4] A connection between this and the growth of 'idols of consumption' irresistibly suggests itself, the idols expressing in ideological form the economic imperatives of society – though the neatness of the connection should perhaps also make us wary.

Success

Albert McLean in his study of vaudeville, *American Vaudeville as Ritual*, has shown how this form was built around the myth of success. The cinema derived the star system from this theatre, and with it the emphasis on the star as a symbol of success.

The general meaning of the myth of success is that American society is sufficiently open for anyone to get to the top, regardless of rank. As Daniel Boorstin puts it: 'The film-star legend of the accidentally discovered soda-fountain girl who was quickly elevated to stardom soon took its place alongside the log-cabin-to-White-House legend as a leitmotif of American democratic folk-lore' (*The Image*, p. 162). The myth of success is grounded in the belief that the class system, the old-boy network, does not apply to America. However, one of the myth's ambiguities is whether success is possible for anyone, regardless of talent or application. Particularly as developed in the star system, the success myth tries to orchestrate several contradictory elements: that ordinariness is the hallmark of the star; that the system rewards talent and 'specialness'; that luck, 'breaks', which may happen to anyone typify the career of the star; and that hard work and professionalism are necessary for stardom. Some stars reconcile all four elements, while with others only some aspects are emphasised. Stardom as a whole holds all four things to be true.

The Hollywood 'biopic' illustrates in its charting of a star's rise to fame these contradictory cornerstones of the success myth. *The Jolson Story* is paradigmatic, managing to hold together all four elements: Jolson is just an ordinary guy from an ordinary Jewish family – he has no 'connections', no wealth; Jolson has an exceptionally beautiful voice, which captivates audiences (e.g. in the early scene where he is attending a vaudeville matinée, singing along in the audience, but so beautifully that everyone else stops to listen); it is just lucky that when a fellow artiste is too drunk to perform, Jolson goes on in his stead on the very night that two leading impresarios happen to be in the theatre; Jolson is a dedicated professional, always inventing new aspects to his act, taking on the challenge of movies, etc. What is suppressed in the film is the activity of the machinery of impresarios, agents, producers, backers – the 'business' of show business. Jolson never gets to be active in that sphere, he is as it were carried up through the machinery. Interestingly, even films *about* producers, such as *The Great Ziegfeld*, suppress examination of this.

The myth of success also suggests that success is worth having – in the form of conspicuous consumption. Barry King[5] has suggested that the stars imply that not only success but *money* is worth having, that the stars 'are models of rapid social mobility through salary'. What they earn (not class connections, breeding, education or 'artistic' achievement) gives them access to the world of good living, to that part of the élite that C. Wright Mills in *The Power Elite* calls 'café society'. Thus, argues King, the stars as successes can be seen as affirming 'in fantasised form' wage earning, selling one's labour power on the market, as a worthwhile goal in life.

Ordinariness – are stars 'different'?

One of the problems in coming to grips with the phenomenon of stardom is the extreme ambiguity/contradiction, already touched on, concerning the stars-as-ordinary and the stars-as-special. Are they just like you or me, or do consumption and success transform them into (or reflect) something different?

Violette Morin suggests that in the case of superstars ('Les Olympiens', the title of her article) they are believed to be different *in kind* from other people. She sees this as stemming from the way stars are treated as superlatives. Stars are always the most something-or-other in the world – the most beautiful, the most expensive, the most sexy. But because stars are 'dissolved' into this superlative, are indistinguishable from it, they *become* superlative, hence they seem to be of a different order of being, a different 'ontological category'. Their image becomes gradually generalised, so that from being, say, the most beautiful they become simply 'the greatest'.

One of Morin's examples is Elizabeth Taylor, and the points she makes about her are similar to those made by Alexander Walker in his chapter on Taylor in *Sex in the Movies*. Whereas other stars may stand for types of people, Taylor stands for the type 'star' – the most expensive, the most beautiful, and the most married and divorced, being in the world. Her love life plus her sheer expensiveness are what make her interesting, not her similarity to you or me.

Walker does not claim that Taylor is typical of all stars, and it is not clear how wide Morin would define her category of 'Olympien'. I am myself not persuaded that a belief in the ontological difference of the stars is at all widespread. Even the case of Taylor seems to me suspect, for it does not take into account the way in which her love life may be paradigmatic of the problems of heterosexual monogamy (see pp. 45–6), nor does it deal with, for instance, the 'common-ness' of her playing in *Cleopatra* or her particular success when playing 'bitch' roles.

The paradox of the extravagant lifestyle and success of the stars being perceived as ordinary may be explained in several ways. First, stars can be seen as ordinary people who live more expensively than the rest of us but are not essentially transformed by this. Second, the wealth and success of the stars can be seen as serving to isolate certain human qualities (the qualities they stand for), without the representation of those qualities being muddied by material considerations or problems. Both of these explanations fit with notions that human attributes exist independently of material circumstances. Stars may serve to legitimate such notions. Finally, stars represent what are taken to be people typical of this society; yet the types of people we assume characterise our society may nevertheless be singularly absent from our actual day-to-day experience of society; the specialness of stars may be then that they are the only ones around who are ordinary! (This is another way of conceptualising the charisma model discussed in Part One.)

The dream soured

Consumption and success, with their intimations of attendant values such as democracy, the open society, the value of the common/ordinary person, are the key notes of the image of stardom, but it would be wrong I think to ignore elements that run counter to this. Through the star system, failures of the dream are also represented.

Both consumption and success are from time to time shown to be wanting. Consumption can be characterised as wastefulness and decadence, while success may be short-lived or a psychological burden. The fan magazines carried articles such as 'The Tragedy of 15,000 Extras' (about people who don't get lucky breaks – 'Struggling to win a place in the cinema sun, they must put behind them forever their dreams of screen success'); 'They, Too, Were Stars' (about big stars who have declined into obscurity); 'Tragic Mansions' (about the superstitions that have grown up around the dwellings that stand as 'monuments of shattered careers'); and 'The Price They Pay for Fame' ('In Hollywood, Health, Friends, Beauty, Even Life Itself, Are Sacrificed on the Altar of Terrible Ambition').[6] These are all from the 30s. The themes of decadence, sexual licence and wanton extravagance emerged more strongly in the 50s and 60s, not only in fan magazines and the press but also in novels and even films set in Hollywood (e.g. *Valley of the Dolls*). Yet even the 'Tragic Mansions' article is subheaded 'the strange story of heartbreak houses in heartbreak town', implying that the idea of tragedy and suffering as endemic to Hollywood was commonplace. These perspectives, and much else of the image of Hollywood stardom, come across in this extract from the semi-pornographic pulp novel *Naked in Hollywood* by Bob Lucas. Carla is on her way to Hollywood, in the company of a second-rate agent named Herb:

> Carla could not recall the precise moment she decided she would become a star. As she grew older it seemed that the dream was born in her. She had no illusions about developing into a great actress. It was the glamour, the make-believe, the beauty, the adulation that were the increments of stardom that bedazzled her. She knew more about Hollywood – that part of it *she* was interested in – than Herb could ever tell her.
>
> The heart-shaped swimming pools, the Rolls Royces, the estates, the mink and ermine. Scotch and champagne – all this she knew as intimately as if she had created the Technicolor paradise where dwelt the screen gods and goddesses.
>
> Rita, Eva, Liz and Marilyn; Rock, Tab, Rip and Frankie – their real names, their broken romances and artistic triumphs, even their pet peeves and favourite foods were part of the movieland lore Carla had crammed into her brain. Books, fan magazines and newspaper columns were the source of her knowledge. Now she was headed for the promised land and had not the slightest doubt that one day in the not too distant future she would join the ranks of the immortals.
>
> Hollywood – it can break your heart, rip out your guts, Herb had warned. Carla was not impressed. To become a star, she was prepared to trade her immortal soul.

The recognition of Hollywood as a destroyer was perhaps most forcibly expressed by the deaths of Marilyn Monroe and Judy Garland, whose ruined lives and possible suicides were laid at the front door of Hollywood's soulless search for profits. Latterly, Monroe has also come to symbolise the exploitation of woman as spectacle in film.

Love

A central theme in all the fan magazines is love. This is achieved partly by the suppression of film-making as work and partly by the overriding sense of a world in which material problems have been settled and all that is left is relationships. These relationships are invariably heterosexual emotional/erotic ones – 'love' – and the magazines carry the implication that these are the only kinds of relationship of any interest to anyone – not relationships of, for instance, work, friendship, political comradeship or, surprisingly enough, parents and children. (Births are featured, it is true, but seldom the developing relationship of a star and her/his child.) One can see this as diverting mass attention away from such areas, as indeed it does, although it is also worth remembering that the majority of the audience was (and still is) placed within the structures and expectations of heterosexual relationships. What is interesting about the fan magazines is that, despite Edgar Morin's views in *The Stars*, love is often not so much celebrated as agonised over.

Morin sees the essence of the myth of stardom as love. For him, love – that is, intense heterosexual passion – forms the substance of writing about the stars, carrying with it the implication that life is about love. This has various manifestations, notably the obsession with physical beauty and youth (caught in the paradoxical pair of clichés that 'the heart is ageless' because it is 'always twenty', p. 175) and the magic of the kiss:

> The kiss is not only the key technique of love-making, nor the cinematic substitute for intercourse forbidden by censorship: it is the triumphant symbol of the role of the face and the soul in twentieth-century love. The kiss is of a piece with the eroticism of the face, both unknown in ancient times and still unknown in certain civilisations. The kiss is not only the discovery of a new tactile voluptuousness. It brings to life unconscious myths which identify the breath from one's mouth with the soul; it thus symbolises a communication or symbiosis of souls. The kiss is not only the piquancy in all Western films. It is the profound expression of a complex of love which eroticises the soul and mystifies the body. (p. 179)

Love then ceases to be a question of physical and practical relations and becomes a metaphysical experience.

Certainly this notion of love is promoted by films and by articles in the fan magazines, but what emerges far more strongly from an examination of the latter is a concern with the *problems* of love. Articles with titles like the following predominate: 'The Inside Story of Joan's Divorce' (Joan Bennett) (pp. 30–1); 'What's the Matter with Lombard? Is it true that her marriage to Clark Gable is responsible for Carole's recent unprecedented behaviour?' (pp. 56–7, 181–2); 'Tarzan Seeks a Divorce' (pp. 106–7, 196); 'Why is Bette Living without Her Husband – after Six Compatible Years?' (pp. 110–12, 198–9); and 'This Year's Love Market' (dealing with 'the marital mergers and tangles, the Blessed and not so Blessed Events of the past year') (pp. 114–15, 199–200). Frequently the attempt is made to blame Hollywood itself for the endless round of marriages, divorces, quarrels, etc. In 'What's Wrong with Hollywood Love?' (pp. 60–2, 183–4) it is suggested that romance cannot flourish under the glare of publicity ('Real Love Thrives on Romantic Secrecy', p. 61). (All quotes from Levin, *Hollywood and the*

45

Great Fan Magazine.) 'The High Price of Screen Love-Making', about the effect of on-screen romance on off-screen relationships, observes:

> Be reasonable. If you spent a day in Ronald Colman's arms, could you forget it? Or, if you are a man, and you had spent eight hours clasping and unclasping, kissing and un-kissing Marlene Dietrich – would you forget it? Could you go home to your sweet, thoughtful, kind loving mate and swear to yourself that such days had made no impression on you! (Gelman, *Photoplay Treasury*, pp. 200–1)

However, putting the blame on Hollywood seems to be a way of disguising the fact that what these articles are really doing is endlessly raking over the problems posed by notions of romance and passion within the institution of compulsory heterosexual monogamy. Thus in addition to the display of romantic-marital agony and the putting-the-blame-on-Hollywood pieces, there are also those that draw a 'lesson' from Hollywood romances – whether it be the value of endurance and suffering ('Don't Be Afraid of a Broken Heart' by Olivia de Havilland; Levin, *Hollywood and the Great Fan Magazines*, pp. 148–9) or tips on keeping a marriage together ('How to Stay Married to a Movie Star – Or to Anybody for that Matter'; Gelman, *Photoplay Treasury*, pp. 134–7 – here the connection with the readers' own problems is made explicit). And the divorce stories themselves also carry messages as to what a proper marriage really consists in, what a woman and a man's correct role and essential needs are. Thus we learn that Joan Bennett

> knew fame and wealth and popularity. She had a beautiful home. She had a husband who was brilliant, fascinating, devoted. She had every outward reason to be happy. But always, despite all that she said in her interviews and tried to believe herself, something was missing from her happiness. In her heart of hearts, she did not have the love that every woman lives to have. (Levin, *Hollywood and Great Fan Magazines*, p. 177)

Bette Davis's marriage to Harmon Nelson is breaking up because:

> It's asking a lot of a man to expect him to be the lesser half of a marital partnership indefinitely – the lesser in income, the lesser in prestige. No matter how much a man loves his wife, it's almost too much to expect him to be happy in the role of just-a-husband, in which people confuse him with just-a-gigolo, say he's living on her salary, and call him by her name with a 'Mr' attached. (p. 112)

5   Stars as Types

Despite the extravagant lifestyle of the stars, elements such as the rags-to-riches motif and romance as an enactment of the problems of heterosexual monogamy suggest that what is important about the stars, especially in their particularity, is their typicality or representativeness. Stars, in other words, relate to the social types of a society.

The notion of social type

The notion of a type – or rather a social type – has been developed by O. E. Klapp, and its ideological functioning is discussed in Part One. Here we are concerned with what social types are.

In *Heroes, Villains and Fools*, Klapp defines a social type as 'a collective norm of role behaviour formed and used by the group: an idealized concept of how people are expected to be or to act' (p. 11). It is a shared, recognisable, easily grasped image of how people are in society (with collective approval or disapproval built into it). On the basis of this Klapp proceeds to provide a typology of the prevalent social types in America, and he frequently provides stars' names to illustrate the different examples. Thus under 'heroes of social acceptability', he lists Will Rogers, Sophie Tucker and Perry Como, and under 'snobs' he lists Grace Kelly, Elizabeth Taylor, Ingrid Bergman, Zsa Zsa Gabor, Katharine Hepburn, Garbo and Davis. (A star may of course be listed under several different, even contradictory, categories reflecting both the ambiguity of their image and the differences in audience attitudes – thus Monroe for instance is used as an example of 'love queen' and 'simpleton', while Liberace is a 'charmer', a 'dude', a 'deformed fool' and a 'prude'.) The star both fulfils/incarnates the type and, by virtue of her/his idiosyncrasies, individuates it. (Critics committed to individualism as a philosophy or tenet of common sense tend to speak of the star's individuation of a type as 'transcendence'.)

There are problems with Klapp's work. Firstly, he does not explore the sources of social types, seeing them simply as 'collective representations'. He sees social types as positive and useful, as opposed to stereotypes, which are wrong and harmful because they deal with people 'outside of one's cultural world' – yet he never examines just who is within and without the 'cultural world'. That is, he never examines the possibility that the cultural world articulated by social types may represent the hegemony of one section of society over another. Yet it is clear from his typology that if you are not white, middle class, heterosexual and male you are not going to fit the cultural world too well – women only fit uneasily, whilst blacks, gays and even the working class hardly fit at all. (I have discussed this in 'Stereotyping'). Secondly, one does rather wonder where his categories come from, and how he arrived at them. There is no discussion of methodology in his writings.

Nevertheless, despite all this, one can I think *use* Klapp's typology as a description of prevalent social types, providing one conceptualises this ideologically (i.e. he is describing the type system subscribed to by the dominant groups in society) and of course allows for modifications and additions since he wrote the work.

Three prevalent social types as defined by Klapp are the Good Joe, the Tough Guy and the Pin-up.

The Good Joe

Klapp takes the 'good Joe' or 'good fellow' as 'the central theme of the American ethos'. He is 'friendly and easy going; he fits in and likes people; he never sets himself above others but goes along with the majority; he is a good sport – but, also a he-man who won't let anyone push him around where basic rights are concerned (p. 108). He is characterised by a 'dislike of bullies, snobs, authoritarians, and stuffed shirts; sympathy for the underdog; and liking for the good Joe or regular fellow who, for all his rough-and-ready air wouldn't try to dominate anybody, not even his wife' (ibid.). And is to be distinguished from squares, sissies and eggheads. Star examples are Perry Como, Bing Crosby, Lucille Ball, Will Rogers, Pat Boone, Eddie Cantor, Bob Hope and William Holden: 'Failure to understand the good Joe complex I believe is a major source of the misunderstanding of Americans by non-Americans' (p. 109).

Klapp is right to pinpoint the good Joe as a central American social type, although we should ask questions as to what it also supresses or conceals, at what cost this good Joe-ism is achieved. Although Klapp maintains that women can be good Joes, his description excludes this (women cannot be he-men, do not have wives . . .); and the implicit, taken-for-granted maleness of the type is reinforced by its opposition to sissies. Equally the opposition to eggheads can also be (as Klapp does hint) a resistance to any attempt to think outside of dominant beliefs and the *status quo.*

Although John Wayne is many things besides being a good Joe, a useful way of studying his image and the good Joe complex is to analyse his films in terms of the way his easy-going, self-contained, male stance is affirmed by (a) differentiating him from other characters (including women, villains and other men who don't 'fit' – see the Hawks Westerns with Wayne for an examination of how a man (or a woman) 'fits' and how s/he does not) and (b) dissolving ideological tensions in the 'unanswerable' good Joe normalcy of his presence (e.g. war films such as *The Sands of Iwo Jima* and *The Green Berets*). It needs to be added, of course, that not all Wayne's roles would meet this analysis, because of, for example, casting against type, villainous inversions, self-reflexive roles, etc., and that there are aspects of his image – his awkwardness with women, his 'hawkish' political stance – that relate ambivalently to it. They may undermine his good Joe-ism – but equally the latter may justify the former.

The Tough Guy

This type is discussed by Klapp in his examination of 'the deterioration of the hero' (see Part One). Klapp's examples are Mike Hammer, Ernest Hemingway and Little Caesar, but he could have supplemented this with film star examples such as James Cagney, James Bond/Sean Connery or Clint Eastwood. What concerns Klapp about this type is not its existence, but its ambivalence. A disapproved type of violence, aggressivity, callousness and brutality would serve a useful function, so 'it is as hero, not villain, that the tough guy is a problem' (p. 149). The tough guy embodies many values that can make him a hero:

> he is like a champ (you have to hand it to him, he licks the others). So long as this is so he has the almost universal appeal of the one who can't be beat. Since he usually fights others as tough as himself, he has a kind of fairness (whereas we should have little trouble rallying against a bully). Another thing that confuses the issues is that sometimes the only one who can beat him is another tough guy ... Tough guys often display loyalty to some limited ideal such as bravery or the 'gang code', which also makes it possible to sympathize with them. Finally, they may symbolize fundamental status needs, such as proving oneself or the common man struggling with bare knuckles to make good. (p. 150)

As a result he confuses the boundaries between good and bad behaviour, presses the antisocial into the service of the social and vice versa. In this instance, the type does not indicate collective approval, disapproval or ridicule, but confusion and ambiguity. Klapp's point is to bemoan the 'corruption of the hero', the collapsing of moral and social categories. I would tend to see it more in terms of the tough guy working through contradictions in the male role, which are disguised in more traditional types (cowboys, swashbucklers, war heroes). This is in some measure borne out by Patrick McGilligan's study of James Cagney (*Cagney: The Actor as Auteur*). He sees Cagney as embodying both the positive and the negative connotations of toughness:

> At worst, Cagney presents the liberal guise of fascist instincts: the drive to be on top, to go solo, to dominate women, to buy one hundred suits, to succeed – the competitive, individualist, capitalist ethic. At best, he represents an optimistic faith in circumstances, hope in the future, a gritty refusal to be dominated in any situation and a stubborn resistance to accepted social standards and *mores* that is exemplary. (p. 181)

What makes McGilligan's account useful is that he moves beyond this statement of an ambiguity or contradiction (which is where Klapp basically would leave it) to make connections with other specific aspects of cultural meaning and to explore the ideological complications these connections bring with them. Thus he links Cagney's toughness to notions of the working class and masculinity. The link with the working class is present equally in the early film roles, the biographies' stress on Cagney's New York East Side Irish background and in his known championing of 'radical' causes. Yet, as McGilligan shows, this working-class toughness – always problematic for middle-class and/or feminist socialists – was easily pressed into the service of right-wing themes in the later films, so that by the time of *One, Two, Three* (1961) 'all the characteristics of the younger Cagney [are] put to the service of the older Cagney persona – patriotic, rightist and complacent' (p. 192). The link between toughness and maleness is yet more ambiguous. Cagney was, says McGilligan, 'outrageously masculine in his every action'. As a result his relations with women are problematic. It is not so much the question of violence (the grapefruit in Mae Clarke's face in *The Public Enemy* – the only caress gesture in his repertoire, a gentle prod from a clenched fist), as the notion that 'Only a woman who is tough [tough like Cagney/tough like a man] is a fitting mate for the male Cagney' (p. 169). In his career only Joan Blondell and Ann Sheridan really come up to this, forming with Cagney examples of the equal heterosexual couple that Molly Haskell admires (on Cagney in particular see her 'Partners in Crime and Conversion'). Quite how one assesses these instances (cf. the Hawksian woman's masculinisation) – as images of equality or as an inability to conceive the feminine – I will leave for now.

A further aspect of the link of tough guy/Cagney with maleness is the role of the mother. As McGilligan suggests, Cagney's closeness (onscreen) to his mother is important because it 'exonerated the nastier actions of the Cagney character'; at the same time, the almost fanatical devotion of the two has an implicit neurosis, so that films in which it is emphasised, such as *Sinner's Holiday, The Public Enemy* and *White Heat*,'show the perversion of the close American family (perhaps unintentionally), not how wonderful such a family is' (p. 109). McGilligan's study is an example of the way that, by following through the chains of association of a star's incarnation of a social type, some of the contradictions elided in that type can be explored.

The Pin-Up

As already mentioned, Klapp's typology is noticeably short on women. He points out that, because 'It is still a man's world when it comes to handing out the medals' (*Heroes, Villains and Fools*, p. 97), there are particularly few women hero types, resulting in the dilemma of modern woman's 'loss of identity' (p. 98). (He does not get very far in asking why this should be so – but he did observe it at a time when few other writers were doing so.) It is interesting to note that when he does propose a predominantly female type, it is one that exists primarily in media representation – the pin-up. (He could perhaps have used the term 'glamour girl'.)

Although he does include some men in his list of synonyms of the pin-up, the emphasis is on women:

> Such a model of bodily perfection need be neither a great lover nor a social lion. Photogenic perfection is enough. It may be surprising to say that a pin-up need not be unusual even in looks (many people have complained of the monotony of American cheesecake and Hollywood beauty). Fashion, cosmetology, and hair styling actually increase the resemblance of pin-up types. (p. 39)

One might say, with heroes like that, who needs villains and fools? As a social model, the pin-up promotes surface appearance and depersonalisation, woman as sexual spectacle and sex object.

The pin-up is an important part of the way a star's image is built up, but we should not confuse this with the pin-up as a social type. All the stars we are concentrating on in this study, men as well as women, have had pin-up photographs taken and used, but of these only Monroe and Fonda were 'pin-ups'. They conformed, in their pin-up photos, to the conventions described by Thomas B. Hess in 'Pinup and Icon':

> By the 1940s, the pin-up image was defined with canonical strictness. First of all, there was the 'pin-up girl' herself. She had to be the healthy, American, cheerleader type – button-nosed, wide-eyed, long-legged, ample hips and breasts, and above all with the open, friendly smile that discloses perfect, even, white teeth. Then there is her costume and pose. These must be inviting but not seducing; affectionate but not passionate, revealing by suggestion while concealing in fact. The legs are carefully posed so that not too much of the inner thigh is shown; the navel is covered and so are most of the breasts except for the famous millimeters of 'cleavage'. The body is evident beneath the costume, but not its details – the bulges of nipples or of the *mons veneris* are scrupulously hidden. There is a dialectical pressure at work, between the voyeuristic public which wants to see more and more, and that same public which, in its social function, supports codes and laws that ban any such revelations. Caught between these two forces, the image tends towards an almost Byzantine rigidity, and assumes some of the symbolizing force of an icon. The pin-up girl and the Virgin in Majesty both are instantly legible visual images of the comforting and commonplace which is also ideal, and thus unattainable. (p. 227)

Much of the sexual charge of the image is carried by symbolism of various kinds. Hess sees this as produced by censorship and puritanism, forbidding any more direct representation of sexuality. A reading of this following Laura Mulvey's analysis in 'Visual Pleasure and Narrative Cinema' would, on the other hand, put a different emphasis – the pin-up as woman represents the possibility of castration for the male viewer (as do all women for him); to avoid this, a substitute phallus is provided in the form of sexual symbols (including various obviously phallic kinds) or fetishes. Unless one chooses to accept that all fetishism is to be explained in terms of phallic substitution, I am not sure how far I would go along with this. Sexual imagery may be fetishistic simply in the sense of being a heightening of erotic/sensual surfaces (fur, leather, satin, etc. being 'more like skin than skin'); at the same time it also links the woman to other images of power and wealth (e.g. fur, etc. as expensive fabrics; frequent linkage to Art, *haute couture*, leisure, etc.). She may thus be seen as an example of wealth (which the viewer in his fantasy possesses), or as being something that can be obtained through wealth.

In terms of films, the pin-up typing of Monroe and Fonda can be analysed in terms of their visual presentation, how they are kept (or not) within the conventions described above and how the association of images pointed to in the last paragraph is developed. Mulvey also indicates a further aspect for analysis. She suggests that one of the aesthetic consequences of woman as spectacle in film is a tension in films centred on glamorous women stars between the narrative (we want to know what happens next) and the spectacle (we want to stop and look at the woman – Mulvey assumes that the only audience position is constituted in terms of male heterosexuality). It is worth examining a film like *Gentlemen Prefer Blondes* or *Barbarella* to see how far this is true, and how they 'manage' this tension.

Alternative or subversive types

Most types discussed by Klapp, and indeed most stars discussed as social types, are seen as representing dominant values in society, by affirming what those values are in the 'hero' types (including those values that are relatively appropriate to men and women) and by denouncing other values in the villain and fool types. Klapp argues, however, that there may also be other types that express discontent with or rejection of dominant values. These types will also be grounded in a normative world-view, but as an alternative to the dominant one.

Klapp calls these other types 'anomic types', and his basic examples are 'beat' heroes and 'square' villains and fools. The concept of 'anomie' was developed in sociological theory deriving from Durkheim. Unlike alienation, a term with which it often confused, anomie is not seen as stemming from inequalities and struggles between social groups (classes, genders, races, minorities). To put the difference between the concepts crudely, people are said to feel 'anomic' because they do not fit in with prevailing norms and/or because they see the latter's pointlessness, whereas people are said to feel 'alienated' because the goals of society and the norms which carry them are the goals and norms of groups other than those to which the people in question belong. You feel anomic because you are outside society in general; you feel alienated because you are outside the ruling groups in society. From a Marxist perspective, then, Klapp's notion of 'anomic types' is problematic because it is based on the notion of anomie and hence is reducible to an inescapable, quasi-metaphysical *Angst* that does not challenge existing power relations in society. At the same time, the notion of types alternative, or in opposition, to types incarnating dominant values is suggestive and worth pursuing. What we have to examine is whether these types are anomic or alienated, in the senses just defined, and to ask whether these represent real challenges to the *status quo* and the dominant ideology or are simply 'holidays' from it.

The Rebel

The type that springs most readily to mind in this context is 'the rebel'. In her article 'The Rebel Hero', a brief survey of this type, Sheila Whitaker lists John Garfield, Montgomery Clift, Marlon Brando, James Dean, Albert Finney, Paul Newman, Steve McQueen and Jane Fonda as representative of the rebel hero. She stresses different relations of rebellion – the immigrant (Garfield), the rebel against his own class (Clift), generation gap rebels (Brando, Dean), the anti-hero (Newman, McQueen, Finney) and the politically conscious rebel (Fonda). The question with these stars is to what extent do they really embody oppositional views (and in what terms)? We can break this question into two parts. First, are they informed by concepts of anomie or alienation? (I do not mean to imply that they or those responsible for their image were students of sociology; but sociological concepts like anomie and alienation can be seen as theoretical abstractions of widely known beliefs and understandings – the common sense and political practice of society throw up the theoretical constructs of sociology which enable us to see that sense and that practice with greater clarity.) Are they grounded in material categories or in a generalised *Angst*? The answer does not seem to be clear cut. Immigration and youth are material categories, and one can see Finney and Fonda as embodying working-class and women's situations respectively. However, not all the rebels Whitaker lists can be seen in similar terms, nor is it clear that the rebellion of those who can is actually cast in terms of that material situation. Are Garfield's films *about* the oppression of immigrants? Is Finney in *Saturday Night and Sunday Morning* a rebel against the middle class? Brando, Dean and Fonda do expressly articulate the situation of youth and women, and could be said to be 'alienated' rebels to that degree.

Second, do these stars, in expressing rebellion, heavily promote it or recuperate it? In answering this question, we would do as well to remember that in terms of 'effect' we do not really know whether Garfield *et al.* made people more rebellious or not. What we can examine is the degree to which the image points to the legitimacy of rebellion or its inadequacy. In general, I would suggest it does the latter, because of the characteristics of the *type* to which the stars belong and because of the film *narratives* in which they are placed. *The type itself* is problematic because firstly, most of the heroes are either actually anomic or largely so, so that in the case of those who are not, the alienated/materialist elements are liable to be subsumed under anomie. (Garfield, Finney and Fonda are not rebelling as immigrant, worker and woman respectively, but because they don't 'fit' even among immigrants, workers and women.) Secondly, the heavy emphasis on youth in the type carries with it the notion of the 'passing phase', the 'inevitable', 'natural' rebellion (often shored up with garbled notions of the Oedipus complex). Youth is the ideal material term on which to displace social discontent, since young people always get older (and 'grow up'). Thus the rebellion of Garfield, Finney or Fonda can be seen as symptomatic of their youth rather than anything else. This process of displacement reflects that analysed in *Resistance through Rituals*,[7] whereby press reaction to youth movements of the 50s and 60s is shown to have consistently avoided recognising these movements as class-specific. Thirdly, the type is very little connected to the basic structures of society. Class really only has relevance in the case of Finney. Most of the heroes are male in very traditional ways (often enforced by generic associations from the Western and the thriller), though I would agree with Jack Babuscio that Clift and Dean, who were both gay, did something to launch a non-macho image of a man.[8] Fourthly, inarticulacy (a symptom of anomie) is the defining characteristic of the type, and it inhibits him/her from any analysis of the situation. (Fonda is, of course, the exception to the last two points. It may be that I am wrong to follow Whitaker's inclusion of her alongside Garfield *et al.* It may be that the cinematic rebel type is defined by being male and inarticulate, and that Fonda is a different type altogether. At the same time, many of the other points that can be made about the 'rebelliousness' of the rebel type do seem applicable to her attempt to embody radical attitudes.) The *narratives* of the films in which these stars appeared tend to recuperate rather than promote the rebellion they embody. This is partly due to the way in which they tend to develop the problem of the hero as an individual, quasi-psychological problem. The fault is liable to be located in him/her and not in the society in which s/he lives (e.g. *The Wild One, Klute*). When there is some suggestion that the problem lies outside the hero, then this problem is often defined as the failure of some persons in her/his world to live up to traditional concepts and dominant values. James Dean's two 'youth' films, *Rebel without a Cause* and *East of Eden*, seem to me to indicate that the character played by Dean has problems that are not only his psychological hang-up but in the family situation in which he lives. This does not mean, however, that the films are critical of the family as an institution, but rather of the failure of the parents of the Dean character to fulfil adequately their familial roles. In *Rebel* he has too weak a father, in *Eden* too charismatic a mother. In other words, the rebellion against family is recuperated because it is against an inadequate family rather than the family as a social institution.

The Independent Woman

Perhaps one of the reasons for the almost implacable recuperation of the rebel type is that s/he is too obviously oppositional to social values. A more covert example is the independent woman type (or series of types) embodied by Davis, Katharine Hepburn, Barbara Stanwyck, Rosalind Russell, Joan Crawford and others during the 30s and 40s. Do these stars represent a more complete alternative or opposition to dominant values?

In *From Reverence to Rape*, Molly Haskell suggests a distinction within these stars between the superfemale and the superwoman. (The same star may be both types at different points in her career.) The superfemale is

> a woman who, while exceedingly 'feminine' and flirtatious, is too ambitious and intelligent for the docile role society has decreed she play. ... She remains within traditional society, but having no worthwhile project for her creative energies, turns them onto the only available material – the people around her – with demonic results. (p. 214)

The chief example of this category is Bette Davis, particularly in *Of Human Bondage, Jezebel, The Little Foxes, Dangerous, Dark Victory* and *Mr Skeffington*. The superwoman is

> a woman who, like the superfemale, has a high degree of intelligence or imagination, but instead of exploiting her femininity, adopts male characteristics in order to enjoy male prerogatives, or merely to survive. (ibid.)

The chief examples here are Joan Crawford as Vienna (in *Johnny Guitar*) and Katharine Hepburn.

This is a suggestive distinction, although it could do with some working-up to be made more directly usable. Is it just a question of the difference between roles within and without the domestic arena? Are there characteristic narrative patterns that structure the representation of the two types? What is the relationship between the star as a total image and the specific character constructed in given films? Are the types carried by physical features, iconography of dress and gesture, modes of performance? These are genuine questions, not disguised attacks on Haskell's distinction. Answering them would be a way of clarifying the distinction and how it operates.

There is a second order of problems with the distinction, and that is how the superfemale or the superwoman actually embodies a radical alternative/opposition to prevalent female types. The 'superfemale' seems inevitably to be shown as demonic in her actions, and it is hard to distinguish her too firmly from other

54

'strong', 'magnetic' types such as the 'bitch' (Davis), the *femme fatale* and the intellectual/aristocratic type (Hepburn), all of which strongly discount the value of female strength and intelligence. At most, the superfemale type seems capable of articulating the damage done when a person of great capacities is confined to a demeaning or over-restricted world.

The superwoman on the other hand raises a more complex set of problems. What exactly is going on when a female character 'adopts male characteristics'? There are perhaps two ways of understanding this.

On the one hand, one can recognise that 'characteristics' of personality are not gender-specific (there is nothing innately male about aggressiveness or innately female about gentleness), but that, for whatever historical-cultural reasons, certain characteristics are associated with one gender rather than the other and that, as a consequence, individual women and men have a great deal invested (in terms of their identities as women and men) in preserving the association between such-and-such a characteristic and one gender or the other. This means that attempts to alter this, to cross gender barriers, to adopt the characteristics associated with the opposite sex, is a matter of negotiation, of working out a way of doing this which both frees people from the constructions of gender-roles and yet does not utterly damage their self-identities. This seems to be the kind of process that Haskell especially admires in Katharine Hepburn. In her relationship with Spencer Tracy, 'Tracy can be humiliated and still rebound without (too much) loss of ego. Hepburn occasionally can defer to him and still not lose her identity' (p. 230). More generally, Hepburn's superwoman

> is able to achieve her ends in a man's world, to insist on her intelligence, to insist on using it, and yet be able to 'dwindle', like Millamant in *The Way of the World*, 'into marriage', but only after an equal bargain has been struck of conditions mutually agreed on. (p. 230)

As Claire Johnston has pointed out, the emphasis in Haskell on 'reconciliation between men and women … flexibility of role playing, "love" and camaraderie' ignores 'the question of the nuclear family [that] has been central to the feminist critique of patriarchal culture' ('Feminist Politics and Film History', p. 121), and treats the problem simply as people deciding to relate better to each other rather than analysing what prevents this and where the roles come from. However, perhaps as a model of how relationships between the sexes might be conducted (a practical ideal rather than a romantic one), as a 'utopian' expression (telling us where we want to get to, rather than how to get there), the negotiated adoption of 'male characteristics' celebrated by Haskell could be acceptable as an alternative/oppositional statement. As she develops it, however, there are I think two further problems. One is that the women seem to have to do all the running, make all the moves (including most of the concessions); it might be worth examining one of the Tracy/Hepburn films to see how far Tracy is prepared to adopt 'female characteristics'. The second is that there is a strain of anti-gayness in her writing, which suggests that the ideal relationship between women and men is also the ideal human relationship – in other words, Haskell is heterosexually normative (or heterosexist).

On the other hand, some feminist theory suggests that in a patriarchal culture there is no such thing as 'the female', only the non-male.[9] That is to say that films are unable to conceive of, or to cope with, anything that is female, which means in effect that the only way a woman can be accepted as a person (except as a demeaned, and still ultimately threatening, sexual object) is for her to become 'non-male': that is, without gender. Although Haskell herself does not work within these terms, some of her accounts of the superwoman stars do support it. Thus the relationship between Joan Blondell and James Cagney in *Blonde Crazy* is based on 'the unspoken understanding that a woman is every bit the "gentleman" – or nongentleman – as a man is and can match him in wits and guts and maybe even surpass him' (p. 130). And she quotes a very revealing piece of dialogue from the Rosalind Russell film *Take a Letter, Darling*, in which Robert Benchley, her boss, complains that her competitors – all men – don't understand her:

'They don't know the difference between a woman and a ...'
'A what?' Russell asks.
'I don't know,' Benchley replies, 'there's no name for you.'

The Hawks women whom Haskell admires are accepted into the male group, as soon as they cease to be womanly – Jean Arthur in *Only Angels Have Wings* is a striking case in point. What seems to me to be happening in the narrative of these films is that there is a contempt for female characteristics yet an obligation to have woman characters. This problem is resolved in the person of the woman who becomes a man (almost). What one thinks about this procedure depends upon one's politics, and in particular whether one does despise female characteristics or whether one sees them as, certainly, oppressed and not, potentially anyway, gender-specific, yet still none the less representing real strengths and values that form the basis and power of the women's movement.

The 'independence' of the stars under consideration here is expressed both in the characters they play and in what was reported about them in magazines (e.g. Davis's fight with Warner Bros. over her contract, Hepburn's intellectual background, Crawford's struggle to the top from a background of poverty). Do the narratives of the films they appear in legitimate and promote this image, or undermine it?

The endings of the films usually involve a 'climb-down' on the part of the star. As Elizabeth Dalton observes, in a survey of Warner Bros. films about working women: 'A woman could be resourceful, intelligent, even cynical, for 59 minutes but in the last two, she would realise that it was love and marriage that she really wanted' ('Women at Work: Warners in the Thirties', p. 17). This dénouement may also involve punishment and humiliation for the star – not only at the hands of the male character(s), but at the hands of the film itself. In *His Girl Friday*,* when Rosalind Russell corners the sheriff who wants to avoid her questions, she is filmed in a way that makes her look comic, not resourceful. *Mildred Pierce** blames Mildred/Crawford for the death of her youngest daughter; despite the fact that the latter is in the care of her father at the time, the film manages to put the blame onto Mildred/Crawford for her independence. Though there are exceptions to the rule, the narratives do not appear to legitimise independence.

* These episodes are included in BFI study extracts from the films.

Haskell, however, has argued that, in a sense, these endings do not matter. What we remember is the independence not the climb-down or the humiliation:

> We see the June bride played by Bette Davis surrender her independence at the altar; the actress played by Margaret Sullavan in *The Moon's Our Home* submit to the straitjacket in which Henry Fonda enfolds and symbolically subjugates her; Katharine Hepburn's Alice Adams achieve her highest ambitions in the arms of Fred MacMurray; Rosalind Russell as an advertising executive in *Take A Letter, Darling* find happiness in the same arms; Joan Crawford as the head of a trucking firm in *They All Kissed The Bride* go weak at the knees at the sight of labor leader played by Melvyn Douglas. And yet we remember Bette Davis not as the blushing bride but as the aggressive reporter and sometime-bitch; Margaret Sullavan leading Fonda on a wild-goose chase through the backwoods of Vermont; Katharine Hepburn standing on the 'secretarial stairway' to independence; Rosalind Russell giving MacMurray the eye as her prospective secretary; and Joan Crawford looking about as wobbly as the Statue of Liberty. (*From Reverence to Rape*, pp. 3–4)

Of course, we cannot know what 'we' – the audience in general – remember, but I think one could argue that in terms of emphasis, weighting within the film, performance, *mise en scène*, etc. the independence elements are stronger, more vivid, than the climb-down resolutions. Two observations support this. One, unlike the rebels, the narratives do not seem invariably to point to inadequacies in the psychology of either the independent woman stars or the people of their immediate environment to explain, and explain away, their independence. Two, because we are dealing with stars, and not just fictional characters, the specific details of what happens in the plot of the film may matter less than the 'personality' that the film as a whole reveals – the star phenomenon emphasises the kind of person the star is rather than the specific circumstances of particular roles.

Marjorie Rosen in *Popcorn Venus* argues that the narratives of the independent woman films always show the star's independence and intelligence in the service of men. It is men who define the social goals and norms; it is to get a man, or for love of a man, that the star acts as she does: 'It's unfortunate that Hollywood could not visualize a woman of mental acumen unless she was fixing up a mess her man/boss had made, covering a scoop to prove herself to a man, or deftly forging a life of dishonesty' (p. 147). It's hard to say how true this really is. Many of the films are about the star's independence *threatening* her relationship with the man she loves, but the pattern suggested by Rosen may also operate, thus effectively denying the woman's independence any autonomy. *Now, Voyager* might be a case in point – the narrative details Davis's liberation from the dowdy spinster role imposed on her, yet it is a man, a psychiatrist (Claude Rains), who 'gives' her the 'means' to be free, and a man (Paul Henreid) who provides her with her ultimate project in life, namely, his daughter. While this element is certainly there, it does not, in my opinion, totally undermine the progressive elements in the film. It is just one of the contradictions of the film, and I suspect this narrative aspect, when it is there, often largely acts as a contradiction rather than an utter denial of 'independence'.

As Molly Haskell herself has pointed out, the independent women stars are often signalled as being exceptional or extraordinary women. Dietrich, Hepburn, Rosalind Russell, Davis, all have strong upper-class, intellectual or, in the case of

Dietrich, exotic associations which make them 'exceptions to the rule, the aristocrats of their sex' (*From Reverence to Rape*, p. 160). Haskell argues this 'weakens their political value'. I am not myself so sure of this. All stars are in one way or another exceptional, just as they are all ordinary. The un-extraordinary 'girl next door' types like June Allyson, Doris Day and Betty Grable are no less characteristic of the star phenomenon than are extraordinary types like Hepburn *et al.* It's worth remembering too that other independent women stars – Barbara Stanwyck, Ann Sheridan, Claire Trevor – do not carry upper-class or intellectual associations.

Many of the stars in the independent woman category were characterised by sexual ambiguity in their appearance and presentation. This can be an aspect of their physical attributes – the broad shoulders of Joan Crawford and Greta Garbo, Katharine Hepburn's height, the 'tough' face of Barbara Stanwyck, Bette Davis's strutting walk – which, in the case of Crawford, could also be exaggerated by the way she was dressed. It can also be a play on costume, sequences of cross-dressing such as:

> Dietrich in white tie and tails, Garbo as the lesbian Queen Christina (although with 'cover' romance), Eleanor Powell in top hat and tails for her tap numbers, and Katharine Hepburn as the Peter Pan-like Sylvia Scarlett; all introduced tantalizing notes of sexual ambiguity that became permanent accretions to their screen identities. (Haskell, p. 132).

This could of course be seen as another instance of cinema being unable to cope with the female and so presenting splendid women as men. However, recent discussion of the cinema in relation to homosexuality has suggested a different emphasis. Janet Meyers and Caroline Sheldon see these stars as an oblique expression of lesbianism:

> The qualities they projected of being inscrutable to the men in the films and aloof, passionate, direct, could not be missed. They are all strong, tough and yet genuinely tender. In short, though rarely permitted to hint it, they are lesbians. (Janet Meyers, 'Dyke Goes to the Movies, p. 37)

Sheldon suggests in 'Lesbians and Film: Some Thoughts' that if we understand lesbianism, not necessarily in purely sexual terms, but in terms of 'woman-identification', then these stars are lesbian. They are 'women who define themselves in their own terms ... playing parts in which they are comparatively independent of domestic expectations and of men'. Meyers and Sheldon are working within a lesbian feminist political perspective that will not be acceptable to many (including many feminists), but their emphasis is a useful corrective to Haskell's heterosexist assumptions. Both recognise that lesbianism (in the erotic sense) may be used in film for the titillation of heterosexual men, but the sense of aloofness, 'otherness', and non-domesticity combined with sometimes quite overtly erotic relationships with women could be seen as subversive of the heterosexual male's pleasure at being titillated.

Jack Babuscio and I have suggested a different emphasis to this, whereby the cross-dressing and play on sexual roles can be seen as a way of heightening the fact that the sex roles are *only* roles and not innate or instinctual personal features. This may be seen as part of the phenomenon of camp in the cinema:

> Camp, by focusing on the outward appearances of role, implies that roles and, in particular, sex roles are superficial – a matter of style ... Finding stars camp is not to mock them ... It is more a way of poking fun at the whole cosmology of restrictive sex roles and sexual identifications which our society uses to oppress its women and repress its men – including those on screen. (Jack Babuscio, 'Camp and the Gay Sensibility', pp. 44, 46)[10]

In this respect then, independent-woman type stars make explicit the life-as-theatre metaphor which underpins the star phenomenon. This can be seen especially in the work of Bette Davis. Davis is one of the most 'mannered' of the independent women – or any other – stars, yet this effectively foregrounds manners as a social code. With most stars, their particular manner is seen as a spontaneous emanation of the personality; but Davis is hard to treat in the same way since her manner is so obviously 'put on'. In certain films – *Jezebel, The Little Foxes, Dark Victory, Now, Voyager, All About Eve* – this sense of the artifice of social performance meshes with notions of social expectations and requirements, of women and/or of class. (Cf. the discussion in Part Three below of her performance in *The Little Foxes*. Another similar instance is Barbra Streisand. I have discussed the possibly subversive effect of her performance in my article, '*The Way We Were*' in *Movie*, no. 22.)

6 Stars as Specific Images

Stars embody social types, but star images are always more complex and specific than types. Types are, as it were, the ground on which a particular star's image is constructed. This image is found across a range of media texts. I want in this chapter to discuss the nature of the different categories into which these texts fall, and then to consider, generally and through an extended example, Jane Fonda, how these texts construct a specific star image.

A star image is made out of media texts that can be grouped together as *promotion, publicity, films* and *criticism* and *commentaries.*

Promotion

This refers to texts which were produced as part of the deliberate creation/ manufacture of a particular image or image-context for a particular star. It includes (i) material concerned directly with the star in question – studio announcements, press hand-outs (including potted biographies), fan club publications (which were largely controlled by the studios), pin-ups, fashion pictures, ads in which stars endorse a given merchandise, public appearances (e.g. at premieres, as recorded on film or in the press); and (ii) material promoting the star in a particular film – hoardings, magazine ads, trailers, etc. Thomas B. Harris has described this in some detail in 'The Building of Popular Images'.

Promotion is probably the most straightforward of all the texts which construct a star image, in that it is the most deliberate, direct, intentioned and self-conscious (which is not to say that it is by any means entirely any of those things).

Promotion can get things wrong. Early promotion may not push the aspects of the performer which were subsequently to make them a star (e.g. both Davis and Monroe were promoted as routine pin-up starlets to begin with). However, this is more the exception than the rule, and either way promotion can be taken as an indicator of the studio's (or its promotion department's), agent's or star's conception of a given star image.

On occasion, promotion of a film may be deliberately untrue to the film itself, in the interests of promoting the star's image (e.g. Marlon Brando's attempts to escape the 'Stanley Kowalski' image of *A Streetcar Named Desire* by playing Napoleon in *Désirée* and Mark Antony in *Julius Caesar* did not deter the promoters of those films from billing his roles in Kowalski-esque terms – see the discussion by Hollis Alpert in his *The Dreams and the Dreamers,* 'Marlon Brando and the Ghost of Stanley Kowalski').

Publicity

This is theoretically distinct from promotion in that it is not, or does not appear to be, *deliberate* image-making. It is 'what the press finds out', 'what the star lets slip in an interview', and is found in the press and magazines (not only the strictly film ones), radio and television interviews, and the gossip columns. In practice, much of this too was controlled by the studios or the star's agent, but it did not appear to be, and in certain cases (e.g. Ingrid Bergman's 'illegitimate' child by Roberto Rossellini) it clearly was not. The only cases where one can be fairly certain of genuine publicity are the scandals: Fatty Arbuckle's rape case, Ingrid Bergman's child, the murder of Lana Turner's gigolo boyfriend, Robert Mitchum's dope charge, Judy Garland's drunken breakdowns, Elizabeth Taylor's 'breaking up' of Debbie Reynolds's marriage with Eddie Fisher. Scandals can harm a career (Arbuckle permanently, Bergman temporarily) or alternatively give it a new lease of life (Turner, Mitchum, Taylor). An unnamed publicity man is quoted by Hollis Alpert to suggest a link between scandal and success and glamour:

> The stars are losing their glamour. It's next to impossible to get Burt Lancaster into columns these days. He's too serious. The public prefers its stars to behave a little crazy. Look what that dope party did for Bob Mitchum! Look how Deborah Kerr's divorce troubles sent her price way up! Who wants to form a fan club for a businessman? (*The Dreams and the Dreamers*, p. 39)

The importance of publicity is that, in its apparent or actual escape from the image that Hollywood is trying to promote, it seems more 'authentic'. It is thus often taken to give a privileged access to the real person of the star. It is also the place where one can read tensions between the star-as-person and her/his image, tensions which at another level become themselves crucial to the image (e.g. Marilyn Monroe's attempts to be considered something other than a dumb blonde sex object, Robert Redford's 'loner' shunning of the attention his star status attracts).

Films

Inevitably, the films have a distinct and privileged place in a star's image. It is after all *film* stars that we are considering – their celebrity is defined by the fact of their appearing in films. However, the star is also a phenomenon of cinema (which as a business could make money from stars in additional ways to having them make films, e.g. in advertising, the fan industry, personal appearances) and of general social meanings, and there are instances of stars whose films may actually be less important than other aspects of their career. Brigitte Bardot is a case in point, and Zsa Zsa Gabor is a film star whose films only a dedicated buff could name. The deaths of Montgomery Clift, James Dean, Marilyn Monroe and Judy Garland (and the premature retirement of Greta Garbo) may be as significant as the films they made, while Lana Turner's later films were largely a mere illustration of her life. It may be as pin-ups that Betty Grable and Rita Hayworth are really important, and as recording stars that Frank Sinatra and Bing Crosby really matter. While in general films are the most important of the texts, one should bear these points in mind when, as here, the focus is the star's total image rather than, as in Part Three, the role of that image in the films.

Particularly important is the notion of the *vehicle*. Films were often built around star images. Stories might be written expressly to feature a given star, or books might be bought for production with a star in mind. Sometimes alterations to the story might be effected in order to preserve the star's image. This is what is implied by the term 'star vehicle' (a term actually used by Hollywood itself).

The vehicle might provide a character of the type associated with the star (e.g. Monroe's 'dumb blonde' roles, Garbo's melancholic romantic roles); a situation, setting or generic context associated with the star (e.g. Garbo in relationships with married men, Wayne in Westerns; as Colin McArthur has noted of stars of gangster films, they 'seem to gather within themselves the qualities of the genre ... so that the violence, suffering and *Angst* of the films is restated in their faces, physical presence, movement and speech' (*Underworld USA*, p. 24)); or opportunities for the star to do her/his thing (most obviously in the case of musical stars – e.g. a wistful solo number for Judy Garland, an extended ballet sequence for Gene Kelly – but also, for instance, opportunities to display Monroe's body and wiggle walk, scenes of action in Wayne's films). Vehicles are important as much for what conventions they set up as for how they develop them, for their ingredients as for their realisation. In certain respects, a set of star vehicles is rather like a film genre such as the Western, the musical or the gangster film. As with genres proper, one can discern across a star's vehicles continuities of iconography (e.g. how they are dressed, made-up and coiffed, performance mannerisms, the settings with which they are associated), visual style (e.g. how they are lit, photographed, placed within the frame) and structure (e.g. their role in the plot, their function in the film's symbolic pattern). (For further discussion of performance and structure, see chapter 8). Of course, not all films made by a star are vehicles, but looking at their films in terms of vehicles draws attention to those films that do not 'fit', that constitute inflections, exceptions to, subversions of the vehicle pattern and the star image. (For further consideration of genre in film, see Edward Buscombe, 'The Idea of Genre in the American Cinema'; the section on 'Genre Criticism' in Bill Nichols, *Movies and Methods*; and Steve Neale, *Genre*.)

One needs also to consider the star's *filmic presentation*, the specific ways in which the star appears, performs and is used in individual films. This is dealt with in Part Three.

Criticism and commentaries

This refers to what was said or written about the star in terms of appreciation or interpretation by critics and writers. It covers contemporary and subsequent writings (including obituaries and other material written after a star's death or retirement), and is found in film reviews, books on films and indeed in almost any kind of writing dealing, fictitiously or otherwise, with the contemporary scene. To this can be added film, radio and television profiles of stars. These always appear after the initial promotion and film-making of a star, although they may act back on subsequent promotion and film activity (e.g. the response of critics to Davis in *Of Human Bondage* legitimated her demand for 'strong' roles; the intellectuals' 'discovery' of Monroe is discernible in the increasingly self-reflexive nature of her last films). We need to distinguish between criticism and commentaries that did that, and those that have been elaborated after the star's active involvement in film-making. The latter may suggest an interpretation of the star at odds with the star's contemporary image (e.g. today's cult of Humphrey Bogart and Monroe – do we see more worldly wisdom in him, more tragic consciousness in her?).

Criticism and commentaries are oddly situated in the star's image. They are media products, part of the cinematic machine, yet it is commonly held that they are to be placed on the side of the audience – the consumers of media texts – rather than that of the industry – the producers of media texts. Critics and commentators are often taken to express rather than to construct the response to a star, and indeed on occasion they may well be expressing a widely held, pre-existing sentiment or view about a star. More frequently, however, they contribute to the shaping of 'public opinion' about a star (and the relationship of what the media call 'public opinion' to the opinion of the public must always remain problematic). Despite this, critics and commentators do not operate in the same space as those who construct the image in promotion and films. This gap between on the one hand promotional and filmic construction of the star image (which is further complicated by the highly ambivalent way publicity relates to promotion and films) and on the other the role of criticism and commentaries in that construction is a real one, and accounts for both the complexity, contradictoriness and 'polysemy' of the star image and also for the capacity of critical opinion to contribute to shifts in careers such as those of Davis and Monroe noted above.

A specific image: Jane Fonda

I want in a moment to look at the way these various media texts come together to form a particular star image, but before doing this we need to ask what exactly the nature of this coming together is.

It is misleading to think of the texts combining cumulatively into a sum total that constitutes the image, or alternatively simply as being moments in a star's image's career (this phrase is used throughout to emphasise the fact that we are talking about a film star as a media text not as a real person) that appear one after the other – although those emphases are important. The image is a *complex totality* and it does have a *chronological dimension*. What we need to understand that totality in its temporality is the concept of a *structured polysemy*.

By 'polysemy' is meant the multiple but finite meanings and effects that a star image signifies. In looking at Jane Fonda's image, I shall not be trying to say what she meant for the 'average person' at various points in her career, but rather to look at her image in terms of the multiplicity of its meanings. This does not mean that these are endless. The possibilities of meaning are limited in part by what the text makes available.

This polysemy is *structured*. In some cases, the various elements of signification may *reinforce* one another. John Wayne's image draws together his bigness, his

3 & 4 (left) *Marlene Dietrich in the 1930s and* (right) *the 1950s.*

association with the West, his support for right-wing politics, his male independence of, yet courtliness towards, women – the elements are mutually reinforcing, legitimating a certain way of being a man in American society. In other cases, the elements may be to some degree in *opposition* or *contradiction*, in which case the star's image is characterised by attempts to negotiate, reconcile or mask the difference between the elements, or else simply hold them in tension. At an extreme – for example the later part of Marilyn Monroe's career – the contradictions threaten to fragment the image altogether.

Images also have a *temporal dimension*. Structured polysemy does not imply stasis; images develop or change over time. In the case of Fonda, the direction is for the most part in terms of change, but it may also in other cases be seen in terms of continuity. Marlene Dietrich is an example of the latter. The image crystallised in her films with Josef von Sternberg (1930–5) has remained the key note of her career – for a sketch of what he calls a 'combination of opposites', see David Shipman, *The Great Stars – the Golden Years*, p. 156. Attempts to break with the image by putting her in Westerns (*Destry Rides Again*, 1939; *Rancho Notorious*, 1952) and other more 'American' vehicles only succeeded in reinforcing her image as the alluring, exotic female 'other'. Her ageing, far from dimming this, contributed to it, partly by the degree to which her beauty remained, partly by her presentation, in films, concerts, records and photographs, in these terms: the 'Eternal Feminine' whose long career is further promise of eternity. Glamour photographs from early and late in her career illustrate this continuity, in particular the way in which she emerges out of a vague background that places her nowhere earthly but rather in some 'other' realm of existence and the emphasis on her almost Oriental eyes that look straight into the camera.

* * *

The illustration on the cover of the paperback edition (1975) of James Brough's *The Fabulous Fondas* provides a useful way into most of the tensions in Jane

5 The Fabulous Fondas, *cover of paperback edition, 1975.*

Fonda's image. Henry Fonda wears cowboy clothes, Peter Fonda those from *Easy Rider*, Jane Fonda is thus situated between the traditional values of her father and the alternative values of her brother. This is, as we'll see, slightly at variance with the emphasis in Jane Fonda's image's career as far as her family is concerned, where the relationship to her father has been seen as of paramount importance. In terms of her image, her brother here reminds us rather of the radicalism she has espoused in the later part of her career. The next point about the cover is that the male Fondas are contained by the strip of celluloid within which their pictures are placed, whereas Jane Fonda is superimposed across the strip and is in no way contained by it. Similarly, her life has been as important to her image as her films, whereas her father and brother are less known as images outside of their films. Finally, Jane Fonda appears nude, in a pin-up pose, while Henry and Peter Fonda are dressed, head and shoulders only showing, in 'character'. Her image is crucially defined by her sexual attractiveness, whereas it is seldom even acknowledged that this may be important to the male Fonda's success. This cover then suggests three important aspects of Jane Fonda's image: the connection with her father, sex and radicalism. I will use these three aspects to structure this account, adding one other to it, 'acting'.

It will already be obvious that Fonda's image is organised around elements that relate awkwardly to one another. While some stars condense such contradictory elements within their image – in a movement that may unite or expose them – in Fonda's case, it is not so much a question of condensing as of negotiating these elements, oscillating between them in what could more purposefully be seen as trying to find a way through them. In particular during her early career, commentators repeatedly asked where she was going. Thus Stanley Kauffmann in a review of *In the Cool of the Day* (1964 – her fifth film) in *The New Republic* observed that she had 'considerable' talent and personality, but 'it is still worth wondering – up to now, anyway – what will become of her' (p. 198; all reviews cited are taken from John Springer, *The Fondas*, unless otherwise stated). Not till her association with Roger Vadim (1965–9) did anything like a clear image develop, and not till the time of *Klute* (1971) did the elements of the image come together in a certain dynamic tension. It is this drama of moving back and forth and eventually through the different elements, rather than simply combining them, that characterises Fonda's image's career.

Father

Throughout her career, Jane Fonda has been discussed and referred to in terms of her father. David Shipman's entry on her in *The Great Stars – the International Years* begins 'Jane is Henry's daughter ...' (p. 159). On the appearance of her first film, *Tall Story* (1960), Ellen Fitzpatrick in *Films in Review* wrote: 'This picture wouldn't be reviewed in these pages but for the fact that Henry Fonda's daughter, Jane, makes her screen debut in it' (Springer, p. 177), while *Time* spoke of her as 'a second-generation Fonda with a smile like her father's and legs like a chorus girl' (ibid.). This emphasis only began to slacken with *They Shoot Horses, Don't They?* (1969) and her entry into radical politics, where her father is still mentioned but not in quite the same defining way.

Much of the discussion of Fonda in relation to her father attempts to discern physical similarities between them. John Springer claims that she has her father's 'electric-blue' eyes and his 'quick, embarrassed smile' (p. 47), while *Life* observed 'by inheritance, [Henry Fonda gave] her a tipped-up nose, blue eyes, a sudden smile – and talent' (quoted in Springer, p. 36). Jean-Luc Godard and Jean-Pierre Gorin go further in their film *Letter to Jane*, arguing that there is a certain expression she uses, especially in relation to political issues, that recalls that of her father (see p. 78). Without recourse to some very precise semiotic categorisation of facial features, it would be hard to prove that any or all of these physical similarities are based on accurate perception. What is important is the repeated assertion of that similarity, the frequent claim that one can see Henry Fonda in Jane, a claim that is widespread and more or less irresistible because she has retained her father's name and any way is so widely known to be his daughter.

These features carry certain connotations over from Henry to Jane, of which the two most important are Americanness and left-wing liberalism. The first of these connotations is clearly indicated by Ronald D. Katz in his interview article 'Jane Fonda – a Hard Act to Follow' (*Rolling Stone*, 9 March 1978): 'She grew up having a father who embodied for an entire nation all of those qualities that are American and middle class and good (pride, honesty, tenacity and a total sublimation of emotions – to name a few) ...' This all-Americanness is present in his films – particularly his roles in Westerns, an indelibly American genre, and as the President (*Young Mr Lincoln*, 1939; *The Longest Day*, 1962; *Fail Safe*, 1964), a presidential candidate (*The Best Man*, 1964) and a prospective Secretary of State (*Advise and Consent*, 1962) in pre-Watergate times – as well as in his background as reported: 'The values and attitudes of small-town America were virtually built into his bones and his blood' (Brough, *The Fabulous Fondas*, pp. 6–7); 'Life in [his] household was as conventional as a Norman Rockwell cover in the old *Saturday Evening Post*' (p. 8). This all-Americanness is supposedly reproduced in Jane Fonda's physical likeness to her father (Katz in *Rolling Stone* even suggests she possesses 'the 'All-American voice'), as well as in other aspects of her career/image. She was brought up on a farm, with all its homesteader connotations, far away from the glamour of Hollywood. She went to Vassar, one of the top women's colleges in the States, and her first film role in *Tall Story* was as a college student and basketball cheerleader. Her costume in this (see Fig. 6) places her clearly as one of the major icons of American normalcy, the majorette. This indelible Americanness has been an important element in her later career, which, with its French sex films and radical politics, has in substance been the antithesis of all-Americanness. Yet virtually all the American critics of *Barbarella* (1968) insisted on Jane's 'normal', 'healthy' performance in this 'kinky' film, and Pauline Kael in the *New Yorker* spoke of her as 'the American girl triumphing by her innocence over a lewd comic-strip world of the future' (Springer, p. 262). In terms of her politics, commentators have seen her Americanness as either the guarantee of her integrity ('it was easy to see that she was not searching for unusual publicity, she was rather letting her whole heart and soul out trying to end this war in Vietnam', David Carlson, *Hollywood Screen Parade*, August 1972, p. 64) or else, in Godard/Gorin's analysis, another instance of the weakness of American liberalism (see p. 78).

6 Tall Story, *1960.*

Nor are Jane Fonda's politics a complete departure from her parental inheritance, as the image emphasises it, because her father also had a reputation for radicalism or 'left-wing liberalism'. His identification with the part of Tom Joad in *The Grapes of Wrath* (1940) most clearly crystallised this in his films, but he had always had an involvement with Democratic politics (particularly the Kennedys) and was outspokenly anti-McCarthy. None of this worked outside the system, as his daughter's politics has (or has tried to), and this is where she has in interviews defined the difference between them, but the sense of a connectedness at this level is also maintained.

As discussed so far, Jane Fonda's relation to her father has been seen in terms of the 'inheritance' of physical, cultural and political traits. This is how publicity and promotion, critics and commentators often posed it, but, as suggested above, the notion of Fonda having to negotiate this aspect of her life is as central to the image. It is a question – posed by reporters and interviewers – of 'what does your father think of this?', and Henry's alleged remark during her early years with Vadim – 'Daughter? I don't have a daughter' (quoted by Brough, *The Fabulous Fondas*, p. 182, no source given) – has served the press for many years subsequently. Equally, Jane Fonda has returned repeatedly in interviews (as they have been written up) to another aspect of her father – his four marriages. The actual content of her remarks is simply that this has made her somewhat of a 'cynic' (*Sunday Express*, 22 March 1964) about marriage. This, and the fact that she was for several years in analysis, has none the less been taken to indicate that her relationship with her father is psychologically problematic. Mike Tomkies's article on Vadim shows this shift: 'Nervous and highly strung, her childhood was unconventional. Her father has been married four times …' (*Showtime*, March 1967, p. 19). He then goes on to indicate the one definite traumatic event in her childhood (she was twelve), when her mother committed suicide. However, although this event is mentioned in most biographical sketches of her, it is with her father that the emphasis lies. This is obviously partly because of his fame, and partly no doubt because of the spread of Freudian ideas in America endowing the image of father/daughter relationships with a greater charge than their mother/daughter equivalent. This, it should be said, is a selective perception of Freud, since he pointed out that for daughters as well as sons the first love object is the mother, thus leading, according to Freud, to the greater capacity for bisexuality among women. All of this gets lost in the predominant, heterosexually normative appropriations of Freud. As we shall see, the question of lesbianism and 'tomboyism' in relation to Jane Fonda's image is both complicated and crucial.

The emphasis on the problematic, 'psychological' aspects of Fonda's relation to her father also leads in the image to an insistence on men as father figures in her life. The supposed difficulties of the primary father/daughter relationship is taken to inform all her subsequent relations with men. Ann Leslie in the *Daily Express* (26 January 1969), implies that with the coming of Vadim, Fonda was completely transformed under his 'Svengali' – often evoked in this context – influence. The logical progression of this line is to subsume all other aspects of her life into this father/daughter one, so that by 1974 the *Sunday Telegraph* (31 March) could quote one of her biographers, Thomas Kiernan, as saying that 'The basic engine for change in her life is men'. In this way, as the article proceeds to do, all her views can be reduced to a relationship in which she surrenders, filially, to the views of a man – Vadim, Huey Newton ('the Black Panther'), Fred Gardner ('a Marxist'), Tom Hayden (her husband).

It is possible to see then how one tendency of the image is to return her personality and her views to her father, via concepts of heredity and/or psychoanalysis. This is, however, only a tendency. It is not picked up in the films, and her more recent career has been read as her establishment of herself as her own person. This means that the other elements in her career – sex, acting, politics – are no longer *reduced* to reproduction of or reaction against her father, as they are earlier in her career. However, it may also be argued that her current image consolidates his *values* while at the same time being cut loose of him as a father or in the form of father figures.

Sex

The question of Jane Fonda's sex appeal was raised from the first. Alongside the reference to her father, there went the other assurance that she was attractive. *Time*'s 'a smile like her father's and legs like a chorus girl', quoted above, makes the point immediately, and there are very few reviews or publicity items that do not make reference to her looks. In promotion for her films she was almost exclusively sold in these terms. Even at the end of a relatively sympathetic account of her political developments, characteristically entitled 'Jane: the Battling Beauty who is Preaching Revolution', Donald Zec writes: 'Hollywood, frenziedly searching for its own backbone, might well study the philosophy of Jane Fonda. Studying the anatomy would be no hardship, either' (*Daily Mirror*, 6 April 1970); while the *Sunday Times* colour magazine's coverage of the making of *Julia* focused on 'Fonda at Forty', with tasteful pictures celebrating the preservation of her beauty.

'Beauty' is a rarefied term, and although not uncommon in writing about Fonda, it is by no means the predominant emphasis. Quite apart from the critics' discussions as to whether she is really beautiful or is rather plain but attractive, it is quite striking how crudely her sex appeal was frequently constructed. She was often photographed in a manner that vulgarised rather than beautified her body. Her bottom, in particular, was focused on – in the early scenes of *Walk on the Wild Side* (1962); in a cut-in close-up of her bottom's movement on horseback, followed by a leering Lee Marvin in reaction shot in *Cat Ballou* (1965); and in the American poster, which she objected to, for *La Ronde/Circle of Love* (1965). Not surprisingly, at the time of *They Shoot Horses, Don't They?* (1969), Pauline Kael in her *New Yorker* review could refer to Fonda as having been hitherto a 'nudie cutie' (Springer, p. 270), while *Variety* commented on her 'previous career as a sex bonbon' (p. 268). The roles sometimes reinforced this crudity – as a tramp-cum-prostitute in *Walk on the Wild Side*; as the 'other woman' in *In the Cool of the Day* (1963); as, in the words of *Time*, 'trollope white Trash' (Springer, p. 223) in *The Chase* (1966); as a 'decadent high-class Southern gal' (Judith Crist, *New York World Journal Tribune*; Springer, p. 236) in *Hurry Sundown* (1967). All but *In the Cool of the Day* are deep South melodramas, a genre particularly given to 'hysterical', 'nymphomaniacal' portraits of women. In this perspective, *Klute* (1971) is a particularly interesting film, since, as Fonda plays the part of a prostitute, it invokes these earlier roles but also tries to inflect them in terms of feminism, so that, in Sheila Whitaker's words, the prostitute can be seen 'as the most honest and most despised of women' ('The Rebel Hero', p. 13). What is not clear is whether the role does cut free from the exploitative quality of the earlier image, or whether the latter contributes to reducing the radical potential of the character. The same problem arises with the discussion of fucking ('baiser') in *Tout va bien* (1973) and the nude scene with Jon Voigt in *Coming Home* (1978). It depends how the audience member reads these films, what sort of interest in or knowledge of Fonda s/he has.

The emphasis on sex in her image was of course increased during her association with Roger Vadim. The very association with him, the 'creator' of Brigitte

7 *Poster for* The Chapman Report, *1961.*

8 *Poster for* Klute, *1971.*

9 Walk on the Wild Side, *1962.*

10 *American hoarding advertising* La Ronde/Circle of Love, *1965.*

Bardot, the director of *And God Created Woman* (1956), already foregrounded sexuality, and the films they made together reinforced this: *La Ronde* (1965), *La Curée/The Game Is Over* (1966), *Barbarella* (1968) and the 'Metzengerstein' episode of *Histoires extraordinaires* (1969). Everything about these vehicles emphasised sex. The very fact that Jane Fonda was doing nude scenes was enough to 'place' these films in terms of both promotion and publicity, but in addition both the narratives and the *mise en scène* reinforced it. She played a 'philandering wife' (Shipman, p. 160) in *La Ronde* and a woman in love with her stepson in *La Curée*. *Barbarella* is entirely a series of sexual adventures, culminating in Barbarella being subjected to a machine that will kill her with erotic pleasure, but for which her sexual drive proves too much, thereby causing the machine to explode. *Barbarella* also threw in perverse, or, as the current jargon had it, 'kinky' elements, such as having sex with a grotesquely hirsute huntsman and being seduced by another woman. This 'kinkiness' was also present in *Histoires extraordinaires*, where the Fonda character is in love with her horse. The erotic treatment of this love is ex-

11 Barbarella, *1968*.

plained by the fact that the horse is really the reincarnation of her beloved cousin. A further twist was given to this by the fact that the cousin, seen in flashbacks, was played by Fonda's brother, Peter. Although she objected, in interviews, that there had been no intention to provide titillating intimations of incest, this is certainly how it was widely taken. The 'kinkiness' of these plots and situations was heightened by the use of dress and decor, most obviously in *Barbarella*. In Fig. 11, we may note such commonplaces of erotic symbolism/fetishism as the hair-textured

12 Histoires Extraordinaires, *1969.*

background, which both mingles with Fonda's hair and yet is itself more akin to pubic hair; the phallic gun; the use of plastic clothing, which both conceals and reveals breasts and belly; and the hint of bondage in the high, stiff neck plate. *Histoires extraordinaires* was also full of such elements, as in Fonda's clothing in Fig. 12 – chains and thigh-length leather boots.

Everything about Vadim's use of Fonda is erotic, and certainly this is how their films together were largely understood. Sheilah Graham's article 'The Fondas: The Papa, the Mamas and the Kids' (published in her 1969 collection *Scratch an Actor*) suggests how widespread was the total identification of Vadim with the sexual use of Fonda: ' "Why are you always undressing?" I asked Jane in Rome, and "Why does Vadim always undress his women?" She protested, "It isn't true. I've only been nude in three films." Why does it seem like three hundred?' (p. 201).

However, the association with Vadim, while intensifying the sex element in Fonda's image, also complicates it. In interviews, both Fonda and Vadim claimed that, in their life together and in these films, he was 'liberating' her. Mike Tomkies, for instance, quotes her as saying 'The moment I realized Roger was only letting me be myself, I trusted him completely' (*Showtime*, March 1967, p. 21) and writes that Vadim says that 'To-day ... it's no longer a problem for women to be sexually free. What interests him now is not the choice of freedom but the true way to it' (ibid.). (This view of Vadim was quite widespread, and Simone de Beauvoir wrote a monograph celebrating Brigitte Bardot's liberatedness – *Brigitte Bardot and the Lolita Syndrome*.) Fonda was also quoted as saying that *Barbarella* was 'a kind of tongue-in-cheek satire against bourgeois morality' (*Photoplay*, February 1968, p. 63). All of this suggested that the relationship with Vadim was not necessarily to be read in terms of sexual objectification – that one could see it in terms of a coming to terms with sexuality.

That this happened in Europe also gave its significance as liberation a certain credibility, in that it belonged to a familiar cultural syndrome, unkindly evoked by Sheilah Graham as 'the American girl gone to sex' (quoted by Shipman, p. 160) and elaborated by Pauline Kael at the beginning of her review of *Barbarella*:

> What would Henry James have made of Jane Fonda, an actress so much like his hero-ines – an American heiress-of-the-ages abroad, and married to a superb example of the Jamesian villain, a sophisticated European (a Frenchman of Russian origins) who is redolent of shallow morals ... (Springer, p. 254)

As was noted above, this sense of Fonda retaining her all-Americanness, even in her 'kinkiest' vehicles, was widely asserted by the critics, and perhaps enabled even the 'Svengali' treatment from Vadim to be seen as one more aspect of her life that she was negotiating rather than being defined or taken over by.

Acting

Throughout her career, Fonda's ability as an actor has been affirmed. Before making her first film, *Tall Story*, she trained for a while under Lee Strasberg, who taught 'the Method' at the Actors' Studio in New York. (See Part Three for a discussion of this and other performance styles.) However, it is hard to discern any of the trademarks of this style in Fonda's performances. (Observers report that Fonda uses the Method approach to performance and character and it may have made the improvisatory feel of some of her later films, discussed below, easier for her.) Her rating as an actor came rather from four more traditional factors.

Firstly, she proved her ability by moderate success in the theatre, always regarded as a 'truer' test of 'acting'. Secondly, there was the range of roles she played in her career, in particular her switching back and forth between high melodrama (*Walk on the Wild Side*, 1962; *The Chapman Report*, 1962; *In the Cool of the Day*, 1963; *The Chase*, 1966; *La Curée*, 1966; *Hurry Sundown*, 1967; *They Shoot Horses, Don't They?*, 1969) and light comedies. The latter constitute the third factor validating her as an actor. Apart from *Cat Ballou* (1965), they all fall within a genre, the only label for which is 'American sex comedy'. This is the type of comedy associated in films with the later career of Doris Day and in the theatre most consummately with the plays of Neil Simon, the film of whose *Barefoot in the Park* Fonda made in 1967. The other films in this category were *Tall Story* (1960), *Period of Adjustment* (1962), *Sunday in New York* (1964) and *Any Wednesday* (1966). All of these were successful Broadway comedies (further theatrical validation) and in them all Fonda, said the critics, displayed her capacity with 'timing', a definite performance *skill*. The fourth confirmation of her acting ability came from her being nominated for an Oscar for *They Shoot Horses, Don't They?* and winning one for *Klute* (1971), and, more convincing in terms of 'acting' as opposed to 'star' quality, gaining the New York Film Critics' Award as 'best actress' for both of them.

Her subsequent career has remained within this definition of acting ability, by doing a film with Godard (*Tout va bien*, 1973),[11] an adaptation of a classic (*A Doll's House*, 1974), a historical personage (Lillian Hellman in *Julia*, 1977), as well as a return to comedy with *Steelyard Blues* (1972) and *Fun with Dick and Jane* (1977).

In addition to an ability to play different kinds of part, rather than just 'be herself' (although one might want to question the validity of this distinction, in general or in the case of Fonda), and the association with non-Hollywood, non-glamorous vehicles and characters, most of the later films (from *They Shoot Horses, Don't They?*) broadly belong to what has been called 'New Hollywood Cinema'. (For a discussion of this see Steve Neale's article 'New Hollywood Cinema'; although Godard is not Hollywood, he is, through his participation in the New Wave, one of the major influences on the new style of American film-making.) From the point of view of performers, this style places greater emphasis upon the elaboration of character within a loose narrative structure and upon naturalistic devices such as interrupted speech, hesitation, mumbling, tics and other techniques that give an air of improvisation to the performance. Fonda has mastered this style – the 'naturalism' of her performance is especially marked in the scenes with the psychoanalyst in *Klute* and throughout *Coming Home* (1978) – and since this is what constitutes 'good' acting in contemporary cinema, it is an index of her reputation as an actor.

Politics

There is already some problem in the critical writing as to whether Fonda is to be considered a sex star or an actor. Some argued that, in *La Curée* especially, she showed a capacity to act out sexuality, but in general the two elements were considered as separate and perhaps contradictory. Her adoption of radical politics raised much sharper contradictions.

There have been major news stories surrounding her political involvement in the four major areas of radicalism recognised by the American mass media – the Native Americans (her trip to the occupation of Alcatraz in 1969), her association with Huey Newton of the Black Panthers, her anti-war (Vietnam) work in GI 'coffee-houses' in one of which she was arrested (1969), and her feminism. In addition, in 1972 she married Tom Hayden, a leading member of the militant student organisation SDS (Students for a Democratic Society) and one of the 'Chicago Seven'. She also promoted two anti-war ventures, the show (subsequently filmed) *Free the Army* (or *Fuck the Army*) (1972) and a documentary film *Vietnam Journey* (1972). Some of her films have also been explicitly radical – in *Tout va bien* she is a radical journalist raking over the inheritance of 1968, *A Doll's House* is Ibsen's classic 'feminist' play; in *Julia* she plays a well-known left-wing liberal, Lillian Hellman; and *Coming Home* deals with a woman's politicisation through working with wounded soldiers during the Vietnam war. In addition, *Klute*, and *Coming Home* in particular, have been read as important in terms of feminism – *Klute* for using prostitution as a metaphor for the sexual treatment of women generally and *Coming Home* for its emphasis on the Fonda character's discovery of her capacity for independent action and for orgasm. (Before sleeping with the Voigt character, she has never experienced orgasm – the contrast, for the woman, between this 'liberated' sex and habitual 'oppressive' sex is shown by an earlier sex scene with her husband, played by Bruce Dern.)

The significance of all of this – the events and the films – is always in terms of the fact that *it is Jane Fonda doing them*. It is not just that the press always handles them in terms of the other aspects of her image – what would her father think? could she not have remained 'the high spirited and rebellious sex symbol who starred in 18 movies' rather than becoming 'the new Jane Fonda [who] is many things, but one thing she is not is "lovable"' (Mike McGrady, *Guardian*, 5 May 1971)? how was all this politicking related to her achievements as an actor? (Donald Zec pointed out in the *Daily Mirror* for 6 April 1970 that her 'dangerous political fling . . . may well deprive her of that Oscar accolade tomorrow night' – and she did not win the Oscar until two years later). This is not just the difficulty the press had in dealing with a revolutionary star. In fact it would be hard for the press to deal in any other way with a star's revolutionary associations. What the star does can *only* be posed in terms of *the star doing it*, the extraordinariness or difficulty of her/his doing it, rather than in terms of the ostensible political issues involved. Thus her visit to Alcatraz did not primarily give publicity to the situation of the Native Americans but rather posed the issue of what a woman like this was doing going to such a place. In other words, it posed the issue of white radicalism.

Fonda-as-star-as-revolutionary dramatises the problem of what role privileged white people can have in the struggles of under-privileged non-whites. (I will reserve the question of feminism for a moment; what is striking is how, in terms of public events and films, although not in some of her actions and statements, the issue of class is only raised in the film furthest removed from her situation and from the public, *Tout va bien*, which is itself a raking over of the problems of bourgeois revolutionaries.) It is this that Jean-Luc Godard and Jean-Pierre Gorin seized on in their film *Letter to Jane* (1974). They suggest that Fonda's politics are imbued with reactionary American values, and hinge their case on a semiotic analysis of a newsphoto of her in Vietnam during the filming of *Vietnam Journey*. As they point out, it is striking that the photo shows her with the Vietnamese rather than the Vietnamese in their own right. (They blame Fonda for this, whereas one could argue that this is inherent in the star phenomenon.) Moreover, they argue, her expression in the photo (Fig. 13) is an expression Fonda often uses in relation to political issues. They detect it in *Tout va bien* ('when as an actress she was listening to one of the film extras singing a text written by Lotta Continua') and *Klute* (when 'she looked at her friend, a policeman played by Donald Suther-

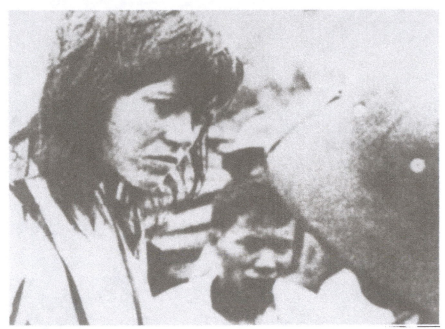

13 *Jane Fonda in Vietnam.*

land, with a tragic sense of pity on her face, and made up her mind to spend the night with him',), as well as in her father's films (including *The Grapes of Wrath* – Fig. 14 – and *Young Mr Lincoln*) and in John Wayne as he 'expresses his deep regrets about the devastation of the war in Vietnam' in *The Green Berets* (Fig. 15). They continue:

> In our opinion this expression has been borrowed, principle and interest, from the free trade mark of Roosevelt's New Deal. In fact, it's an expression of an expression and it appeared inevitably by chance just as the talkies were becoming a financial success. This expression talks but only to say how much it knows about the stock market crash for example. But says nothing more than how much it knows. (From a transcript made by Nicky North)

This negative view (which, incidentally, remains purely formalist – it does not examine the situation within which Fonda works), not so much of the political issues Fonda is involved in as of Fonda-as-politico, is widespread on the left and on the right. As an example of the latter, it is interesting how often the press quote Henry Fonda's remarks, such as: 'She's the instant cause girl, working for the right causes for what I think are the wrong reasons. She won't be satisfied until they burn her, like Joan of Arc' (*Sunday Mirror*, 24 September 1972).

Something of the same unease can be found in feminist views of her feminism, although much feminist writing is largely supportive of her. This ambiguity is perhaps because feminism puts the nature of personal involvement in politics very much more centrally on the political agenda than do traditional politics, where the 'personal' is discarded in the face of the actual 'issue' of struggle. It is not

14 *Henry Fonda in* The Grapes of Wrath, *1940.*

so much that feminists all acknowledge her as a model, as that she dramatises what it is like to be political – she does not dramatise an issue, but the question, itself political, of involvement with an issue. Tracy Young develops this point. She compares Fonda to other contemporary women stars who may embody something of the 'new' woman, but: 'Unlike Faye Dunaway ... Fonda has a willingness that isn't sharp. Unlike Lily Tomlin ... Fonda seems infinitely straighter, seems to still believe in the positive aspects of Ego ... unlike Diane Keaton ... Fonda is not insecure' ('Fonda Jane', p. 57). Ambiguously she concludes:

> In many ways [Fonda's] current box-office appeal is an indirect result of the women's movement, a movement that has been in constant search of role models, and a movement that was up until recently (and like the left-over Left) composed mainly of the well-intentioned middle class. And in many ways it is their values she both celebrates and validates all over again. (ibid.)

Like Helen Reddy, Fonda can be seen to reconcile the aims of the women's movement with 'acceptable', 'normal' behaviour. The all-American connection here is important, as is the validation of her as a good actor, but perhaps most important is the sexual connection. Throughout the 'kinky' French films, her 'healthy', 'American' qualities were applauded, and Fonda has remained unerringly 'normal', i.e. heterosexual. The importance of this became particularly clear with *Julia* (1977). As Jennifer Selway observed in a *Time Out* blurb (7–13 July 1978), in *Julia*: 'no-one bothers to mention that lesbianism is central to *The Children's Hour*, which Hellman tries to write while, as per synopsis, "her memory returned again and

80

15 *John Wayne in* The Green Berets, *1968.*

again ... to Julia"' (p. 39). And in an interview in *Télérama* (18 December 1976), Fonda herself says:

> On m'a dit à Londres qu'il s'agissait d'homosexualité. Je ne le crois pas: c'est seulement l'histoire d'une amitié profonde. D'ailleurs, c'est moi-même qui me suis proposée pour le rôle. [They told me in London that it [*Julia*] was about homosexuality. I don't think so; it's just a story of a deep friendship. Besides it was me who put myself forward for the part.]

One of the biggest 'taints' that the women's movement has acquired, courtesy of the mass media, is that of lesbianism. While many women in the movement have discovered lesbianism in themselves through the movement and while the movement is certainly formally committed to the defence of lesbianism, it clearly remains a stumbling block to many women (and men). I do not wish to propose that Fonda's image is an anti-gay one, but it is certainly an ostensibly *non-gay* one, and this, together with her parentage and acting skill, makes her politics, especially her feminism, seem more ordinary and normal. (In this context the omission in

16 *Jane Fonda in* Cat Ballou, *1965.*

the popularisation of Freud, noted above, of the Freudian understanding of mother/daughter relationships in terms of lesbianism is particularly suggestive.)

Fonda's image's career can be seen as representing the journey of Fonda-as-person through various possibilities and problems that I have organised under the headings of father, sex, acting and politics. The argument of the last few pages suggests that her image in the period discussed reconciles these various elements, that the 'journey' has come to an end. Clearly I cannot get into predictions on this score here, but it does seem that, with *Julia* and *Coming Home*, her standing as a star has reached a peak, and the theory of charisma advanced in this book places particular emphasis on the star as the reconciler of contradictions. Beyond this, I'll end by noting a further possible element that provides a certain continuity to her image and that one might call 'tomboyism'. Several women stars have had this quality – compare Fonda (Fig. 16) with Debbie Reynolds and Nancy Sinatra (Figs. 17 and 18) – and Fonda's most successful roles with the public before *Klute* were basically tomboys, as in *Walk on the Wild Side, Cat Ballou* and *Barbarella*. Images

17 & 18 (left) *Debbie Reynolds: 'Just one of the boys!'* (right) *Nancy Sinatra in* Wild Angels, *1966.*

from different points in her life have emphasised this element, from promotional photographs of the Fonda family to depictions of her at political meetings with cropped hair and wearing jeans (Fig. 19). Tracy Young also suggests that in playing Lillian Hellman in *Julia* she was playing a 'legendary tomboy' ('Fonda Jane', p. 57), and her scenes with Dashiell Hammett/Jason Robards Jnr are played with her dressed in sweater and slacks shouting and cursing at him. This is not the place to enquire into the roots of the acceptability of the tomboy image in general, but the following observations can be made. It clearly is acceptable for a girl to be a tomboy (whereas it is not acceptable for a boy to be a sissie), presumably because it is admirable for a person to wish to take on the attributes of the superior sex but not vice versa; the woman as tomboy retains something of the 'immaturity' of a boy, hence she does not prove a threat to a grown man. When, as with Fonda, the image is highly charged sexually we may want to speculate on this psychically in terms of phallic substitution (see the discussion by Laura Mulvey, in the section on the 'independent woman') or upon the homosexual appeal of this to heterosexual male fans – and to other women, thus providing a possible contradiction at the level of appeal to the non-gay element of her image at the level of representation (i.e. she embodies a non-gay woman, who may none the less make an appeal to gay feelings in the audience – for further discussion of this, not specifically in relation to Fonda, see Caroline Sheldon in 'Lesbians and Film: Some Thoughts'). Such speculations are risky, but it may be that her charisma – which evokes extremes of hate as well as love[12] – can be accounted for not only in the reconciliation of radicalism and feminism with Americanness and ordinariness but also in her ability to suggest (as a tomboy) redefinitions of sexuality while at the same time overtly reasserting heterosexuality.

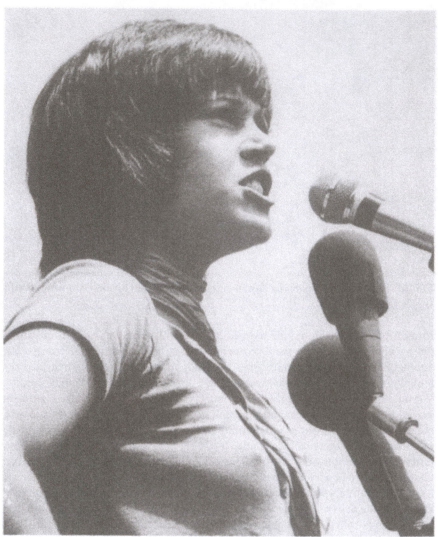

19 *Jane Fonda addresses a political meeting.*

Notes
1. Richard Griffith (ed.), *The Talkies;* Martin Levin (ed.), *Hollywood and the Great Fan Magazines;* Barbara Gelman (ed.), *Photoplay Treasury.*
2. *Film Pictorial,* 30 September 1933; reprinted by Peter Way Ltd. in 1972 as part of the series 'Great Newspapers Reprinted'.
3. Griffith, *Talkies,* pp. 106–7, 302–4.
4. Solutions to the production of surplus include the expansion of overseas markets and war, but also the stimulation of home consumption through advertising, product differentiation, etc., all leading to an emphasis on consumption, hence the tag, 'the consumer society'. See J. K. Galbraith, *The Consumer Society* and Paul Baran and Paul Sweezy, *Monopoly Capital.*
5. See note 1 to Part One concerning King's work.

6. Griffith, *Talkies*, pp. 136–7, 331; Griffith, *Talkies*, pp. 140–2, 337; Gelman, *Photoplay Treasury*, pp. 144–7; Levin, *Great Fan Magazines*, pp. 94–6.
7. In Tony Jefferson *et al.* (eds.), *Resistance through Rituals*, originally published as *Working Papers in Cultural Studies*, 7/8.
8. See Jack Babuscio, 'Screen Gays' in *Gay News* nos. 79 (Dean) and 104 (Clift).
9. The *locus classicus* of the view that 'culture is male' is Simone de Beauvoir: *Le Deuxième Sexe*. For a discussion of more recent, psychoanalytically oriented theorisations, see Elizabeth Cowie, 'Woman as Sign'.
10. See also Richard Dyer, 'It's Being So Camp as Keeps Us Going', pp. 11–13.
11. Godard does not use performers in an 'actorly' way – the point here is that the fact of Fonda being in a film directed by a name European director would be widely taken as indicating an 'acting' job.
12. See Ronald D. Katz, 'Jane Fonda: A Hard Act to Follow', *Rolling Stone*, 9 March 1978.

PART THREE

Stars as Signs

Stars as images are constructed in all kinds of media texts other than films, but none the less, films remain (with the qualifications noted in the previous part, p. 61) privileged instances of the star's image. This final part is concerned, then, with the more precise and detailed question of how stars function in films themselves.

This question is examined principally from two points of view. Firstly, in 'Stars and character', it is assumed that one can conceptualise a star's total image as distinct from the particular character that s/he plays in a given film. This chapter is concerned with the relationship between these two entities, and this in turn involves a prior consideration of the notion of character itself.

Chapter 8, 'Stars and performance', works from the assumption that although stars signify in films by virtue of being an already-signifying image and by being given a character partly constructed by script, *mise en scène*, etc., none the less all of this is only there on the screen in its enactment or performance. This section is then concerned with how performance signifies, and with the relationship between the signification of performance and of image and character.

A final, much shorter chapter, is concerned with setting the understanding of how stars function in film texts in relation to the most established contextual mode of film study, namely, authorship.

7 Stars and 'Character'

In films, stars play characters, that is, constructed representations of persons. To understand how stars 'are' in films, we need to understand what is meant by character in film and how it is achieved.

This understanding is made peculiarly difficult by the fact that, in so far as there has been any theoretical consideration of character in fiction (in any medium), it has primarily been directed to exposing its fallacious aspects – having demonstrated that characters are not real people, that they are an effect of the text constructions, critics and theorists have not proceeded to an examination of how this effect, so widely known and understood, is achieved, and just what the rules of construction are.

In a discussion of critical ideas about character in *The Dynamics of Literary Response*, Norman N. Holland points out that discussion of characters as real people has 'in our time . . . fallen into disuse'. Yet he goes on to suggest that 'Mostly it survives only in high-school teaching, in the *New York Times Book Review*, and the writings of Miss Mary McCarthy . . .' (p. 264 – the reference to McCarthy is presumably her essay on characters in fiction in *On the Contrary*, in which she regrets the demise of the character in modernist fiction). What this means, though Holland does not seem to see it, is that in the mainstream of discussion about literature, in educational practice and middlebrow writing, assumptions about character persist untouched by the avant-gardist discourse of New Criticism. (For a survey of the main lines of attack on the notion of character see W. J. Harvey, *Character and the Novel*.) In this chapter, I am attempting to examine these assumptions and their realisation in film texts.

Exceptions to the rule that stars always play characters may seem to be revue films, in which stars do their turn, and guest appearances such as Ava Gardner in *The Band Wagon* or Bing Crosby, Gene Kelly and Milton Berle in *Let's Make Love*. In the case of the revue films this is partially true – in doing their turn, stars project their image, although they may also participate as a 'character' in a sketch or playlet. The 'guest appearances' are more ambiguous. Gardner as 'herself' recognises Fred Astaire as 'Tony Hunter'; the scene is there moreover to tell us about Hunter's has-been status as a star and the camaraderie of show business personalities. Gardner is thus wholly enmeshed as a character, albeit a very minor one, in the film, and, by playing herself, contributes to the illusion of the other character's existence. What we have is a perfect fit between Gardner as an image and Gardner as a character. (The same is true of Crosby et al. in *Let's Make Love* and other such instances.) It is on the question of the fit between star image and character that much of the subsequent discussion must hinge.

I have throughout this section used the word 'character' to refer to the constructed personages of films and the word 'personality' to refer to the set of traits and characteristics with which the film endows them.

To discuss character we need to discuss the *notion* of character and the *construction* of character, and the relation of stars to both.

The notion of character

In the most general sense, all fictions have characters, that is, fictional beings, whether human, animal or fantastic, who carry the story, who do things and/or have things done to them. However, how those beings are conceptualised has altered in the history of fiction. This has been most clearly shown by Ian Watt in his *The Rise of the Novel*, a very useful reference here in that it both reveals the historical and cultural boundedness of notions of character and opens up the particular notion of character that dominates in our particular socio-cultural period. This section is accordingly organised around a discussion of these two themes (Sections A and B), followed by a brief discussion of attempts to move beyond the dominant conceptions of character operative in our time (Section C). The relevance to stars will be examined as we go along.

A – The cultural-historical specificity of notions of character

In *The Rise of the Novel*, Ian Watt argues that the novel form arose in the period it did in accord with changes in western thought. He takes each of the major formal characteristics of narrative fiction – plot, characterisation, the representation of time and space, prose style – and shows how in each of these respects the novel marks a radical break with previous modes. In terms of characterisation, the most significant feature is the 'particularisation' of characters, that is, fiction is no longer dealing with 'general human types' embodying broadly moral or intellectual concepts, but with 'particular people in particular circumstances'. This is signalled by, among other things, 'the way the novelist typically indicates his [sic] intention of presenting a character as a particular individual by naming him [sic] in exactly the same way as particular individuals are named in ordinary life' (p. 19). In previous literature, characters were given either historical or type names: 'In either case, the names set the characters in the context of a large body of expectations primarily formed from past literature, rather than from the context of contemporary life' (ibid.).

Other aspects of novel form – the representation of time and of space – also relate to the novelistic notion of character. In the novel, time and space were particularised, thus reinforcing the sense of the characters' particularity. The awareness of time, and of change over time, was accompanied by the novel interesting itself 'more than any other literary form in the development of its characters in the course of time' (p. 23). The attention to the particularity of space also allows for the novel's examination of the interaction between an individual and her/his environment (although this concern develops somewhat later in the novel's history than the other elements just discussed).

That the novel, in general and in its promotion of a particular notion of character, is a product of bourgeois society has become a truism of literary history. Thus in *Character and the Novel* W. J. Harvey observes:

> One of the few Marxist generalizations about literature to hold up reasonably well when put to the test of detailed historical examination is the thesis that the development of the novel is intimately connected with the growth of the bourgeoisie in a modern capitalist system. (p. 24)

The novel may be taken as the bourgeois narrative form *par excellence*, but its general features have also been aimed at by other forms. J. L. Styan's discussion, in his *Drama, Stage and Audience*, of different notions of acting and character in the theatre illustrates this, as does Leo Lowenthal's study of post-Renaissance literature, *Literature and the Image of Man*. (For further discussion of the social implications of this, see Elizabeth Burns's *Theatricality*.)

Before turning to an examination of the characteristics of this novelistic conception of character, we need to consider the extent to which star images and film characters belong to this conception.

It is worth noting that stars are themselves a peculiarly characteristic feature of bourgeois theatre (and only subsequently cinema). The emergence of stars in the theatre is usually dated from the 18th century with such actors as Garrick, Peg Woffington, Sarah Siddons, Edmund Kean, Schröder and Rachel. This relates to the emergence of the theatre as both a viable economic enterprise and a respectable profession (neither dependent on patronage nor itinerants regarded as little better than rogues and vagabonds). Along with this went a change in the conception of what theatres and actors were. In earlier theatre, the actors either were recognised to be playing prescribed roles which were more important than themselves or, in early professional companies such as the *commedia dell'arte* troupes, were completely identified with their roles. As Burns points out in *Theatricality*, Garrick and those following him took familiar characters (notably from Shakespeare) but promoted themselves as well as the character in the process. The felt naturalism they introduced was 'a means of realising both the character and his [the actor's] own personality so that the audience would remember Kean's Hamlet, Kemble's Macbeth and Irving's Shylock' (p. 171). In this way the early stars are not only embodiments of triumphant individualism but also already raise the notion of the difference between self (Kean) and role (Hamlet).

There is a sense in which the history of stars in the cinema reprises the history of the change in concepts of character and the individual as defined by Watt et al. As has been discussed in Part One (pp. 21–3), the conventional wisdom concerning the history of stars in the cinema is that there has been a shift from stars as ideals, gods and goddesses, to stars as representations of ordinary life, mortals, just like you and me. This is a shift similar to that from characters as embodiments of moral or intellectual principles to characters as 'particular people in particular places' (although only the early stars were believed to *be* absolute qualities). This implies considerable cultural lag in the formation of the early cinema, but fits in with Edgar Morin's assertion of the gods-to-mortals shift in the stars as an aspect of the cinema's embourgeoisement.

It has also been argued that there is a parallel history in the changes in predominant conceptions of character in the cinema (in cinematic traditions that use stars and in those that do not). Thus from a cinema focused principally on heroic or emblematic characters, who represent, respectively, ideals or ideas, there has been a shift to a cinema that deals with individuated characters. The kind of evidence that is adduced for this view is the changing nature of the cowboy in Westerns – the cowboy of the early silent Western is either chivalric or a figure of (recent) myth, and the polarisation of values in characters is fairly complete (according to Panofsky in 'Style and Medium in the Motion Picture', down to the clothes they wore: black for villains, white for heroes). With the various innovations in the genre's development – history (e.g. *The Iron Horse*), psychology (e.g. *The Left-Handed Gun*), naturalism (e.g. *Will Penny*) – the characters have become more individuated and less easily labelled good and bad. In *The World in a Frame*, Leo Braudy takes this discussion a step further by arguing that, as this 'individualisation' of character has developed, film has become more and more centred on character and correspondingly less so on plot. Where in the 30s–40s, films in both Hollywood and Europe subordinated character to the working out of a plot, films since the early 60s have concentrated more and more on 'character'. (Braudy's examples include the image and roles of stars such as James Dean and Marlon Brando and directors such as Truffaut and Altman.) This can be seen as a logical progression of the novel's concern with particular characters in particular situations, a progression that the novel itself has taken. That is, whereas the early novels/films were still using character to illustrate aspects of the overall design of the plot, later novels/films, it is argued, use the plot to illuminate aspects of character. If this is broadly true, then – since at the level of 'high art' and criticism this emphasis on character was brought to a head by, and largely went out with, Joyce, Woolf and Proust, among others, in the earlier part of this century – we have the remarkable (but actually very common) phenomenon of the most modern of the arts lagging several decades behind its seniors. A particularly important aspect of this model is whether it in fact applies only to half the characters/stars in films, i.e. only to men. In her discussion of stereotyping in the cinema, Claire Johnston extends Panofsky's discussion of iconography in the early cinema:

> Iconography as a specific kind of sign or cluster of signs based on certain conventions within the Hollywood genres has been partly responsible for the stereotyping of women within the commercial cinema in general, but the fact that there is a far greater differentiation of men's roles than of women's roles in the history of the cinema relates to sexist ideology itself, and the basic opposition which places man inside history, and women as ahistoric and eternal. As the cinema developed, the stereotyping of man was increasingly interpreted as contravening the realisation of the notion of 'character'; in the case of woman, this was not the case; the dominant ideology presented her as eternal and unchanging, except for modifications in terms of fashion etc. (*Notes on Women's Cinema*, pp. 24–5)

There are arguable (and hotly debated) exceptions to Johnston's rule – the woman's film; Howard Hawks; certain films identified by Jeanine Basinger in 'Ten That Got Away' as 'a considerable minority of Hollywood pictures with positive portraits [of women]' (p. 61); recent 'character studies' such as *Klute*, *Alice Doesn't Live Here Any More* and *Julia* – but all these are undoubtedly *exceptional*, thus suggesting the broad truth of the rule. What makes them exceptional is that these all feature women as central characters. This immediately involves the films in reconciling the stereotyping of women in general and the individuated requirements of protagonists. (In general, secondary characters of either sex are types, for reasons of economy as much as anything else – it takes longer and requires more detail to establish and develop an individuated character.) Whether the female *star*'s image also conforms to Johnston's rule is less clear – it is hard to see that Davis, Garbo, Monroe or Fonda are less individuated, or more type-based, than Wayne, Brando and Redford.

B – The novelistic conception of character

The following qualities may be taken to constitute an abstract of the novelistic conception of (or prescription for) character:

— particularity
— interest
— autonomy
— roundness
— development
— interiority
— motivation
— discrete identity
— consistency.

Particularity

This has already been discussed as the defining characteristic of novelistic conceptions of character. A more frequent, and extreme, term for this is 'uniqueness' of character.

Interest

W. J. Harvey argues that the emphasis on particularity rests on the 'liberal' humanism of the novel, that is, 'an acknowledgement of the plenitude, diversity and individuality of human beings in society, together with the belief that such characteristics are good as ends in themselves. It delights in the multiplicity of existence and allows for a plurality of beliefs and values ...' (*Character and the Novel*, p. 24). This means that the novelist 'must accept his [sic] characters as asserting their human individuality and uniqueness in the face of all ideology (including his own limited point of view) ...' (p. 25). As a result, Harvey suggests that it is impossible to reconcile novelistic character with 'monistic' commitments, such as Christianity and Marxism.

Autonomy

It is assumed that characters should have, or appear to have, 'a life of their own'. Precisely because they are no longer representatives of ideals or ideas, they must not appear to be merely a part of the design of the text, whether that be a thematic structure or simply a plot. We should not be aware of a character's construction, nor her/his function in the text's structure. We should have the illusion of 'life' in front of us. For many critics this illusion of 'life' is not an illusion. For characters do 'escape' the constructing activity of authors. Here, for example, is Bernard J. Paris in an extract from his *A Psychological Approach to Fiction*:

93

there is a character-creating impulse which has its own inner logic and which tends to go its own way, whatever the implied author's formal or thematic intentions may be. As critics we demand, indeed, that the central characters of realistic fiction be like real people, that they have a life of their own beyond the control of their author. (p. 9)

Roundness

The notion of 'round' as opposed to 'flat' characters is most familiar from E. M. Forster's *Aspects of the Novel* (1927). Forster is not claiming a rigid distinction between the two nor denying the usefulness of 'flat' characters, but roundness is clearly for him what novels 'are about'. Roundness means that characters cannot be understood in terms of one particular trait but rather in terms of a multiplicity that fuses into a complex whole. Round characters have the capacity to surprise the reader by the revelation of unexpected layers of character. Round characters are neither good nor bad, but a complex mixture of both.

Development

At a minimum, characters in novels should change. The fact that the novel can show 'life by time' (Forster) means that it can – and should – show a character's movement through time and how s/he changes. Scholes and Kellogg in *The Nature of Narrative* suggest that there are two forms of what they call 'dynamic characterisation':

> the *developmental*, in which the character's personal traits are attenuated so as to clarify his [sic] progress along a plot line which has an ethical basis (as in *Parsival, The Faerie Queene* Bk.1, *Pilgrim's Progress, Great Expectations* and *The Power and the Glory*); and the *chronological*, in which the character's personal traits are ramified so as to make more significant the gradual shifts worked in the character during a plot which has a temporal basis. (p. 169)

Scholes and Kellogg clearly regard the former as the more primitive, and explicitly identify the latter with the novel. A further distinction that may be made is between 'genuine' and 'apparent' development – that is, between revelations of character traits that constitute an alteration in the personality of the character as opposed to revelations of traits that are taken as having been present all along, but concealed from the reader/audience. J. L. Styan argues that the latter is in fact always the case: 'the development of character is in fact nothing but a finer definition of the features of the mask. It is properly the development of the image that deludes us into seeing a development in the character' (*The Elements of Drama*, p. 513).

Interiority

It is in the capacity of the novel to reveal what is in the heart and mind of a character directly – that is, without necessary recourse to inferences from what s/he says aloud, does or looks like – that the novel's special greatness is held to lie. Thus Paris claims that the novel 'gives us an immediate knowledge of how the world is experienced by the individual consciousness and an understanding of the inner life in its own terms' (*A Psychological Approach to Fiction*, p. 23). Devices such as authorial comment and internal monologue are held to give the reader access to a character's 'interiority' in a way closed to theatre, film and other forms of narrative fiction. As Leo Braudy points out, the specificity of the novel's access to interiority has been raised into a principle of its superiority, with which to bash film, especially, on the head:

> When critics say film allows no psychological complexity, they are drawing their standards from the nineteenth-century French and English novel, with its omniscient look into the inner thoughts of its characters, its decision to place the reader in a detached position about those thoughts, and its didactisim about the right kind of character and understanding one should have. (*The World in a Frame*, p. 183)

Motivation

The actions of characters should be motivated. This requirement involves both particularity and interiority, since what is understood by motivation is 'psychological' reasons for doing things. As Jeremy Hawthorn, in an attack on this aspect of characterisation, puts it: 'Anything the character ... does ... is ... explained in terms of that character alone in abstraction from his [sic] situation, and never in the particular, concrete context which called out some potentialities rather than others into the realm of action' (*Identity and Relationship*, p. 60).

Discrete identity

By this is meant the sense of characters having an existence and an identity independent of what they say and what they do – a self as well as roles. This is a problem for any narrative form, in that character logically only exists in the detail of the medium, in 'the words on the page'. This is granted by most literary theorists, yet the sense of an independent existence is none the less seen as requisite:

> if character manifests itself only in action, can we say it exists apart from action? This seems to be what we do say and believe with all our hearts – that character *is* absolutely, quite apart from what it does at any time. (Charles C. Walcutt, *Man's Changing Mask*, p. 5)

Consistency

The notion of a character's consistency is somewhat tricky. The fact that a character is discrete involves the assumption that, while character may be round, may change, surprise or reveal unexpected qualities, all this takes place within broad parameters of personality, the existence of which is guaranteed by the character's discrete identity. Harvey discusses this problem in terms of 'the idea of a stable ego': 'one aspect of our notion of identity lies in our sense that the self is discrete, isolated, unique; to this we may add the common assumption that it is a constant, stable thing' (*Character and the Novel*, p. 119). While admitting, following the trajectory of bourgeois philosophy since Hume, that this notion is philosophically unsound, Harvey none the less relates the idea of a stable ego – and thus of character consistency – to the 'commonsensical, unanguished, philosophically unsophisticated notion of the self' (p. 120). (The role of common sense as the cement of ideology should be borne in mind.)

How this consistency within roundness and development is achieved has not been much discussed. Kenneth Burke in *A Grammar of Motives* proposes the notion of 'repetitive form' as the means of securing coherence within rounded characterisation – that is to say that a formal pattern is discernible, and endlessly repeated, beneath the apparent changes in a character's behaviour. The notion of 'placing' discussed below (p. 121) also relates to this – through various techniques (dramatic irony, hierarchisation of discourses, use of stars), the different facets of a character may be 'explained' in terms of one, or a few, that are taken to be essential and defining.

The persistence of the notion of coherence/consistency in relation to character is clear in the following quotation from Cleanth Brooks and Robert Penn Warren, taken from a frequently reprinted, widely used, basic textbook on literary criticism. The use of 'obvious' in the first sentence is a good indication of how unchallenged this idea of character feels itself to be:

> An obvious test of fiction ... is that the motives and actions of its characters are rendered coherent. It is the glory of fiction that the great artists have been able to render coherent so many strange and out-of-the-way, often apparently self-contradictory, examples of human nature. (*Understanding Fiction*, p. 173)

It should be stressed that while it is appropriate to call these aspects 'bourgeois', this is not because any category of the individual is necessarily bourgeois, as certain anti-individualism polemics may appear to suggest. The peculiarities of the bourgeois conception of the individual/character are, first, that the stress on particularity and uniqueness tends to bar, or render inferior, representation of either collectivity and the masses or the typical person/character (types being relegated to a merely functional role in promoting the central character); and second, that the concern with interior motivation reinforces a model of history and social process in which explanation is rooted in the individual conscience and capacity rather than in collective and/or structural aspects of social life. (For a discussion of Marxist conceptualisations of the individual see Jean-Paul Sartre, *Search for a Method*, and the journal *Ideology and Consciousness*.)

Identification

The bourgeois conception of character intends to produce characters that are unique and individuated. Yet, clearly, not *so* unique and individuated as to be beyond comprehension or representativeness. For all their individuation, Hamlet, Elizabeth Bennett, the narrator of *Remembrance of Things Past* and Martha Quest are figures of identification, figures with whom the reader can, and is almost required to, empathise or at least feel some sense of familiarity. While the psychology of identification has been little explored (for a Freudian account, see Holland, *The Dynamics of Literary Response*, Chapter 10), it is clear that, as Joan Rockwell argues in *Fact in Fiction*, identification depends upon a fit between the traits of the character and those traits known about, understood, delimited by and available to the wider culture.

In the context of the bourgeois conception of character, we can discern two kinds of ideological work that identification is made to do. The first is what Rockwell identified as a general aspect of identification within all ideological systems, namely the reinforcement of norms:

Fiction not only legitimates emotions and aspirations, it also ... particularly since the appearance of the novel with its devotion to the minutiae of personal relationships, gives models and patterns of acceptable and unacceptable behaviour ... if the reader or watcher of drama can recognise enough of himself [sic] in a fictional character to make identification possible, identification with a literary character may be quite decisive in transmitting norms and influencing personal behaviour. (pp. 80–1)

The second is that the specific emphasis of bourgeois characterisation on the individual serves to mask the ideological role of character. By feeling that we are identifying with a unique person, we ignore the fact that we are also identifying with a normative figure. It needs only to be added that ideology works better when we cannot see it working.

(There is nothing intrinsically bourgeois, or wrong, with identification. See Rockwell for a discussion of identification in other cultures; for a discussion of the uses of identification in radical film-making see Christine Gledhill, 'Whose Choice?': Teaching Films about Abortion'. Recent theorisation stemming from Lacanian psychoanalysis sees – though it is not a position that is elaborated so much as assumed in passing – all identification as locking people into ideology through the construction of them as 'imaginary subjects outside contradiction'. By seeing 'whole and unified people' on the screen and identifying with them, we imagine that we are ourselves whole and unified people, and since this fiction of 'subjects' as whole people is one of the basic strategies of ideology, identification is one more barrier in the way of our breaking free from ideology. While most of this may be taken as a possible theorisation of identification, this last point does stray from the Althusserian/Lacanian insistence that one cannot live outside of ideology. One may be able to change ideology, but one cannot do without it altogether. For a discussion of this position see Colin MacCabe, 'Theory of Film: Principles of Realism and Pleasure'.)

Star images and character

Star images are constructed personages in media texts. In discussing them in Part Two emphasis was placed on them as types, yet they also bear many of the hallmarks of novelistic character. This is not as surprising as it may look. As the process of identification demonstrates, it is in fact perfectly possible, and indeed fundamentally inherent in the form, for a fictional character in the novelistic mode to be both normative with respect to social types and individuated with respect to the specific realisation of those types in a given character. The individuation of types is even taken to be the mark of 'greatness' in literature. Thus S. W. Dawson describes Harpagon in the climactic scene of Molière's The Miser as: 'the type ... invested with an individual life; it is the combination of the typical with the individual which makes this a great and memorable scene' (Drama and the Dramatic, p. 52).

From this point of view, star images do in many respects correspond to novelistic notions of character. They are particular and interesting. (The aspect of particularisation that Watt discusses most fully is the use of proper names to replace emblematic ones. However, a residue of the emblematic remains in the names of characters in the most 'realist' fiction and this element is probably even stronger with stars – hence John Wayne rather than Marion Morrison, Marilyn

Monroe rather than Norma Jean Baker. The fact that Fonda and Redford have retained their real names may relate to the cinema's becoming increasingly 'character-oriented'.) They are autonomous, although the notion of 'manipulation' is fairly widespread and this tends to undercut the illusion of the star's autonomous existence. Their existence in the real world is a guarantee of their independent identity.

Other aspects are more of a problem. That is, with regard to roundness, development, interiority, motivation and consistency star images aspire to the condition of novelistic characterisation in a medium not altogether developed to this end. Roundness, development and consistency may be taken together here, since all involve the nature of *change* in a star's image. Certainly there is no requirement that a star image should change, and a star's apparent changelessness over a long period of time can be a source of charisma. Apart from growing older, the image of Cary Grant or Bette Davis has not really 'deepened' since the period in which they were established as stars. Equally, attempts by a star to change may meet with box-office failure – Ingrid Bergman is the *locus classicus*. (Her popularity with American audiences was killed stone dead – for a few years – by her decision to make films with Roberto Rossellini and have their child without marrying him.) Some star image's careers do change (Joan Crawford, Jane Fonda) or at any rate 'deepen' (John Wayne, Marilyn Monroe). All these work within the notion of consistency – there must at least be traces of Crawford's flapper in her working women, of Fonda's sex-pot in her radical portraits – and the careers of Wayne and Monroe can be seen as disquisitions on the West and sex, respectively. With most stars this emphasis on consistency (or *apparent* consistency, since on investigation most images can be seen to condense conflicting values) may in fact go further than suggested in the abstract of the novelistic concept of character above, so that *sameness* becomes the overriding feature.

This is probably best explained by considering stars' appearances as serials. Just as Charles Dickens found in publishing his novels in serial form, and as contemporary soap opera also finds, changes in character are hard to handle in this form since they and milieu, rather than plot, are the form's anchors. Because stars are always appearing in different stories and settings, *they* must stay broadly the same in order to permit recognition and identification. (In this respect, star images as characters may be closer to how Scholes and Kellogg describe Homer's characterisation, where, for example, Odysseus always remains the same, fixed, simple character, indicated by repeated formulaic epithets, despite the fact that he plays an enormous variety of roles. See *The Nature of Narrative*, p. 164.)

Where interiority is concerned access to the inner thoughts of stars is also problematic, especially as they are always appearing in different roles. However, interviews and articles about or by them ('ghosted' or otherwise) may be read as granting such access, and the belief in the transparency of the face as a window to the soul is also widespread. What these elements lack is the precision and detail available to the novel, and the authority of the author's 'voice' to tell us the 'truth' about the character. (Cf. section on 'placing' below, p. 121.)

As to motivation, it may be worth recalling the discussion above of the paradigmatic nature of *The Jolson Story*, as revealing how stardom is conceptualised. Here both the decisions and desires of the protagonist are seen to motivate his actions, and yet certain other elements – the 'lucky break', the system – are also present. Similarly with star images generally: the star's ambition and success are shown to be rooted in her/his psychology, yet her/his lifestyle is one of passive consumerism (Lowenthal) and awareness of the manipulation of the image has become more widespread. In terms of motivation, then, stars are very often on the raw edge of the individual-versus-society, self-versus-role nexus.

What is abundantly clear is that stars are supremely figures of identification (for the various modes of this see Andrew Tudor, *Image and Influence*) and this identification is achieved principally through the star's relation to social types (and hence norms) as discussed in Part Two. What are the forms of the relationship between the star's uniqueness and her/his social normativeness? As a general rule, the star's uniqueness, seen as the only true locus of lived life, is a guarantee of the ideological truth of the type to which s/he belongs. One of the types that stars embody is the type of 'the individual' itself; they embody that particular conception of what it is to be human that characterises our culture. The specific relation of a star to her/his type may be conceptualised in terms of *transcendence, maximisation, inflection* and *resistance*. By transcendence it is assumed that the 'great' stars transcend the type to which they belong and become 'utterly' individual. That this is how many stars are experienced and that it is a condition to which the whole apparatus of the star system aspires are crucial aspects of the system's particular ideological flavour. However, the notion of a pure individuality, untrained by common social characteristics, is unsound both as a theory of personality (cf. Burns, *Theatricality*) and as a theory of characterisation, since an utterly unique personality/character/star in a film would be indecipherable (since decipherment/comprehension of any meaning/affect depends on shared, and therefore to some degree generalisable, signs).

Lawrence Alloway in the discussion of stars in his book *Violent America* suggests they are 'maximised types': 'In the movies we are faced with figures that embody in terms of contemporary references maximum states of age, beauty, strength, revenge or whatever' (p. 12). He instances Burt Lancaster as 'an ex-convict but a loyal friend with a code of honour' and Kirk Douglas as 'socially acceptable but faithless and corrupt' in *I Walk Alone*:

> The two men are maximized symbols, one, as Agee pointed out, for old-fashioned entrepreneurial elan (Lancaster as good bootlegger), and one for modern executive skills (Douglas as corrupt behind a corporate shield). Both attitudes to business (i.e. life) are appropriate in the 'capitalistic' United States.

Alloway deliberately talks here of the stars and the characters they play as one, and it is not clear whether he regards the stars as maximised types or just characters in Hollywood movies. The notion of maximised types would seem to tell us something about a star like John Wayne, who can be read as the Westerner par excellence, the man of the West taken to his logical conclusion. However, this perhaps only tells us about a tendency of stars' images – even Wayne has weaknesses and complexities that counteract this maximising tendency, and equally a star as profoundly contradictory as Monroe was also at the same time the 'ultimate' dumb blonde.

In the case of inflection, the star is seen to be within a distinct type mould and yet sufficiently different from it to be experienced as an individual variation on it.

The most obvious examples are the line of cowboys from William S. Hart to John Wayne, or Draculas from Max von Schreck to Christopher Lee. The variation may be little other than adding a few superficial idiosyncrasies to the type, but it may also exaggerate or foreground aspects of the type to such an extent that the type itself changes (e.g. the gradual emphasis on the *attractiveness* of the vampire, explicit in the literary sources but initially repressed in the cinematic versions until Christopher Lee, since when it has become a stock feature of the type). This introduction of new elements may, on examination, be seen to put the type at risk, either by introducing a contradictory element (e.g. Garbo/Christina's erotic attachment to her maid-in-waiting in *Queen Christina*, whereas the type traditionally either poses female royal rule as a choice between asexuality and heterosexuality – Davis as Elizabeth I – or else conflates female power with heterosexual manipulation – Dietrich as Catherine the Great); or by revealing the contradictoriness of the type (e.g. the male fascist, isolated pitch to which Clint Eastwood has taken the tough guy image) or, as in the Lee example, by bringing out a repressed element of the type.

In some cases the star's image's career has been centrally about attempts to overthrow the type to which s/he belongs. This has usually been done in the name of individuality, and the star's struggle to assert individualism in the face of typicality then becomes central to their image. (Cf. also Hollis Alpert's discussion of Marlon Brando in *The Dreams and the Dreamers*.) However, such resistance may also act to expose the oppressiveness of the type. Although 'individualism' can be seen in the contradictory development of Marilyn Monroe in relation to the dumb blonde sex-symbol type to which she belonged, this development can also be read in terms of suggesting how demeaning this type is.

Characters in films

Setting aside for the moment the question of the relationship of star image to the character constructed in film, we need to ask of the latter whether it too conforms to the novelistic conception of character. Here in the remarkable absence of any extended study of the matter (with the exception of Braudy, discussed overleaf), I shall have to risk generalisation even more than with the stars.

Characters in the kind of films stars usually appear in are certainly particular people in particular situations, with interesting traits and problems. We do not see their construction (unless we deem the film to have 'failed'), and they appear to have a life of their own. (This is confirmed by almost any off-the-cuff conversation people have about films.) Whether they are more predictable than 'roundness' would allow is impossible to generalise, but certainly the plot habitually involves a 'change of heart' somewhere along the line that is either the revelation of a hitherto unsuspected quality or a growth of those 'human' qualities that permit the happy end. (It would seem that character development in movies is closer to what Scholes and Kellogg call 'developmental' than to 'chronological' dynamic characterisation – see above.) Interiority and discrete identity are rather harder to assert; there are, as we shall see, devices to construct them but they are often felt to be exceptional (even though, as with voice-over, quite widespread at certain periods) and 'clumsy'. Consistency may be aimed at, but in films in which the plot is most important (which according to conventional wisdom is up to the late 50s), such consistency may be sacrificed in the interests of a concise and dynamic narrative. In this respect, although most actions are seen to be motivated by individual impulse, design or whatever, the consistency of this motivation is often in considerable disarray.

As with star images as characters, so film characters *per se* can be seen as character construction trying to be novelistic and yet not quite pulling it off. This problem of the *unsatisfactorily* novelistic quality of film characterisation underpins the discussion of the subject by Leo Braudy in *The World in a Frame*. He starts from the position that film characters *should* be individuated and then seeks to rescue character construction in films by showing how, by other means, films construct the novelistic notion of character.

Braudy emphasises that characterisation in films deals with the way people inhabit roles rather than those roles themselves. This can be seen as one inflection of the self/role opposition discussed by Elizabeth Burns in *Theatricality*. This he does through the questionable assertion that 'stage characters always exist in a society, and the great plays are almost all plays about the problem of living within a social context' (p. 195). Whereas:

> In films, the theatrical emphasis on the importance of the role is replaced by the authenticity of feelings, the preserved human being with whom we have come into contact. Film acting expands the ability of art to explore the varieties of the intimate self, apart from social awareness, outside of ceremonial or semi-ceremonial occasions, with a few others or even alone. (p. 196)

Braudy bases these observations on a conceptualisation of the 'nature' of film. He asserts that 'in films we tend to see characters alone, separate bodies before our eyes' (p. 185) and that 'films are obsessed by the human face, yet constantly collide with its final inscrutableness' (p. 187).

It is this that leads to his concern with 'the intimate self, apart from social awareness'. This may be an accurate description of how the dominant tradition in film has presented character, but it is also clear that nothing in the medium demands the use of 'isolating' close-ups while the inscrutablness of the human face rests on a certain 'naturalist' conception of the image which is opposed to any notion of the codification of the image (including the image of the human face). Braudy draws on assertions about film's 'essential nature' to describe particular, and ideologically determined, uses of film.

Having said that, however, it is still worth presenting Braudy's subsequent thesis on the varieties of film characterisation, since it is a stimulating discussion on different ways in which film has dealt with the issue of individuation. Braudy distinguishes between three types of characterisation (to which both star images and the construction of character by scenario, etc. conform): the double, the theatrical character and a synthesis of the two. All of these are constructed around the problem of role and self discussed above. They are in other words interesting distinctions within the problematic relationship between imposed norms of behaviour and the discrete persons who perform them.

The distinction between the double and the theatrical character rests on a distinction Braudy makes in an earlier section of his book between closed and open films:

> In the open films we experience character momentarily included by the limits of the film, with a life that extends beyond those limits. We believe that characters in such films pre-exist the specific events of the story and will exist after the story has completed its particular rhythm. (p. 218)

> The closed film, on the other hand, considers character to be only another element in the visual pattern of the film ... Character has no potential beyond what the film illustrates. It is character manipulation, because the closed film is a totally coherent system in which visual effects echo and re-echo, creating an aesthetic order that parallels the order in which their characters are caught. (pp. 219–20)

Renoir's work is Braudy's prime instance of the open film, and Lang and Hitchcock of the closed. The double and the theatrical character are the two dominant versions of characters corresponding to this distinction. With the double in the closed film it is the anguish of the powerfully oppressive nature of social roles that is articulated. Either the character is split between her/his inner self and outward appearance (e.g. the former surfacing in distorted forms, as in *M*, *The Wolf Man*, *I Was a Teenage Frankenstein*) or else two characters are shown to represent opposing facets of the same personality type (e.g. *Shadow of a Doubt*). With the theatrical character in the open film, on the other hand, codified social roles are seen as identities that the character is free to choose, select, try out at will. Renoir's *La Grande Illusion* and *La Règle du jeu* are adduced here, as well as *To Be or Not to Be*, *Lola Montès*, *Notti di Cabiria* and *Il Generale Della Rovere*.

Braudy is less clear on the synthesis of these two kinds of characterisation. He suggests that the 'new' (essentially post-New Wave) use of actors and characters consisted first in the recognition of 'the potential of character to escape total interpretation' and second in a self-consciousness about the fictionality of character and star images that threw assumptions about them into relief (and question). As a result the actor/character no longer has an instantly recognisable and definable personality but appears 'to have a wealth of possibility within, a complexity beyond the surface':

> The concept of a real movie face had been redefined, often through unconventional looks like those of Jeanne Moreau or Jean-Paul Belmondo, to prevent the audience from stopping at the surface and to make them wonder what in this face and behind it was worth exploring. (p. 251)

Braudy here lapses again into naturalism, implying that with Belmondo, Moreau, *Persona*, Brando in *Last Tango in Paris*, we are getting some closer contact with the actor/character precisely because their enigma and elusiveness is stressed. Yet these instances are just as much constructions as any other, and simply accord with another conception of what people are.

There are, clearly, considerable theoretical and methodological problems with Braudy's thesis. Braudy works within a theoretical opposition of liberalism and determinism (the classic oppositions of bourgeois philosophy). Either the individual is free to do what he (or she?) wishes (the 'open' film) or s/he is trapped in the 'forces' of 'society' (the closed film). Happily, for Braudy, the 'synthesis' he points to is also the defeat of 'the closed-film definition of *society*' by 'the open-film definition of *character*' (p. 258, my italics; Braudy slips in this give-away opposition without acknowledgment: it clearly signals the triumph of the individual over the social). Certainly we cannot lightly dismiss or skirt around this opposition, which is why Braudy's elaboration of its presence in films is so interesting; but the lack of any concept of dialectic between self and role or of any notion of the collective is a crucial one.

Regarding methodology, generalisations about the use of a given aesthetic feature in the whole of an art form obviously raise the question of evidence. There is no way round this question, but equally there can be no lapsing back into either empiricism ('the evidence speaks for itself' – it doesn't) or particularism ('every text is different' – it isn't, much). Braudy's thesis should be regarded heuristically, something to be tried out and worked with, fully recognising that where it is wrong and inapplicable may be as illuminating as where it is right and appropriate.

C – Alternative conceptions of character
Characterisation in film approximates to or tries to be like the novelistic conception of character. The qualifications to this are important. The special emphasis a commercial medium must put on identification (and hence on individuation within typicality), the problem of interiority (in a medium developed for narrative economy and spectacle), the supremacy of plot (in given periods), the fairly widespread knowledge of and cynicism about image manipulation; all suggest the problem film, as a mass art, has in sticking to bourgeois norms.

Before turning to the specificity of the filmic construction of character, it may be useful to indicate some other conceptions of character that have been used by film and their possible relevance to stars.

The 'world-historical individual'
Georg Lukacs's notion of the world-historical individual attempts to inflect the role/self aspects of character in such a way as to construct a character which articulates a given socio-historical conjuncture within a fully realised individual experience of that conjuncture. Thus history and society – both their detail ('extensiveness') and their movement ('intensiveness') – are revealed through a character who is chosen by the author because s/he is deeply involved with their 'social work', that is, the particular tasks their social situation sets them, tasks and a situation which are themselves capable of expressing the essential extensiveness and intensiveness of the given historical social moment. Thus there must be a: 'deep ... inner connexion ... between the persons at the centre of the drama and the concrete collision of the social-historical forces ... These characters [must be] engaged with their whole personality in the conflict' (*The Historical Novel*, p. 114).

Lukacs's attempt to re-articulate the individual/society, self/role oppositions has been deemed problematic, partly because of his adherence to the 'great tradition' of bourgeois literature, his hostility to modernism and the vague humanist rhetoric of his writing. However, his real weakness seems to me to be his failure to elaborate more clearly (that is, less by assertion and more through analysis) how this articulation of history/society through the individual character works, how one knows it when one sees it. Although utterly outside anything that would have appealed to Lukacs's temperament and without this evaluative emphasis, it is hard not to feel that a character like Monroe, Wayne or Fonda does not (or cannot be read as doing), through their typicality and individuation as well as through the obvious fact of people's identification with them, precisely dramatise such general social situations as the sexual objectification of women, the symbolic cluster of the West, the opposition between sexuality and politics respectively. This link between Lukacs's theory of character and the stars is explored by David Morse in 'The American Cinema: A Critical Statement'. There is also an interesting discussion of Lukacsian characterisation in films, including reference to the choice of performers, in Geoffrey Nowell-Smith's account of *Rocco and his Brothers* in his book, *Visconti.*

Types

As noted above, type characters are acknowledged to have a place in novelistic fiction, but only to enable the proper elaboration of the central, individuated character(s). In this respect, no star could be just a type, since all stars play central characters. (It may even be a rule that where the central character in a film is constructed by all other means as just a type, then the 'individuality' of the star masks this just as it does her/his image's typicality.)

Types have been used deliberately in the cinema in two ways. First, in the various notions of *typage*, stemming from the theories of Eisenstein, Kuleshov and Vertov. Here, performers were selected for roles on the basis of the appropriate-ness of their physical bearing to a particular, socially defined category of persons. (This 'appropriateness' is a matter of correspondence between a given performer and the tradition of representing the given social category, although Eisenstein for one tended to overlook this point and see the correspondence as between the performer and the social category, in reality.) Types in this tradition are often inflected to express the category's relative political desirability – e.g. the rough-but-noble face of the peasant, the over-sophisticated appearance of the bureaucrat – although this does not generally mean that the types are endowed with psychological traits.[1] Second, types may be exaggerated, reversed or otherwise foregrounded in order, in Claire Johnston's words, 'to provide a critique' of the 'ideological tradition' to which the types belong (see *The Work of Dorothy Arzner*). I am bound to say that my experience of teaching this line of argument, to which I felt broadly committed, has raised considerable doubts as to its validity. Very few students, even when acknowledging the thesis in principle, have felt they could see it at work in the supposed instances of it, e.g. the work of Arzner and Rothman. While this does not wholly undermine the thesis, it does make it harder to sustain. The relation to stars renders the issue even more complex. Whenever I have used *Dance Girl Dance*, for instance, students have found Bubbles/Lucille Ball the most interesting character, whose 'vitality' or 'charisma' makes her more than a stereotype. This goes against the argument, which reads Bubbles as a mere 'foregrounded' stereotype. (This does not mean that *Dance Girl Dance* is any less remarkable, but it may mean that we have to talk in terms of Ball, as much as Arzner, in relation to the stereotype and the way that her performance foregrounds the stereotype by resisting it. Equally problematic is the role of Judy/Maureen O'Hara and, as it seems to me, her unquestioned relationship to stereotypes such as the winsome ballerina and the hot-blooded Irish colleen.)

Deconstruction

Much of the argument against 'character' in literary criticism has come from a formalist position. This has moved from the obviously correct position that characters are not real people and only exist in their construction in the text to a position that suggests the only interest of literature is in the formal qualities of the text and its structuring. The radical variant of this position in relation to character suggests that texts should cease to construct the illusion of lived life in the use of characters and show how characters are simply devices that are part of a wider design. Thus Ben Brewster writes approvingly of *Justine* (by the Film Work Group) that its 'aim is a fictional space not dominated by narrative and actors speaking without projecting character (Edinburgh International Film Festival News, 1976); while Stephen Jenkins in his NFT programme notes (February 1978) rescues Fritz Lang for this view by celebrating the fact that in his later films we find 'characters stripped of humanity and reduced to concepts' (p. 19). Stars are of course wholly incompatible with this since they always bring with them the illusion of lived life, and indeed are often used to achieve this with films that are in other ways, admirably or not, schematic in their use of character. (E.g. in the case of Lang, Edward G. Robinson in *Woman in the Window*, Gloria Grahame in *The Big Heat* or Joan Fontaine in *Beyond a Reasonable Doubt* threaten, at any rate, to inform their role with the reverberations of their image, just by being in them; similarly Marlene Dietrich outlives Sternberg's calligraphic use of her.)

Brecht

Brecht's views on character have often been wrongly collapsed both into types and into deconstruction. Brecht's aim was not anti-realist, but rather to reinvent realism according to historical-materialist principles. In terms of character this included, first, a rejection of casting actors because they 'looked right' (the very basis of typage):

> It is pure folly to allot parts according to physical characteristics. 'He has a kingly figure'. Do all kings have to look like Edward VII? 'But he lacks a commanding presence'. Are there so few ways of commanding? 'She seems too respectable for Mother Courage'. Have a look at the fishwives. (*Brecht on Theatre*, p. 243)

Second, it involved a rejection of psychological, rounded character construction in favour of characters seen as, in John Willett's words:

> an inconsistent bundle of conflicting motives and interests, as inconsistent as himself [Brecht], or as the world in which we all live. Such characters are never 'rounded': they have to be presented as a jagged mass of broken facets, clear and hard and often transparent, offering many irrelevancies and distortions to the eye. (*The Theatre of Bertolt Brecht*, p. 55)

> the actor ... has to be able to show his [sic] character's coherence despite, or rather by means of, interruptions and jumps. (*Brecht on Theatre*, p. 55)

It is too great a simplification if we make the actions fit the character and the character fit the actions: the inconsistencies which are to be found in the actions and characters of real people cannot be shown like this. (ibid., p. 195)

Third, there was an emphasis on 'showing' or 'presenting' a character rather than embodying it, so that the actor sometimes steps out of character, comments on it, plays it a different way, etc. It is this last that has been interpreted as a mode of 'deconstruction', which to a certain extent it is. However, Brecht does not advocate the destruction of character through deconstruction, but rather the restructuring of character according to the principles outlined in the previous paragraph. The stepping out of character is not intended to destroy the reality of the character, but rather to give the performer/audience the opportunity of seeing the character in a new light, discovering a new contradiction, analysing the character's social, historical or political significance, etc. This breaks novelistic realism, but does not throw the baby of character out with the bathwater of psychologism and individualism.

The possibility of using stars in a Brechtian fashion resides in the star's embodiment of given social values which, if s/he performed with 'interruptions and jumps' and if the fit between her/his image and the character in the film was suitably manipulated, could break down the psychologistic, individuated assumptions of the star's image's character. In this way, various latent aspects of star images could be foregrounded: the contradictions they mask and condense, the anti-individualism aspects of typicality, the problem of interiority, and the knowledge of manipulation. This would not mean that the star as an entity ceased to exist, but that the nature of him/her as an entity would be radically altered, becoming 'an inconsistent bundle'. Examples of this that might be worth following up include comedians of various kinds – the Marx Brothers, Gracie Allen, Jerry Lewis – and Godard's use of Marina Vlady in *Two or Three Things I Know about Her* and of Jane Fonda and Yves Montand in *Tout va bien*. (I think one could also make a case for a Brechtian effect with Rita Hayworth in *The Lady from Shanghai*, Bette Davis in *Jezebel* and Barbra Streisand in *The Way We Were* – but the making of those cases will have to wait for another day.)

The construction of character

A character's personality in a film is seldom something given in a single shot. Rather it has to be built up, by film-makers and audience alike, across the whole film. A character is a construct from the very many different signs deployed by a film (within the context of cinema). (Cf. Roland Barthes's discussion of character and the 'semic' code in his *S/Z*.) The overall principle of construction is the conception of character outlined above, but within that we first have to ask what signs are used in the construction of character, and how; and second, what specific problems of character construction film poses.

Signs of character

In this section, I shall write principally from the point of view of the audience/reader/decoder of films. In other words, the question posed is, what are the signs that we as viewers latch on to in constructing characters? (I do not assume thereby a complete reciprocity, in terms of film-makers/audience, encoder/decoder understandings of the medium, but nor do I assume complete disjunction either.) In detailing these, I have also indicated what seem to me the largely unproblematic and immediate inferences that we draw from these signs, although the more difficult issues of inference I leave to the discussion of the problems of character construction in film.

The signs of character in film include:

— audience foreknowledge
— name
— appearance
— objective correlatives
— speech of character
— speech of others
— gesture
— action
— structure
— *mise en scène.*

(It will be clear that we have different orders of signs here, audience foreknowledge and action in particular referring to much larger sign-clusters than the rest. And even with the rest, we shall only be concerned with the sign's articulation at an already fairly high degree of complexity; for example, I shall take it that discussion of speech will not involve us in discussion of phonetics.)

Audience foreknowledge

We may come to the cinema with certain preconceptions about a character. These may be derived from:

— familiarity with the story. Many films are based on pre-existing books, often best-sellers or classics, plays, television series, or else on traditional stories. There will thus be members of the audience who have expectations about the character derived from their knowledge of the film's source. (The most famous example is probably Rhett Butler in *Gone with the Wind*, but in terms of the stars in this book, consider Brando as Stanley Kowalski, Zapata, Mark Antony, Fletcher Christian and Sky Masterson.)
— familiar characters. Certain characters exist across a span of films, or of films and other media, and may be incarnated by different stars: e.g. Sherlock Holmes, Tarzan, Dracula. (Are there any female examples?) Characters may also be biographical; e.g. Fanny Brice in *Rose of Washington Square*, *The Great Ziegfeld*, *Funny Girl*, *Funny Lady.*
— promotion. Advertising, posters, publicity, etc. may also set up certain expectations about character. (E.g. what sort of person would we expect Monroe and Brando to be playing on the evidence of the posters for *Niagara* and *Reflections in a Golden Eye?*)

20 *Poster for* Niagara, *1952.*

21 *Poster for* Reflections in a Golden Eye, *1967.*

— star/genre expectations. We expect John Wayne to play a certain kind of character, and we expect anyone playing the male lead in a Western to fit broad parameters of cowboy characterisation. This may be less (but seldom more) clear cut with other stars/genres.

— criticism. Accounts of films – and the characterisation in films – by critics and reviewers may also lead us to try to read a character in a certain way.

N.B. All of these forms of foreknowledge are expectations which may or may not be fulfilled. They do not have the prescriptive rigidity that holds for traditional character/stories in so-called 'traditional' societies. (Cf. Thomas F. Van Laan's discussion of character in Greek tragedy in *The Idiom of Drama*, pp. 72–6.)

Name

The character's name both particularises him/her and also suggests personality traits. Although names in films seldom have the effect of 'fixing' a character clearly from the word go, as in the classic 'charactonym' of morality plays and comedy (see Van Laan, *The Idiom of Drama*, p. 76), they do usually imply quite a lot about character. This may be material – the class and ethnic backgrounds of Stanley Kowalski and Blanche Dubois – or 'psychological' – the harsh consonants of Kowalski and the open vowels of Dubois, the connotations of Blanche (French = 'sophisticated'; denotes white, meaningful in the context of her background in the South, and also in the traditional opposition of white/pale skin = feminine; dark/brown skin = masculine). Names can be foregrounded in relation to identity. Thus the Monroe character in *Bus Stop* has chosen the name Cherie for its charming connotations, just as the Don Murray character mispronounces it Cherry for his lubricious view of her. Similarly the Murray character's name Beauregard charms Cherie, although his embarrassment at it leads him to call himself Bo. Another example is the Davis character in *Now, Voyager* who discusses with Tina (the daughter of her lover Gerry) what name she (Tina) should call her by. These include 'Aunt Charlotte', recalling her earlier, old-fashioned self, and 'Camille', the glamorous name Gerry has given her, as well as such 'obviously' inappropriate names as Carlotta and Charlie. Tina chooses Camille.

A star's own name can be similarly analysed, as suggested above, and it is very common for people to speak of a character in a film as having the star's name. This may be because names are harder to establish in films than in the novel or even, courtesy of the programme, the theatre, since it depends upon characters saying them repeatedly.

Appearance

What a character looks like indicates their personality, with varying degrees of precision. (When it is misleading – as in Mary Astor's superb plausibility in *The Maltese Falcon* – this becomes an issue in the narrative.) Appearance may be divided into the categories of physiognomy, dress and the image of the star.

We are able to place people's physiognomy according to such broad cultural oppositions as masculine:feminine (applied to both sexes), old:young, handsome:ugly, sensitive:crude, generous:mean, nice:nasty, etc., as well as to ethnic

22 *Robert Redford in* The Way We Were, *1973*.

types. There are also types of face and build thought to be characteristic of groups such as mothers, businessmen, lesbians, cowards, intellectuals and nobility.

Clothes and aspects of dress such as hairstyle and accessories are obviously culturally coded and widely assumed to be indicative of personality. (For considerations on the meaning of dress see Roach and Eicher, *Dress, Adornment and the Social Order*.) Dress is usually taken to point both to the social order in general and to the temperament of the individual concerned. Thus Robert Redford's clothes in *The Way We Were* place him in terms of period, age-group, class, occupation, etc., at the same time indicating certain personality traits, both stereotypic (the all-American boy) and relatively personalised (clean, warm-looking clothes, comfortable-but-not-sloppy). This 'dual' articulation of dress can be used in films to raise the issue of 'identity': e.g. the play on dress, both Chance's and Feathers', in *Rio Bravo*; *Now, Voyager*, with its protagonist's 'progression' through different dress styles/self-definitions, imposed by her mother (shapeless 'spinster's

23–25 *Character development constructed through dress. Bette Davis as Charlotte Vale in* Now, Voyager, 1942: *from 'dowdy spinster' (23, top left), through 'woman of fashion' (24, top right), to 'a whole person' (25, above). Note how the pattern of the first is integrated with the stylishness of the second in the final synthesis.*

dresses'), her sister (glamour), her lover (camellias), and, perhaps, herself (an amalgam of all three styles). (Figs. 23–25.)

The image of the star playing the character is carried in the star's physiognomy. This has been discussed by Lawrence Alloway in relation to Frank Sinatra in his article 'The Iconography of the Movies'.

Objective correlatives

In *The Nature of Narrative*, Scholes and Kellogg discuss Flaubert's use of 'physical correlatives to symbolize mental states', instancing Emma Bovary's dog, her bridal bouquet, Binet's lathe, etc. This may be considerably extended in film through the use of decor and setting, montage and symbolism. A character's environment – whether a home or a general landscape – may be felt to express him/her. (E.g. Bree's room in *Klute*, John Wayne's West. A film like *The Courtship of Eddie's Father* uses this with a fair degree of schematisation.) As in the classic example of Kerensky and the peacock in *October*, montage may also, by association of images, indicate aspects of character. Then again a character may be associated with a particular object or an animal (consider Hitchcock's use of birds of prey in relation to Norman/Anthony Perkins in *Psycho* and caged birds in relation to Tippi Hedren in *The Birds*). W. J. Harvey in *Character and the Novel* suggests that objects do not only reflect or express character, as proposed by Scholes and Kellogg, but may also reveal personality by the character's attitude to and 'control' over things. A very clear example of this in the cinema is the contrast between James Stewart and John Wayne in *The Man Who Shot Liberty Valance*. The difference between them in the ability to handle a gun (shown in the awkward dangling of the weapon from Stewart's hand in his confrontation with Liberty Valance as compared to Wayne's elegant poise with a gun in the flashback of the same scene), and the different placing of them in the restaurant kitchen (Wayne massively standing in the centre of the bustling activity, Stewart clumsily trying to read while washing up), help to establish their position in the world.

Speech of character

What a character says and how s/he says it indicate personality both directly (what a character says about him/herself) and indirectly (what a character betrays about him/herself). Importantly, we are more inclined to trust our perception of the latter than the former. (Cf. Erving Goffman, *The Presentation of Self in Everyday Life*.) A special case of the former is voice-over, whether in the role of narrator or just as a device for the expression of inner thoughts. These we are more inclined to believe, since the former is grounded in the convention of the (more or less) omniscient narrator and the latter in a belief in the truth of the 'private'.

Speech of others

What other characters say of a character, and how they say it, may indicate a personality trait of that character and/or of the characters speaking. Again, the question of who we believe and why is problematic. It is important to note that these last two categories include dialogue, that is, speech between characters and not just isolated statements.

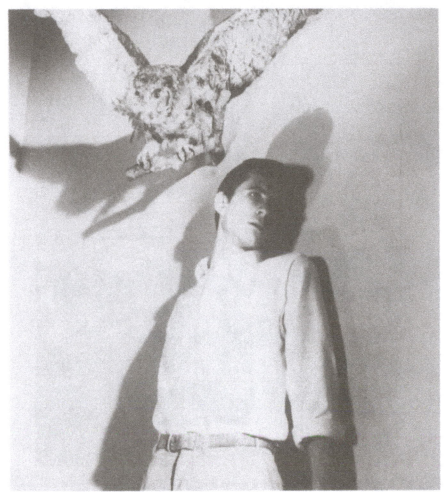

26 *Anthony Perkins as Norman Bates, a bird of prey,* Psycho, *1960.*

Gesture
The vocabulary of gesture may be read according to formal (that is, recognised to be governed by social rules) and informal (or involuntary) codes. Both may be taken as indicative of personality and temperament, although only the former recognises the social dimension of personality. For this reason, the latter are often taken as giving particularly privileged access to a character's 'true' self. (E.g. one could examine the obvious 'tough' stance assumed by Bree in her first meeting with Klute and the way it is 'betrayed' by slight nervous facial grimaces and finger movements.) This will be discussed in the section on performance.

Action
Action is not always easy to distinguish in practice from gesture. It refers to what a character *does* in the plot. A rule of thumb might be that an action furthers the

27 *Tippi Hedren as Melanie, a caged bird,* The Birds, *1963.*

narrative in some way and points towards plot, whereas a gesture does not further the narrative and points towards character. (In an intimate narrative situation, a raised eyebrow may constitute an action, since, for example, it furthers the development of a relationship.) In terms of Bree in the scene discussed in the previous paragraph, the action is that she does not let Klute in.

Structure
The notion of action already points towards the question of plot, one of the most familiar kinds of structure that film may have. The role of structure in character may, however, extend beyond plot. This involves us in a brief discussion of different concepts of structure in relation to character, and consequently this subsection is considerably longer than those above.

The notion of the structure of a narrative fiction involves a crucial assumption about the way we read such fictions, namely, that we are able, at the end of reading, to construct what the structure(s) of the text is (are). Narrative is linear, one thing follows another, and we therefore read it sequentially; but we can also grasp its overall shape, after we have read it. W. J. Harvey calls this distinction that between temporal or sequential reading and spatial reading. Roland Barthes, in *S/Z*, has inflected this distinction in terms of two reading codes, the hermeneutic and the proairetic. The former is sequential; it is the questions the narrative poses, and the reader poses of the narrative, as it/he/she goes along. The latter is the overall shape of the narrative as one understands it at the point at which one stops reading (which may or may not be before the end of the story). The relationship or tension between these codes is as important as the codes themselves; it is not the either-or that the sequence/space opposition tends to pose.

The important problem posed by this distinction is how far one accepts an emphasis on structure as something that corresponds to the actual practice of reading (and not just to critical ingenuity). On one's answer to that depends on an assessment of what structure can reveal about character and the importance of structure *vis-à-vis* other signs of character.

The notion of function in relation to character and structure revolves around an issue that has been debated since Aristotle, but with special insistence since the emphasis on character in the nineteenth-century novel. Baldly, the issue is whether characters are to be seen as functions of the structure, their personality determined by the requirements of the plot (or other structural principle) or whether, on the contrary, structure is to be seen as emanating from character, the plot in particular expressing the personality of the characters. As Martin Price puts it: 'Is a character a person living a free and spontaneous life or part of a plot ... ? Does the person dissolve into an agent of plot, or does the plot seem, at some level, the working out of the characters' inherent natures?' ('The Other Self', p. 271).

This issue invokes wider debates. Within a Marxist frame of reference, two polemical positions can be outlined. A polemic in favour of structure over character sees the reverse as expressing bourgeois individualism (the discrete self seen as the motive of both individual action and the course of human history) and, in a modernist inflection of the polemic, sees undue emphasis on character disguising the facticity of structure that is an inescapable element of any work of fiction. The polemic in favour of character over structure identifies an emphasis on structure with myth, fatalism or crude determinism, and rejects the notion that a fiction's facticity must necessarily be foregrounded in order for audiences to know that they are watching a fabrication. However, it seems to me that the emphasis on character can also be an emphasis not only on the individual but also on human activity, while the emphasis on structure can also be an emphasis on the determinations that act on a human life. This suggests that some way of articulating the relation between structure and character, determinations and human activity, may lead out of the reactionary implications of adhering too exclusively to either side of the dialectic.

With this in mind, further issues arise. First, how does one identify where the emphasis lies in terms of structure or character (and their functional relationship)? At present, we shall have to rely on intuition and plausible arguments, since as far as I know no theorisation of this has been undertaken.

Second, the fit between a character's personality and the demands of plot/ thematic structure, etc., or between the shape of the plot and the personality traits it is required to express, may be more or less good. Fitting the star image to this adds a further complication. In a discussion of Lana Turner's role as Cora in *The Postman Always Rings Twice* in 'Four Films of Lana Turner', I have suggested that one can see three uneasily combined elements: (i) Cora's function in the plot (and it is a very strongly foregrounded plot) as the instrument of Frank's tragic destiny; (ii) the motivations ascribed to the character by dialogue which appear to motivate the plot in some degree; (iii) the image of Lana Turner. I argue in the article that the contradictions between (i) and (ii) are masked by the presence of Turner, whose image itself contains and reconciles other, and relevant, contradictory elements. I think the three elements I isolate that contribute to the construction of Cora/Turner are correct, although I am less certain that the way the viewer combines them to make sense of the character is necessarily the one I argue for. The important point here is to be aware of the *problem* of fit, and, to fulfil the sacred requirement of coherence, of the film's necessary apparent resolution of that problem.

Third, this question of fit, and of emphases on character and structure, can lead to some interesting articulations of the problem of the individual and the determinations that act upon him/her. It may be a way of coming to grips with the idea of a star's 'transcending' their material, as posed by Molly Haskell among others. For instance, *Now, Voyager*, in common with most 'women's pictures', uses coincidence, repetition and convoluted narrative in its plot, in such a way that the protagonist's role becomes passive: she is a 'function' of the 'plot'. However, by virtue of the fact that the protagonist is Bette Davis (i.e. the carry-over of her battling independent image) and that it is her performance which imposes, as we watch it seems as if character dominates and the plot is therefore an expression of her development (repressed spinster to glamorous independent woman). Whether in the final analysis one decides structure or character dominates depends on how you read the film; and perhaps precisely the point of the film is that it is about the tension between the two, that is, between determinations and human action.

Most critics who have devoted attention to structure have tended to regard character as a function of it. Their difference lies in the ways in which structure is conceptualised.

Some critics treat the structure of a given fiction as particular to it. However, most critics of structure have seen a given work's structure as an instance of more generalised structures, whether across particular genres or bodies of works (e.g. auteur studies or, potentially, star vehicles) or across narrativity in general. Two broad differences of conceptualisation may be discerned: *linear* structures and *relational* structures. Linear structures are for our purposes plots (although in principle they could be logical patterns such as syllogisms or musical ones such as sonata form), that is, a progression of events, one following another in an ordered sequence. This may be very simple (as in the horror film structures outlined by Andrew Tudor in *Image and Influence*, pp. 203–11) or very complex (as in Vladimir Propp's sequence of functions in Russian fairy tales; cf. Peter Wollen on *North by Northwest* in '*North by Northwest*: A Morphological Analysis'). In either case, what

116

the critic has tried to do is to establish the basic pattern upon which a host of seemingly different stories are built. (This pattern may be 'transformed', it may 'generate' other patterns – cf. Claude Brémond's discussion of Propp[2] – but the notion of sequential ordering none the less remains.) Relational structures are identified not in a linear sequence but in certain root relationships or oppositions. The most popular version of this has been that of binary oppositions (e.g. Wollen, Kitses[3]), but another instance is the set of 'base predicates' that Tzvetan Todorov identifies in his analysis of *Les Liaisons dangereuses*, 'Categories of the Literary Narrative'. (These predicates are forms of relation between the characters – desire, communication, participation – that 'generate' the book's plot by means of various narrative 'rules' of transformation, reversal, combination, etc.) Whether using linear or relational concepts of structure, most critics have been content to locate characters as functions of those structures. As Seymour Chatman observes, discussing Propp's view of character: 'it is as if the differences in appearance, age, sex, life-concerns and so on were *mere* differences, and the similarity of function were the only important thing' ('On the Formalist-Structuralist Theory of Character', p. 57).

This question of the relation between a character's function and the traits attributed to him/her takes us back to the questions raised in the discussion of function.

Mise en scène

The cinematic rhetoric of lighting, colour, framing, composition and the placing of actors that is usually referred to as *mise en scène* can be used to express the personality or state of mind of characters. For example, V. F. Perkins discusses a scene in *The Courtship of Eddie's Father* in which, on Eddie's first day back at school after his mother's death, he is 'perched on top of a kitchen stool, taking down a cup and saucer from the wall-cupboard'. Perkins suggests various meanings that are expressed by the decision to place Eddie in this position for this conversation with his father, including one related to Eddie's character: '[it] takes us graphically inside Eddie's mind and feelings by stressing the instability of his emotional balance. Eddie's precarious physical position on the stool, his careful handling of two fragile objects, counterpoint his attempt at emotional balance' (*Film as Film*, p. 76).

J. A. Place and L. S. Peterson in an article on visual style in film noir attempt to systematise in some degree the *mise en scène* of a particular filmic tradition, and this again includes the way *mise en scène* contributes to the construction of character. They compare, for instance, the 'soft' and 'vulnerable' effect on lead actresses of diffused lighting in standard Hollywood lighting with the use of 'harsh lighting of the low-key *noir* style' on their film noir counterparts: 'the *noir* heroines were shot in tough, unromantic close-ups of direct, undiffused light, which create a hard, statuesque surface beauty that seems more seductive but less attainable, at once alluring and impenetrable' ('Some Visual Motifs in *Film Noir*', p. 328).

Mise en scène analysis raises more acutely than the other signs of character considered in this section the problem of interpretation and inference. At the same time, it also points to the very basic fact that all the other signs are perceived through and in *mise en scène* and that we have somehow to come to grips with this level of analysis.

Problems of character construction in film

Inference

The problem of inference is not a problem specific to the cinema, but is common to all fictions that use characters. Although anathema to all brands of formalist critic, it is a fact of the reading process in whatever medium that we infer what a character 'is like' beyond the definite information supplied about him/her in the signs listed above. We may guess at why a character does such and such, what s/he would do in other circumstances, what her/his childhood was like. The bases of these guesses may be conceptualised in different ways:

Most commonly the universals of human nature are invoked. We infer that a character feels so-and-so because that is what people – or people like that – would feel in such-and-such circumstances. A sophisticated version of this is Norman N. Holland's discussion of character and identification in relation to the universal processes postulated by psychoanalysis (see *The Dynamics of Literary Response*).

That notions of human nature are used by us in inferring aspects of character is undoubtedly the case – what we have to do is to be very careful about the cultural, historical specificity of such notions and their ideological provenance. In terms of character analysis in films, this means attempting to situate the constructed character in relation to the assumptions about human nature (and the different character types that embody them) prevalent at the time the film was produced.

The inferences that we make may be outward, to universals or cultural specificities. They may also be, as it were, inwards, to the place of the character in the overall scheme of the film. As Price observes, in a discussion of character in novels:

> Character may be said to exist within a novel as persons in a society, but the 'society' of the novel is one with intensive and purposive structure. We read the novel immersed in its complexity, it is true, but with confidence in its resolution and its ultimate significance. This sense of a total structure inevitably qualifies the attention we give to the characters; it need not diminish that interest, but it complicates it. ('The Other Self', p. 269)

Price is not arguing here for the ascendancy of structure over character, but rather for the subjection of both to a work's overall 'purpose'. It is in this sense that we may infer a character's personality from our sense of a novel's/film's overall purpose. As students, we would need to bear in mind questions of multiple or contradictory purposes, or on what grounds one could establish a dominant purpose, etc. Thus if we take *Last Tango in Paris* to be 'about' the male menopausal problem of Paul/Brando, we will infer different meanings from his treatment of Jeanne/Schneider than if we take the film to be 'about' the relation between them. Whether these meanings are complementary or contradictory is a different question.

Interiority

The biggest problem facing film in trying to construct character along more or less novelistic lines is how to render a character's 'inner life'. Leo Braudy sees this as constituting film's break with the norms of the novel:

28 *Reaction shot – Barbra Streisand as Katie, the moment she catches sight of her old flame Hubbell, in* The Way We Were, *1973.*

> The basic nature of character in film is omission – the omission of connective between appearances, of references to the actor's existence in other films, of inner meditation, in short, of all possible other worlds and selves except the one we see before us. (...) The visible body is our only evidence for the invisible mind. (*The World in a Frame*, p. 184)

However, film does have access to certain methods for expressing interiority. Quite apart from the connotations of 'invisible' character traits carried by all the signs listed above, certain devices have been particularly developed.

The notion of the truth 'revealed' by the close-up has been discussed in Part One (p. 15). In relation to character, Scholes and Kellogg assert that 'In a movie the close-up provides a way of revealing more of the psyche than can be managed on the stage through mere expression and gesture ...', but add that 'in narrative only (i.e. written and spoken narrative) is the inward life of characters really accessible' (*The Nature of Narrative*, p. 171). What they are getting at here is the absence of any discursive consideration of a character's inner thoughts and feelings (whether achieved by narrative intervention or interior monologue) in the close-up. In fact, in so far as the notion of seeing into the character's 'psyche' may be invoked by close-ups, it is so within a conception of the essentially indefinable, mysterious and ineffable nature of the human psyche. The paradigm of this is Greta Garbo (cf. Roland Barthes's short article 'The Face of Garbo' in *Mythologies*).

A shot may also show us the reaction of one character to an event or another character. If this shot is clearly signalled as being something that only we, the audience, have been permitted to see, then it is read as giving us an insight into the inner thoughts/feelings of that character. For example, the shot of Katie/Streisand as she catches her breath at seeing Hubbell/Redford in the night-

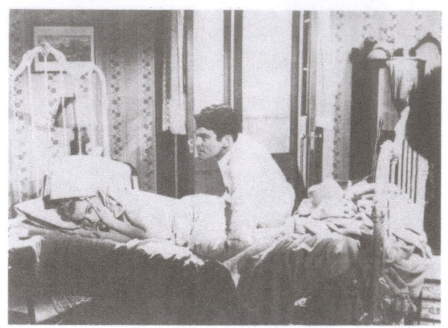

29 Bus Stop, *1956: Marilyn Monroe as Cherie and Don Murray as Bo. He has one feeling about their future together, she has another, negative one. Placing allows us to see both feelings.*

club in the pre-credit sequence of *The Way We Were* (Fig. 28). This is a medium shot, cut on her turning away from the man she has come in with and cross cut with shots of Hubell/Redford asleep at the bar. Her visible reaction, because it is clearly not addressed to another character, is then read as telling us unmediatedly about her inner feeling. A particularly striking example of the reaction shot, taken to lengths perhaps only possible in silent films, is the long take (in *True Heart Susie*) of Susie/Lillian Gish's reaction to her beloved's apparent infidelity with the town floosie, which she overhears outside his door. By the most delicately modulated facial mime, Gish conveys the conflict within her/Susie of utter distress at his betrayal and a determination not to be brought low by it or to show her pain. It should be added that such private reactions can be registered within a shot, as for instance Cherie/Monroe's horror at Bo/Don Murray's early morning call on her in *Bus Stop*, shown by her reaction lying across the bed bottom left of screen while he walks about oblivious at top right.

The most obvious form of access to a character's inner thoughts is the voice-over. As an example, there is the sequence of Jerry/Paul Henreid's first meeting with Charlotte/Davis, travelling incognito as Miss Beauchamps, in *Now, Voyager*. Half-way through the sequence, Jerry leaves her to make a phone call, having just said that he wants to know who she really is. Looking after him, her voice says (over), 'He wants to know', twice – the first time with an inflection suggesting that she too would like to know who she is, the second with a slight hint of irritation at his presumptuousness.

A shot taken from the point-of-view of one of the protagonists in a scene is part of the basic narrative grammar of film. Given that this means we are seeing through the eyes of a character, it may be said to afford us a certain access to the (constructed) interior of that character. (In a discussion of the way point-of-view (POV) shots are established and how they work, Edward Branigan suggests that POV shots, because they 'belong' to a character, thereby point to 'the presence – the existence – of character' and are thus one of the ways by which the construction of character as an apparently autonomous existence is achieved. See 'Formal Permutations of the Point-of-View Shot'.)

Such shots in general do little more than allow us to see what the character sees, and this may of itself be of little significance. In most cases, we already know what the character sees and all that the POV shot does is confirm that s/he sees it (e.g. POV shots in dialogue confirm that the characters are seeing each other as well as looking at each other). However, there are two exceptions to this. First, where a POV shot reveals that a character is seeing something other than that which we know s/he is seeing. This may constitute a distraction or a revelation for the character, or else reveal to us that the character's mind is elsewhere than we suppose (e.g. a POV shot in which it is revealed that a person is not looking at the person they are speaking to but at a picture of someone else on the wall). Second, properly subjective shots, where we see not only what the character sees but, through a well-known rhetoric, how s/he sees it: e.g., the skewed angle shot of Cary Grant that expresses Ingrid Bergman's sense of hangover near the beginning of *Notorious*.

The examples of Gish and Davis above both needed to refer to performance in addition to reaction shot and voice-over respectively in order to describe what was conveyed in each about character. More generally, it seems to me that Braudy and Scholes and Kellogg underestimate the degree to which performance can signal inner thoughts, even in interactions with another character. Performance will be considered at greater length below, but the following examples may be worth citing here. Bette Davis's ability to convey (to us), largely through use of the eyes, that she is lying and thinking about something else, even while she is telling the lie (e.g. in the scene in *Dark Victory* where she tells George Brent, a doctor, that there is nothing wrong with her; and numerous examples throughout the films she made with William Wyler: *Jezebel, The Letter, The Little Foxes*); the apparently spontaneous and untrammelled expression of emotion embodied in Judy Garland's performances (cf. especially the single long take of her discussing Norman/James Mason with Oliver/Charles Bickford in her dressing room in *A Star is Born*); the use of irrelevant but 'revealing' gestures or tics by Method actors, including Brando and, most manneredly, Rod Steiger.

Placing

Nearly all forms of narrative fiction attempt to 'place' the reader/audience in relation to the characters, in terms both of the understanding we are to have of a character and our judgment of or feeling for him/her. This involves the notion of coherence. Out of the mass of details about personality that we may be given about a character, we construct a coherent character and attitude towards him/her. We decide that certain aspects are 'true' and correspondingly likeable, approvable or otherwise, and use these aspects to comprehend and judge the other aspects. It seems that this is a tendency of both texts and readers, but it should be pointed out that (i) what the text tries to get the reader to construct may not in fact be what s/he constructs; and (ii) it may be our job as students of film to construct the totality of traits, in all their complexity and contradiction, and attempt to work out which of these is signalled as the 'true' and 'positive' aspect(s) of the character without ourselves reducing the polysemy of traits to that (those) anchoring trait(s).

Much placing depends upon the way a film associates a character with cultural/ideological values and attitudes. Such cultural assumptions are partly to do with stereotypical views of the social group to which a character belongs. That is to say, we judge a character to a certain extent on how s/he fits with our previous assumptions of what members of that group are like. This judgment in turn differs according to whether, first, we take our assumptions as unalterable and therefore take those traits of the characters that conform to our assumptions as the essential and defining ones against which to place all the others; or second, we may tend to consider cases where characters seem to break with stereotypes as traits thereby more individuated and hence more 'real'. (Cf. Christine Geraghty's analysis of *Alice Doesn't Live Here Any More* in *Movie*, no. 22.)

Cultural assumptions may also be of a different order, concerned with the circumstances under which 'transparency', 'sincerity', 'authenticity' and hence 'the true person' are to be found. These have been mentioned in passing above, and seem in our culture to cluster around notions of the private and the uncontrolled. That is, when people are not in public, and especially in circumstances defined as intimate (the family, bed), they are held to be more 'real' than otherwise; and when people 'let themselves go', pour forth their thoughts and feelings in an untrammelled flow, then they are being their 'true selves'. (The latter also relates to popular psychoanalysis, the notion of the Id, or that which is repressed, always threatening to burst forth and somehow, by its very force and intensity, being thought of as more 'real' than the super-ego that controls it.)

These cultural assumptions 'get into' films via iconography of social personality types and conventions of *mise en scène*, montage, performance, etc. Let me briefly exemplify all this from *All About Eve*. Margo/Davis has an ambitious admirer in Eve/Anne Baxter, who acts as her devoted slave while secretly desiring to usurp her star status. Equally, Margo is torn between her devotion to the theatre and her desire for a permanent heterosexual relationship. The film tries to place us in relation to this tension such that we acknowledge and feel it as a real and legitimate tension, and yet ultimately feel the second should have supremacy over the first. Two scenes illustrate how this is achieved. The first occurs when Margo arrives late for the audition of Miss Caswell (Marilyn Monroe) for a small part in a play she, Margo, is currently starring in. She meets Miss Caswell in the foyer, where the latter explains that Eve has stood in for her, knew her lines perfectly and was 'wonderful'. Margo goes into the auditorium and pretends not to know what has happened. She goes onto the stage as if to start the audition and then feigns surprise, followed by anger, when she is told that Eve had taken her place. By having Margo delay her anger and then 'deliver' it on a stage in a display of histrionics (a brilliantly witty speech, delivered with expert timing and thrust), the film

30 *Plain and simple Anne Baxter, as Eve, faces overblown and monstrous Bette Davis, as Margo, in* All About Eve, *1950 – but appearances are deceptive.*

effectively undercuts the legitimacy and authenticity of her anger. This has been achieved by the refusal through *mise en scène* of the private (it is on a stage) and through performance of the uncontrolled (it is superbly 'played').

In a later scene, Margo has been in the country with a couple who, because they also like Eve, fix their car so that they run out of petrol when running Margo to the station in time for a performance (hence Eve, her understudy, has to go on for her). The man leaves the car to find petrol, and Margo talks to the woman about being an actress and how, if you haven't got a man, no matter how famous you are, you are not really fulfilled as a woman. Whereas the first scene undercuts what Margo says through *mise en scène* and performance, this scene uses these features to substantiate what she says. Thus the fact that the man leaves turns the situation into a private conversation between women friends (itself a paradigm of an occasion for authenticity, unburdening one's heart, and also in this film clearly within the tradition of the protagonist and the confidante, to whom the former always speaks her heart and mind), while the long held close-up bespeaks a rhetoric of truth already discussed. In this scene, the 'truth' of the tension – that in the end for a woman marriage is more important than career – is asserted, assisted, it need hardly be added, by the massive resonance of that 'truth' in patri-archal culture. Further complexity is added to this if one places Margo and Eve iconographically. The former is 'monstrous', tough, bitchy, in her first scene shown with her face plastered in cold cream and her eyes moving about neurotically. The latter on the other hand is a 'sweet girl' with a soft voice, pretty features and modest appearance (she wears a mac in the first scene, and afterwards very simple dresses). This iconographic contrast is also clear in the party scene in the middle of the film (Fig. 30). The film however, in its course, cheats these iconographic implications. Eve is revealed as hard as nails underneath, and as having only her career at stake; while Margo is revealed as easily hurt, vulnerable, ultimately wanting to settle down with a man. This iconographic reversal is a departure from stereotypes and thus may be read as 'realism'. Equally the fact that it meshes so powerfully with the ideology of a woman's place also secures it the label of 'realism' (i.e. conforming to prevailing norms). The fact that Bette Davis plays Margo allows the tension to appear to be 'authentic' (i.e. not decided in advance in favour of one term over the other), in that she was someone who put her career before her private life while at the same time insisting that beneath it all she was just a woman in need of a man. (However, her autobiography, *The Lonely Life*, which echoes some of Margo's sentiments in the car scene, was published eleven years after the release of *All About Eve*.)

Hierarchy of discourses

In an article entitled 'Realism and the Cinema: Notes on some Brechtian theses', Colin MacCabe suggests that the formal operation of what he calls the 'classic realist text' (which includes '*The Grapes of Wrath* and *The Sound of Music*, *L'asso-moir* and *Toad of Toad Hall*', p. 12) consists in placing the various discourses of the text (e.g. the construction of characters) in a position of subservience to the 'narration of events':

> Through the knowledge we gain from the narrative we can split the discourses of the various characters from their situation and compare what is said in these discourses with what has been revealed to us through narration. The camera shows us what happens – it tells the truth against which we can measure the discourses. (p. 10)

MacCabe illustrates this from *Klute*. He suggests that Bree's (Jane Fonda) 'subjective discourse' in her talking to the psychiatrist 'can be exactly measured against the reality provided by the unfolding of the story', and that the final shot of the film counterposes (in a voice-over from her last meeting with her psychiatrist) 'her own estimation of the situation ... that it most probably won't work' with 'the reality of image [which] ensures us that this is the way (i.e. settling down) it will really be' (p. 11). It is hard to know how MacCabe gets this meaning from the *image* of an empty room with a telephone in it; and because his analysis remains formalist, without cultural situating, he does not consider the 'privileged' status as 'truthfulness' of enclosed conversations between psychoanalysts and their clients. However, the primary narrative expectation that heterosexual couples will get together at the end of the film (cf. Joan Rockwell, *Fact in Fiction*) may be powerful enough for us to read into the film's end that this is what has happened and therefore that Bree's talk of her desire to be independent is just talk.

In fact, MacCabe's example is more ambiguous than he allows. While this does not diminish the interest of his general thesis, it does raise the question of how one knows it to be correct. Let us go back to the 'rebel heroes' and 'the independent women'. If MacCabe's thesis is correct, then these categories can only be granted even partial progressive force if the narrative outcome coincides with what the characters declare themselves to be and to desire. As we have seen, this is almost never the case – narrative events nearly always undercut the rebel/

independent woman *as* rebel or independent woman. To counter MacCabe, we would need to argue *either* that other levels of discourse (*mise en scène*, performance, star image) can be as decisive as narrative events; *or* that (a) texts are contradictory, a structured polysemy which have the ambition to be an expressive totality (reducible to one discourse) but seldom achieve it and (b) audiences read texts differently, not 'freely' certainly, but not uniformly either. MacCabe's thesis returns to the problem of reading and of validity in interpretation. Nevertheless, its heuristic value should not be overlooked – to pose the question of the hierarchy of discourses in relation to a given film can enable one to attain a particularly useful engagement with its ideological operation.

Star identification

The phenomenon of audience/star identification may yet be the crucial aspect of the placing of the audience in relation to a character. The 'truth' about a character's personality and the feelings which it evokes may be determined by what the reader takes to be the truth about the person of the star playing the part.

In a discussion of *Last Tango in Paris* ('The Importance and Ultimate failure of *Last Tango in Paris*') E. Ann Kaplan suggests that the intention of the film, as evidenced by *mise en scène* and the character of Tom (Jean-Pierre Léaud), is to act as a critique both of two dominant film styles (50s American and French New Wave), including the appropriate acting style, and of the ideological values that go with them (broadly categorisable as, respectively, Hemingway-tough male dominance and anguish, and chic and 'modern' irresponsibility and permissiveness). The film's method involves putting a distance on the characters in order to be able to see their cinematic/ideological representativeness – and this includes the Brando character, Paul. However, argues Kaplan, because it is Brando and because he employs an acting style which 'has the effect of drawing the audience in close to the character', the film's aim of placing us at a critical distance to him does not come off. Instead Brando/Paul's view (and Kaplan suggests they are almost identical in this instance) comes to dominate the film and thus seems to be legitimated. For all the subtle undercutting and irony that Bertolucci deploys and that Kaplan draws attention to, Brando – as image (the reverberations of *Streetcar Named Desire* and *On the Waterfront* still remaining) and as performer (the compelling interiority of the Method) – is so powerful that 'it was logical for people to take Brando's consciousness for the consciousness of the film'. Since Brando's view – a hatred of 'the false middle-class way of being' which is taken out on women – becomes identified as the truth about the character and the film, the seemingly anti-sexist intentions of the latter are overturned by the (very complexly) sexist attitudes of the former. It would be wrong to deduce from this example that it is always the case that the star image is the ultimate locus of truth about character. Partly the search for one truth about character (on our part) may do violence to the contradictoriness and polysemy of character, partly each case needs to be argued as carefully as Kaplan argues hers. As with the MacCabe thesis, it is as much a heuristic device as anything.

31 *Mia Farrow and Robert Redford in* The Great Gatsby, *1974 – both equally glamorously lit.*

Stars as characters in films

What then is involved in studying a film text in terms of a star and the character s/he plays?

We may note first of all the points at which the star is effective in the construction of character. These can be considered from two points of view: the fact of a star being in the film, and their performance in it. Performance is discussed in chapter 8. As regards the fact that a given star is in the film, audience foreknowledge, the star's name and her/his appearance (including the sound of her/his voice and dress styles associated with him/her) all already signify that condensation of attitudes and values which is the star's image. Perhaps this is most blatantly demonstrated by Marlene Dietrich's appearances in *Around the World in Eighty Days* (1956) and *Touch of Evil* (1958). The former is, with its string of cameo appearances by stars, testimony enough to how much a star's mere presence in a film can signal character. When Dietrich tells Quinlan/Orson Welles his sombre fortune, towards the end of *Touch of Evil,* her presence is enough to give it a mysterious and faintly erotic authority. The Dietrich example is particularly interesting, in that the enigmatic-exotic-erotic complex which her image signifies and which is irresistibly read into her appearances is sustained principally by vague memories of the Sternberg films, glamour photographs and her cabaret act, and not by the substance of her films or interviews. Her face, her name even, carries the 'mystique', no matter what films she makes or what she says.[4]

The star image is used in the construction of a character in a film in three different ways:

126

32 Butch Cassidy and The Sundance Kid, *1969 – glamour lighting, including halo effect, for Redford's role as love interest.*

Selective use

The film may, through its deployment of the other signs of character and the rhetoric of film, bring out certain features of the star's image and ignore others. In other words, from the structured polysemy of the star's image certain meanings are selected in accord with the overriding conception of the character in the film.

This selective use of a star's image is problematic for a film, in that it cannot guarantee that the particular aspects of a star's image it selects will be those that interest the audience. To attempt to ensure this, a film must use the various signifying elements of the cinema to foreground and minimise the image's traits appropriately. For us it is not enough simply to say that such-and-such a film uses such-and-such an aspect of a star's image: we have to show *how*. Let me take a conveniently narrow example, the use of one signifying element, lighting, in relation to Robert Redford. We might begin by considering the way he is lit in *The Way We Were* and *Butch Cassidy and the Sundance Kid* as compared to in *All the President's Men*. In the first example, Redford is primarily the film's erotic/romantic focus and he is accordingly glamorously lit, with light from behind that both creates the warm glow of classic Hollywood glamour photography and also makes

127

33 All the President's Men, *1976 – plain, high-key lighting reflecting Redford's role as the serious, questing journalist.*

his already fair, all-American hair still more golden. More surprisingly, perhaps, this lighting is also used on him as Sundance, and not only in the scenes with Katherine Ross. This suggests that the interest of Redford as Sundance is still in his erotic/romantic aspect. (It is interesting to speculate on who for.) Effectively both films also minimise Redford's 'political' side: he is uneasy about Katie/Streisand's commitments in *The Way We Were*, and as Sundance is basically a good-time outlaw. *All the President's Men* on the other hand is entirely concerned with his political side and accordingly not at all with the erotic/romantic. He is lit in standard 'high-key' lighting which, as J. A. Place and L. S. Peterson note, was developed in the 40s 'to give what was considered an impression of reality, in which the character's face is attractively modelled' ('Some Visual Motifs of *Film Noir*', p. 327). As Woodward, Redford is not filmed in any mock *cinéma vérité* lighting; he is still the 'attractively modelled' classic film hero, but without the glamorous, erotic/romantic emphases of *The Way We Were* and *Butch Cassidy and the Sundance Kid*. It would be interesting to extend this analysis of the lighting to *The Candidate*, where the Redford character is simultaneously political for himself and erotic/romantic for the political machine that takes him up.

Perfect fit

In certain cases, all the aspects of a star's image fit with all the traits of a character. That is, all the various signs of character, including those achieved through the use of stars, accord. (Probably some aspects of the star's image will not be especially important, but they will not be incompatible either.) There are cases of this working with already known characters – Clark Gable as Rhett Butler in *Gone with the Wind*, Gérard Philipe as Julien Sorel in *Le Rouge et le noir* – and one would expect it to be the case with films not based on previous material but written and developed expressly for a given star. For example, John Wayne. While most Wayne films simply use, and celebrate, his relaxed, masculine, Westerner/leader qualities, certain films have also brought in his awkwardness with women and his 'authoritarian self-sufficiency' (Leo Braudy): *Red River, Rio Bravo, The Searchers, The Man Who Shot Liberty Valance*. Equally a film like *The Sands of Iwo Jima*, by eliminating women from the scene and setting the narrative within an accepted authoritarian social structure, capitalises on the Wayne image without having to criticise it. As Lawrence Alloway observes in *Violent America*: 'His authority, physically massive, more at ease with men than women on the screen, makes him a natural for action pictures with teaching situations' (p. 37) (such as *The Sands of Iwo Jima*). 'A natural' here indicates the perfect fit between image and character.

Some auteurist critics have considered the question of fit in terms of directorial choice of stars for parts. In Leo Braudy's words: 'The wise director, recognizing the contribution to characterization an actor brings, uses the casting to create meaning inarticulately' (*The World in a Frame*, p. 207). V. F. Perkins instances Alfred Hitchcock's use of Cary Grant, an actor of whom Leo McCarey observed that he always 'seeks out the humour in a dramatic situation':

> Hitchcock recognizes this in casting Grant for films (*To Catch a Thief, North by Northwest*) whose tones are predominantly light and in which Grant's presence acts as our guarantee that all will turn out well. At the same time, he centres his meaning on the moral weakness of the hero's disengaged attitude. (*Film as Film*, p. 182)

Problematic fit

Although good cases can certainly be made for both a selective use of a star image and perfect fits between star images and film characters, it seems to me that the powerfully, inescapably present, always-already-signifying nature of star images more often than not creates problems in the construction of character. As Leo Braudy observes: 'Without an awareness of the aesthetic weight of a film star's accumulated image, a director can easily make mistakes that destroy the unity of his [sic] film' (*The World in a Frame*, p. 210). And he instances Yves Montand in *State of Siege* after his politically sympathetic roles in *Z* and *The Confession*.[5] (It is of course not necessary to think this problem within Braudy's auteurist perspective.) The contradictory and polysemic nature of the images makes it hard either to delimit a few aspects or to fully articulate the whole thing with the character as constructed by the other signs in the film. Since this is my view, I have already offered several examples of problematic fits between star images and characters – Lana Turner in *The Postman Always Rings Twice*, Bette Davis in *Now, Voyager*, Marlon Brando in *Last Tango in Paris*. These examples all specify the particular point of signification (i.e. through which of the signs of character) where the contradiction may be discerned. In certain cases, the contradiction may be at all points, such that one can conceptualise the problem in terms of a clash between two complex sign-clusters, the star as image and the character as otherwise constructed. A prime example of this, in my view, is Monroe as Lorelei in *Gentlemen Prefer Blondes*. Everything about Anita Loos's character (in the best-selling novel and in Carol Channing's acclaimed interpretation of her in the smash-hit Broadway musical) as well as the script of the film (e.g. what Jane Russell/Dorothy says about Lorelei), other performances and casting (e.g. the obvious manipulability of 'wet' Gus/Tommy Noonan and 'dirty old man' Piggy/Charles Coburn, the suspicion of 'straight man' Malone/Elliott Reid) and the structure of the film (Dorothy and Lorelei as polar opposites, in name, hair colour, interests in men and money; the basic hermeneutic of the Lorelei plot being whether or not Gus will realise Lorelei's true intentions) – all of this constructs Lorelei as a cynical gold-digger, who fully understands how to use her sex appeal to trap rich men and is motivated above all by cupidity. Her dialogue as written is self-aware and witty, signalling (to us and to herself) amusement at what she is doing even while she is playing the *fausse-naive*. The weight of the Monroe image on the other hand is on innocence. She is certainly aware of her sexuality, but she is guiltless about it and it is moreover presented primarily in terms of narcissism – i.e. sexuality for herself rather than for men. At this stage in her image's development, her motivations were taken to be 'spiritual', either in the magic, 'little-girl' aspirations to be a movie star or in the 'pretentious' interests in Acting and Art.

There is thus a quite massive disjunction between Monro-as-image and Lorelei-as-character. They only touch at three points: the extraordinary impact of their physicality, a certain infantile manner and a habit of uttering witticisms. Yet even these points need to be qualified. Lorelei is quite definitely in control of her physicality whereas Monroe (at this stage in her image) was equally clearly not; Lorelei pretends to be infantile, Monroe was by and large taken to be so; Lorelei's wit expresses an intelligent but cynical appraisal of the situation, whereas Monroe's remarks to the press (known as Monroeisms) were regarded far more, at this point, as wisdom on a par with that 'out of the mouths of babes and sucklings' (i.e. wise by chance rather than by design). As a result of this disjunction (and one would need to demonstrate through close analysis the full complexity of the two image clusters we are talking of, Monroe's and Lorelei's), the character of Monroe-as-Lorelei becomes contradictory to the point of incoherence. This is not a question of Lorelei/Monroe being one thing one moment and another the next, but of her being simultaneously polar opposites. Thus, for instance, when Lorelei/Monroe says to Piggy that she had expected him to be older, him 'being a diamond miner and all', the lines as written and situated (in particular by Russell/Dorothy, straight-woman and confidante, thus in some measure privileged with respect to the truth of narrative and characters) indicate her manipulative propensities, but, because they emanate from Monroe's mouth, they also at the same time indicate innocent pleasure in being sexy.

Where there is such disjuncture, analysis will be concerned to specify how, and with what particular ideological significance. At the same time we also need to ask to what degree it 'shows' as a disjuncture. Various possibilities suggest themselves in this regard.

First, the disjuncture may indeed be glaring (as I find it in *Gentlemen Prefer Blondes*). Such disjunctures need not only be evident after analysis; we are after all speaking of a familiar enough idea, miscasting. Second, the star may be thought to rejig the contradictions so as to make them more reconcilable. (In the words of Maurice Zolotow: 'In her characterization of Lorelei Lee, Marilyn put together a sympathetic portrait of a girl who mingles tenderness of heart with a greed for status symbols'; *Marilyn Monroe*, p. 143.) Third, the placing of the audience in relation to the characters, through the hierarchy of discourses, may deny the truth of the star's image *vis-à-vis* the character. For example, it might be argued that the fact that in *Niagara* we see Monroe/Rose with her lover kissing passionately behind the Falls makes it impossible to read any legitimacy into her behaviour with her husband. (It seems likely that this can only happen when the audience is unaware of the star's image, or when the film is deliberately having a joke at the expense of the star's image, as with the utterly evil doings of Henry Fonda in *Once Upon a Time in the West*.) Finally, the star's image is so powerful that all signs may be read in terms of it. From this perspective, all Lorelei's manipulative lines and actions would be read as genuine and innocent. In this connection, it is worth quoting Michel Mourlet's celebrated words on Charlton Heston, that Heston 'means' Heston regardless of what the film is trying to do with him:

Charlton Heston is an axiom. By himself alone he constitutes a tragedy, and his presence in any films whatsoever suffices to create beauty. The contained violence expressed by the sombre phosphorescence of his eyes, his eagle's profile, the haughty arch of his eyebrows, his prominent cheek-bones, the bitter and hard curve of his mouth, the fabulous power of his torso: this is what he possesses and what not even the worst director can degrade. It is in this sense that one cay say that Charlton Heston, by his existence alone, gives a more accurate definition of the cinema than films like *Hiroshima mon amour* or *Citizen Kane*, whose aesthetic either ignores or impugns Charlton Heston. (Quoted by Colin McArthur in 'The Real Presence')

What analysis is concerned to do is both to discover the nature of the fit between star image and character, and, where the fit is not perfect or selective, to work out where the contradictions are articulated (at what level(s) of signification of character) and to attempt to see what possible sources of 'masking' or 'pseudo-unification' the film offers (such as the irresistible unifying force of a star image).

8 Stars and Performance

Trends in the study of performance

In relation to the stars, the study of performance is inextricably linked to the study of character. There have been other performance traditions – *commedia dell'arte,* music hall, dance – and radical performance theorists – Meyerhold, Brecht, Grotowski – but these have either dispensed with character or at any rate not operated with the novelistic notion of character discussed in the previous chapter. Predominantly performance has been concerned with the creation (the word favoured over 'construction' by writers on performance) and presentation of character.

Two kinds of writing may be found which deal with this. First, there is writing from the point of view of the performer, i.e. how to create and present a character. This is found equally in the reflections of performers on their art and in the writings of performance theorists. One of the few books devoted to performance in film,[6] Michael Pate's *The Film Actor,* is written entirely from this point of view, and it is the main emphasis of V. I. Pudovkin's *Film Technique and Film Acting.* Interestingly, both write from a broadly Stanislavskian perspective, a perspective which is almost defined by its absence of any theorisation of 'effect', 'audience' or 'communication'.

Such work may be divided into two broad schools of thought, classically associated with Diderot and Coquelin on the one hand and Stanislavsky on the other. Diderot and Coquelin, with differing emphases, maintained that the performer should never lose him/herself in a role and should base the performance on the observation of others or on traditional skill. (Cf. Ralph Richardson's account of how he constructs a character, given in John Russell Brown's *Effective Theatre.*) If you want to perform a person unhappy, you either observe unhappy people in the world and base your performance on how they behave, or you draw upon the stock of theatrical conventions for expressing sorrow.

Stanislavsky on the other hand felt that the performer should come to 'live' the character s/he plays as fully as possible and should base the performance on how s/he feels inside. If you want to perform a person unhappy, you remember how you felt when you were unhappy. By building on or diminishing that feeling (in relation to the play's circumstances) you attain the appropriate inner degree of feeling and your performance behaviour follows from this.

The Diderot/Coquelin–Stanislavsky opposition is sometimes referred to as acting from the outside in *vs* acting from the inside out. In principle both approaches may produce the same result, but in practice this is rarely the case since both (even when, as with Stanislavsky, explicitly against this) are historically allied with given and various performance conventions.

Second, there is writing from the point of view of the audience. In any sustained form (i.e. other than from journalistic critics), this is surprisingly thin on the ground. The vast majority of texts on performance deal with it from the point of view of the performer. Moreover, of the few of any substance that do not, most are essentially concerned with a polemic against any notion of performance communicating 'naturally'.

The need for this polemic is great enough. Terms like 'magic' and 'getting it across' abound in the discussion of performance. This quotation from Lee R. Bobker may stand as an example of what the polemic is directed at: 'The great actor transmits inner conviction and knowledge of the character across the barrier of celluloid and reaches directly into the consciousness of each member of the audience' (*Elements of Film*, p. 196). Such writing (and teaching) is by no means rare.

Against this kind of thing, Umberto Eco demonstrates how even an actual drunk man put on a stage is already a 'sign', no longer signifying his own drunkenness but either a character's drunkenness or drunkenness in general; while the meaning of drunkenness in this context depends upon who put him there, a brewery or the Salvation Army. Richard Schechner with Cynthia Mintz, in a review of the development of kinesics in relation to performance ('Kinesics and Performance'), stress repeatedly that no kind of movement or gesture has meaning of itself but only by virtue of its cultural context. (For a full discussion of the debate over the nature of human non-verbal communication, see Ted Polhemus, *Social Aspects of the Human Body*.)

This kind of work is obviously important in clearing the ground, but at present leaves us with the problem of interpreting, and discussing interpretations of, performance. Kinesics may yet elaborate a useful notation system for more precisely describing movements and gestures (as has been developed for dance – e.g. Labanotation, choreutics – and cf. Tony Harrild's application of dance terminology to performance in an article on '*Killer Elite*: Emotion Expression'). But, as currently projected, this will only enable us to describe with greater precision; it will leave us with the same problems of interpretation.

These problems may at first sight appear trivial. We all know that shaking hands is a sign of greeting, and while we may acknowledge its cultural specificity, do we really need any further theorisation on how to interpret it? Again, we all know anger when we see it and hear it. Yet any attempt to analyse performance runs up against the extreme complexity and ambiguity of performance signs. This is illustrated by Lawrence Shaffer's consideration of Chaplin's smile at the end of *City Lights*:

> the no longer blind heroine touches Chaplin's hand and 'recognizes' him as the kind stranger who had befriended her when she was blind . . . Chaplin's facial response to the flower girl's . . . is a screen-encompassing, transcendent smile that, over the years, has assumed mythic proportions. What does the smile signify? Pride? Sheepishness? To know all is to accept all? What else can one do to the naked face of truth but smile? ('Reflections on the Face in Film', p. 4)

It is to tackling such issues of interpretation that this section is devoted.

Performance signs

Performance is what the performer does in addition to the actions/functions s/he performs in the plot and the lines s/he is given to say. Performance is how the action/function is done, how the lines are said.

The signs of performance are: facial expression; voice; gestures (principally of hands and arms, but also of any limb, e.g. neck, leg); body posture (how someone is standing or sitting); body movement (movement of the whole body, including how someone stands up or sits down, how they walk, run, etc.). Of these the first is often held to be the most important, on analogy with its primary importance in interpersonal communication in everyday life. Yet just as its importance may be greatest, so too is its ambiguity. Shaffer points out that we hold, despite arguments to the contrary, to the illusion that the face is supremely expressive of personality: 'A face that looks "lived in" is a face that *seems* to comprise (or reprise) its past in any of its momentary expressions. Fredric March's sensibility did not somehow "inform" his features osmotically ... And yet that was the illusion' (ibid., p. 3). At the same time, when it comes to deciphering facial expression we are at a considerable loss (as in Shaffer's example of Chaplin's smile quoted above). Aside from films that use this ambiguity in the service of the notion of the eternal ineffability of the face as the window to the soul (cf. Balazs discussed in Part One), most films do, through the use of codes discussed below, narrow down the range of meanings that a facial expression considered in isolation may have. None the less, as the analyses of *Fort Apache* and *The Little Foxes* below reveal, ambiguity is seldom totally eliminated.

This ambiguity needs to be understood in terms of the relation between the performer and the audience in film. This can be considered by comparing the character of Maurice (Montgomery Clift) in *The Heiress* with the same character in the novel the film is based on, *Washington Square* by Henry James. In the latter, we are clearly told from the word go that Maurice is deceitful. In the film, however, we are in the same position as Catherine (Olivia de Havilland) in this regard; we have to work out from our observation of him whether he is sincere or not. This is further complicated by the particular relation we have to Clift as a star. In these ways, film and especially performance in film fabricates a relationship to, rather than a telling about, the characters.

How we read performance signs

Our reading of performance signs depends in the first instance on our very general knowledge of what intonation, gesture, eye dilations, etc. mean. This knowledge is culture- and history-bound. As Ray L. Birdwhistell insists, no gesture is intrinsically meaningful but only culture makes it so. His discussion of the smile (*Kinesics and Context*, pp. 29–38) and of 'masculinity and femininity as display' (pp. 39–46) provide evidence of this, and his general model of communication is as follows:

> I have posited communication as a multi-channelled system emergent from and regulative of the influenceable multi-sensory activity of living systems. Within such a frame of reference, spoken and the body motion languages are *infra*-communicational systems which are *interdependently merged* with each other and with other comparable codes utilizing other channels to become communicative. (Quoted in Schechner and Mintz, 'Kinesics and Performance', p. 104)

134

34 *Olivia de Havilland as Catherine Sloper and Mont-gomery Clift as Maurice Townsend in* The Heiress, *1949. Can she – can we – trust him? We have only what he says and does, and how he looks, to go on.*

The signification of a given performance sign is determined by its place within culturally and historically specific codes. In other words, in terms of film, to read Bette Davis's eye movements or John Wayne's walk, we cannot refer to a general and universal vocabulary of eye and walking movements, but to specific vocabularies, specific to the culture and specific within it. (For more discussion of this, see Ted Polhemus, *Social Aspects of the Human Body*.)

It should be added that while such limited vocabularies can be established (e.g. in Julius Fast's *Body Language*) they by no means exhaust the signification of most performance signs. This is because performance signs are analogical rather than digital:

> Analogic codification constitutes a series of symbols that in their proportions and relations are similar to the thing, idea or event for which they stand ... Such a form of codification deals with continuous functions, unlike digital codification which deals with discrete step intervals. (Jurgen Ruesch and Weldon Kees, *Non-Verbal Communication*, p. 8)

This means that the attempt to break down performance signs into discrete units that would clearly constitute a vocabulary will be very limited indeed, confined only to particularly formalised styles (e.g. Japanese greetings, stage melodrama). More usually, the signification of a performance sign is determined by the multiple codes in relation to which it is situated, and also by its place in the totality of the film.

The determining codes

What then are the codes in relation to which stars' performance signs have to be placed?

As has already been stated, in the first instance it is the general codes of the culture that produced the film which have to be understood. To a large degree, we may in the practice of analysis take this for granted. As an Englishman looking at Hollywood films often made before I was born, I may already misread more than I realise, due to both geographical and temporal distance from them. It is good to be on one's guard in this respect, and it is an important theoretical point to make but, to put it bluntly, there is little in practical terms that one can do about it.

A second level that can again only be discussed theoretically (at the moment) is the relationship between the actual kinesic and vocal codes of a culture and those codes in that culture's films, taken as a whole. That is, it seems likely that we read movement and speech in films according to specifically filmic, culture-bound but general (i.e. not confined to genres, studios, etc.) codes of movement and speech. These will be in relation to but not the same as the codes in the wider culture. This is an area for research.

Types of performance

Where we can begin to make headway in the area opened up in the previous paragraph is in the different kinds of performance tradition that (Hollywood sound) cinema has used. (For accounts of different performance traditions in the cinema as a whole see Raymond Durgnat 'Getting Cinema on the Right Wavelength' and James F. Scott, *Film – the Medium and the Maker.*)

Different types of performance can in principle be described in formal terms. I shall try to do this in a moment, but two points should be made about it first. First, very little work on formal description of the differences between performance traditions has been done, and what follows is not based on any very prolonged analysis or research. Second, it *may* be a characteristic of performance signs that how they are read depends importantly on what we know of how they are produced. That is, there may in some instances be little formal difference between given performance traditions, yet the theory of performance that informs them may be sufficiently widely known for this to inform in turn how they are read. I am thinking particularly of the widespread ideas about the Method that arose in the 50s. It may be that the formal differences between the Method and, say, the repertory/Broadway style are less clear than the known differences between how the performances were arrived at. (Brando, Dean and Steiger all constitute a distinctively, formally different tradition, but the Method also covers Woodward, McQueen, (Jane) Fonda and Keir Dullea, all much more 'ordinary' performers.) Part of what follows them necessarily deals with the assumptions that were made about the different ways performers work.

The different types of performance I am going to suggest all fall within the broader historical category of the novelistic conception of character, with the qualifications to it in terms of film noted above. I have named them according to their origin outside film. This is partly for convenience, but partly because the study of signs needs to be rooted in the specific history of signs at their point of production. (I have elaborated this point with reference to tap dance in an article on 'Entertainment and Utopia'.)

Vaudeville and music hall

These styles operate chiefly in the realm of comedy ('business', 'patter', 'timing') and song and dance. Their stylisation, their use of non-realist, even distanciating, devices aimed at 'pointing' a gag or a number tend to render them problematic in relation to novelistic character. Even in comedies and musicals they are virtually used only to be actually funny or for numbers. Thus there are shifts of perform-ance gear between comic and/or musical sections of a film and the rest of it. (It is particularly interesting to study such shifts of gear for the mischief they may do to the assumptions of the non-comic or non-musical aspects of a film. The havoc wreaked by the Marx Brothers on the conventions of their MGM films is the most obvious example.) It should be added that comedy and song and dance can be 'naturalised' by abandoning vaudeville performance traditions (e.g. the singsong in *Rio Bravo*); and that there are other comic styles; cf. Robin Wood's comparison of the aristocratic performance style of *To Be or Not to Be* with the vaudeville style of *Once Upon a Honeymoon* ('Acting Up', pp. 23–4).

Melodrama

The importance of melodrama in the early development of the cinema has been discussed by several writers including Vardac, Fell and O'Dell (see Bibliography). Thomas Elsaesser in 'Why Hollywood?' and 'Tales of Sound and Fury' has shown how this influence helped define what kind of cinema Hollywood was and traces its continued importance well into the 60s. Lev Kuleshov's description of how Griffith expanded the gestural repertoire of film also shows how this remained within the aesthetic of melodrama:

> With Griffith, actors did not merely bulge their eyes, say, in terror, but created other movements, which communicated their states of being more truthfully. Lip biting, fidgeting, wringing of hands, touching of objects, etc. are the characteristic signs of Griffithian acting. It is not difficult to surmise that they are approaching moments of extreme emotion and even hysteria. (*Kuleshov on Film*, p. 94)

Melodramatic performance may be defined as the use of gestures principally in terms of their intense and immediate expressive, affective signification. In melodrama, these emotions are also moral categories, and it is this that sets melodramatic performance apart, at the level of meaning, from Method acting, although *both* give primacy to a character's emotional life.

The development of a repertoire of gestures in melodrama was such that François Delsarte was able to build a whole theory of expressive performance on it. He described a limited vocabulary of melodramatic signs (e.g. hand signals for 'simple affirmation', 'emphatic declaration', etc.; see Fig. 35) as well as analysing

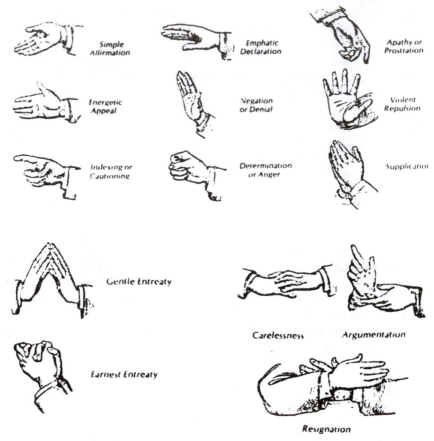

35 *The Delsarte codification of melodrama's repertoire of gestures.*

posture and gesture in terms of certain expressive norms, e.g. a 'normal' upright position as compared with an 'eccentric' (active or forward) and 'concentric' (passive and backward) position. The interest of Delsarte is, as E. T. Kirby points out in 'The Delsarte Method: Three Frontiers of Actor Training', partly his attempt to systematise performance signs, and partly the record it constitutes of melodramatic performance practice.

Radio

I do not know that the radio had a direct influence on performance in the cinema, but it seems likely and a subject worth researching. Radio developed in America between 1919 and 1922, and by the coming of sound in the cinema had already established a number of distinctive kinds of programme without any real precedent in the history of the arts. These included soap opera, the interview and programmes such as the enormously popular Fibber McGee and Molly, who just chatted over breakfast every morning. One of the most important stars of the radio (and of stage and screen) was Will Rogers, who just talked *ex tempore* about what he thought about the world. (See Llewellyn White, *The American Radio.*)

The mode of performance thus developed by radio was characterised by three things: (i) domestic immediacy, radio seen as just another member of the family; (ii) instantly recognisable characters, recognisable that is both as types and as individuals; and (iii) the use of people playing 'themselves', and themselves being plain ordinary folk.

In sound cinema, performers nearly always played characters, yet with stars (and even arguably with character actors) the tendency also at the same time to play 'themselves' was equally strong. A style of performance that seems more like day-to-day interaction and the adaptation to social types facilitated this process. (That radio performance *could* be described as formally as melodrama is almost certainly the case, cf. Merton's discussion in *Mass Persuasion* of the sincerity 'register' used by performers.)

It is from this style of performance, which James F. Scott in *Film – the Medium and the Maker* identifies as 'the Hollywood studio style', that the notion of film performance not being 'acting' stems. Scott quotes Henry Fonda's words, that in film acting, unlike theatre, 'You do it just like in reality' (p. 241). Although Scott does not appear to believe this is the case, he does not in so many words define what this style consists in other than the combination of 'stereotypic appearances with personalised speech and manner' (p. 240). However, his discussion of Humphrey Bogart and Greta Garbo suggests that the style consists in the repeated use, within films and through the films of a star's career, of certain mannerisms, which do the job of personalising the type the performer plays. These may be relatively 'naturalistic' mannerisms, but they are different and repeated enough to constitute idiosyncrasies. These form the basis of the individual star's performance style.

'Radio' or 'Hollywood Studio' style meshes with the various star/audience relationships to construct performances which we experience analogously to our relationship to others in everyday interaction. (Cf. the discussion of Shaffer above.) There has been no charting of the rules that govern this. Perhaps the nearest to it, though in a very different field, is Erving Goffman's *The Presentation of Self in Everyday Life*. Although not providing descriptive tools comparable to Delsarte's, Goffman does detail some of the assumptions we use to decipher others in face-to-face interactions, and it would be interesting to see how these relate to the presentation of character through 'radio' performance in films. Of particular interest here is Goffman's distinction between signs that we 'give' and those that we 'give off' (p. 14). The former are what we want people to think, the latter are what we betray about ourselves. (We may, however, be adept at manipulating the latter.) In film, both these kinds of signals are used consciously to construct character. It may, however, be that the signals a star gives off are sometimes not deliberate (on her/his part and/or on the part of whoever selects the shots of him/her in a particular film), and yet constitute a major part of her/his interest and image. Monroe's parted lips give the signal 'yielding sexuality', but the quivering upper lip (in fact quivering to hide her high gum line) may also be read as giving off the signal 'vulnerability'. (On the link between sexuality and vulnerability in female star images, Susan Brownmiller has some thought-provoking words in *Against Our Will*, pp. 333–6.)

36 *The archetypal Marilyn Monroe pose.*

Repertory/Broadway

With the coming of sound, many performers were recruited from the 'straight' theatre. As Scott's example of Henry Fonda shows, most of these stars unlearnt their theatrical performance style in accord with what I have called the radio style:

> Henry Fonda claims he learned his lesson about film acting the day director Victor Fleming accused him of 'mugging'. Shocked and hurt, he says 'I then realized that I was giving a stage performance that I had been giving for months in New York'. After that, apparently, Fonda knew that in film acting, 'You do it just like in reality'. (*Film – the Medium and the Maker*, p. 241)

However, certain stars – Paul Muni, Bette Davis, Katharine Hepburn – were able to draw on their theatre background, and Lee R. Bobker stresses the importance of British stage actors in Hollywood in the 50s (*Elements of Film*, p. 190).

The key point about this style is that it stands as the very opposite of the 'radio' style, in emphasising above all that the performer should be hidden behind the character s/he constructs and in no way play him/herself. Frequently this tradition is compared to the 'classic Hollywood studio style' as real 'acting' versus just 'being', and the special esteem in which this style is held will be familiar to anyone who has got into discussions as to whether such-and-such a star can 'act'.

Acting, in the mode established by Broadway and the English repertory theatre movement, means the ability of a performer to be different in every part s/he plays. This difference is achieved, within the Diderot/Coquelin theory of performance, through observation and convention. It is the paradigm of performance 'from the outside in'. It is characterised, firstly, by 'careful attention to detail' (Bobker, *Elements of Film*, ibid.). This means both a meticulous concern with 'naturalist' accuracy over period manners, class and ethnic accents, etc. and the construction of character through the accumulation and elaboration of such details (rather than through the broad, repeated strokes of other approaches). Secondly, it displays a particularly conscious aesthetic of coherence, such that every detail must tell and nothing must be redundant; in practice, this means that every performance sign must be clearly motivated *and* relevant to the plot (e.g. in *The Heiress*, left alone in the drawing room on the day of Catherine's return from France, Maurice/Clift walks behind the sofa and looks at the walls and ceilings; this is not just a filler, nor is it the redundant tics of Method acting, but it is rather a reminder to the audience of the suspicion of Maurice's fortune-hunting character at the point when it seems most likely he and Catherine will marry). Thirdly, a greater stress is placed on verbal fluency and articulateness than with other styles, which makes it possible for characters to speak at greater length and with greater self-knowledge or what Lukács terms 'intellectual physiognomy' (i.e. reflecting on the wider implications of what they are doing, feeling or thinking) than is usual with the other styles.[7] Finally, in many cases, a certain detachment between the actor and her/his role is evident, as noted by Lawrence Shaffer in an article ('Some Notes on Film Acting') that attempts in part to delineate this kind of performance, which he calls 'character acting':

> In the finest character acting – Maggie Smith in *The Prime of Miss Jean Brodie*, Brando in *The Nightcomers*, Vanessa Redgrave in *The Seagull*, Steiger in *On the Waterfront*, Olivier in *The Entertainer* – the audience is still vaguely aware that strings are being pulled, that the actor has concocted special traits for his role. Effort also shows when an actor tends to impose certain facial and vocal mannerisms, as is often the case with Olivier. Such mannerisms are evidence of strain and stress on the acting apparatus. The actor is not 'with it' but straining to 'do it'. Identification and involvement are at an ebb. (p. 104)

The 'Method'

'Method acting' was the name given to the approach to performance taught by the Actors' Studio in New York, which was founded in 1947. It was an adaptation of the teaching of Konstantin Stanislavsky, and involved the performer feeling her/his way into a role from the inside, temporarily identifying with a character or, in a widespread distortion of the approach, actually becoming the character while playing him/her.

Like melodrama, Method acting privileges emotional meaning over all other aspects of character (such as social behaviour and 'intellectual physiognomy'), but where melodrama returns emotions to moral categories, the Method roots them in broadly understood psychoanalytic categories. The Method constructs a character in terms of her/his unconscious and/or inescapable psychological make-up. Although in principle the Method could be used to express any psychological state, in practice it was used especially to express disturbance, repression, anguish, etc., partly in line with a belief that such feelings, vaguely conceptualisable as the Id and its repression, are more 'authentic' than stability and open expression. (I suspect that analysis would also show a sexist bias whereby disturbance and anguish were reserved for men and repression for women – men as the Id, women as its repression ...) In this perspective, character itself becomes more important than plot or structure, and as a result much of the performance is 'redundant' in these terms. Scott's description of Brando in *A Streetcar Named Desire* indicates these elements: the reduction of performance to a given 'basic' psychology, the accumulation of redundant performance signs, the emphasis on raw and violent emotion which is further validated as 'authentic' in this case by its opposition to the falsity of Blanche (both as played by the British repertory actor Vivien Leigh and as the dénouement 'proves' her to be):

> In *Streetcar* Brando evidently built the part around his sense of Stanley Kowalski's animal aggressiveness. Sometimes this is innocently canine, as when his incessant scratching of back and belly remind us of a dog going after fleas. But the Kowalski character is also destructive, as we are told in Brando's use of the mouth: he chews fruit with loud crunching noises, munches up potato chips with the same relentless jaw muscles, washes beer around in his mouth and then swallows it with physically noticeable gulps. These two Brando-generated metaphors come together in the scene where Kowalski rummages through Blanche's trunk, his clawlike hands burrowing furiously and throwing velveteen dresses and fake fox fur back over his shoulders with fierce determination. These apparently insubstantial bits of stage business prepare us for the climatic scene in which Kowalski, having worked havoc upon Blanche's wardrobe, at last destroys the woman herself, devouring her futile illusions of Southern gentility. (*Film – the Medium and the Maker*, p. 249)

Scott maintains that the Method is equally adaptable to performers (such as, he suggests, Brando) who are essentially the same in every film (for, despite 'fabricating an astonishing array of ethnic accents' he is always 'the surly proletarian who suspects every smell of middle-class decorum' (ibid.); cf. also Kaplan's discussion of *Last Tango in Paris* referred to above), and to performers (Rod Steiger is Scott's example) who 'put aside [their] own personality to think [their] way into an alien psyche' (p. 251). In either case, the fact that many people did and do believe that the Method performer 'got inside the character' or 'became' him/her gave such performances a mark of authenticity that made other styles seem correspondingly artificial or stilted.

The star's performance style
As has already been mentioned, a star will have a particular performance style that through its familiarity will inform the performance s/he gives in any particular film. The specific repertoire of gestures, intonations, etc. that a star establishes over a number of films carries the meaning of her/his image just as much as the 'inert' element of appearance, the particular sound of her/his voice or dress style. An example is provided by G. Hill who quotes ('John Wayne', p. 7) from a reviewer of *The War Wagon*: 'It is worth seeing to watch John Wayne wrap his horse's reins round a hitch post!' It is not only that it happens to be Wayne doing it or that the action is always redolent of meaning, but that the particular way Wayne habitu-

ally does it sums up a particular aspect of his image. (The relish with which men tell me of this example suggests that what it sums up above all is Wayne's easy and confident masculinity.)

Part of the business of studying stars is to establish what these recurrent features of performance are and what they signify in terms of the star's image. They will usually only sum up an aspect of that image. The example just given does not remind us of everything about Wayne – in particular its joyous appeal operates because he is in the saddle in the West, not in Vietnam, not with a woman. (For an example from Bette Davis's performance repertoire see the analysis of *The Little Foxes* below, pp. 147–50.)

Montage and mise en scène

One of the few debates about film performance that has recurred in film theory is the degree to which performance may be considered an expressive element of any significance. While everyday critical talking about film tends to concentrate on performance (e.g. 'What was so-and-so like in the film you just saw?'), an important tradition in film theory has tended to deny that performance has any expressive value: what you read into the performer, you read in by virtue of signs *other than* performance signs. The classic exponent of this view is generally held to be Kuleshov. In particular, his view of the decisive role of editing in determining the significance of facial expression, gesture, etc. is often referred to. This is his account of his discovery of this effect:

> We had a dispute with a certain famous actor to whom we said: Imagine this scene: a man, sitting in jail for a long time, is starving because he is not given anything to eat; he is brought a plate of soup, is delighted by it, and gulps it down. Imagine another scene: a man in jail is given food, fed well, full to capacity, but he longs for his freedom, for the sight of birds, the sunlight, houses, clouds. A door is opened for him. He is led out onto the street, and he sees birds, clouds, the sun and houses and is extremely pleased by the sight. And so, we asked the actor: Will the face reacting to the soup and the face reacting to the sun appear the same on film or not? We were answered disdainfully: It is clear to anyone that the reaction to the soup and the reaction to freedom will be totally different.
>
> Then we shot these two sequences, and regardless of how I transposed those shots and how they were examined, no one was able to perceive any difference in the face of this actor, in spite of the fact that his performance in each shot was absolutely different. With correct montage, even if one takes the performance of an actor directed at something quite different, it will still reach the viewer in the way intended by the editor, because the viewer himself will complete the sequence and see that which is suggested to him by montage. (*Kuleshov on Film*, p. 54)

Gianfranco Bettetini takes this view further by suggesting that not only montage but also the decisiveness of visual as opposed to verbal signs in the cinema (a very debatable point; it depends on *which* cinema you mean), the two-dimensionality of the screen and the function of the performer in the film's diegesis all reduce the performer to 'an instrument in the hands of the director' (*The Language and Technique of Film*, p. 83). Although not quoted by Bettetini, the most famous instance of this is probably the final shot of Garbo in *Queen Christina*. She stands on the prow of the boat taking her away from Sweden and after the death

37 *Greta Garbo in* Queen Christina, *1934 – the last shot.*

of her lover. She stares ahead and into the wind which ruffles her hair. Much can be read into this shot – of resignation, melancholy, profound feeling. Yet it is well known that the director, Rouben Mamoulian, told Garbo to do nothing for this scene, and she did as she was told. (In itself, one should say, a considerable feat of performance.) The meaning of her face in this shot thus derives entirely from its place in the film's narrative, the way it is shot and the resonances of Garbo's image carried by her face.

Such examples are, however, more the exception than the rule, and Kuleshov himself was never so extreme as Bettetini in this regard. Although he did refer to actors as 'models' or 'mannequins', and argued consistently against 'theatrical' performance and in favour of the use of 'types' and of 'real people', none the less he also saw action, what was done, as 'the main element in cinema film' (*Kuleshov on Film*, p. 71), and much of his writing is concerned with the training of performers for the cinema. There is besides to Kuleshov an evaluative emphasis: Bettetini implies that performance *can* have *little* expressive significance in film, Kuleshov argues that it *ought* not to have *too much* (since this leads to humanist or individualist expression). Although one may not agree with the latter, it is an acceptable argument, whereas Bettetini's denial of the possibility of expression through performance cannot be sustained by examining films.

Let us consider John Wayne in relation to the last point. Wayne is a performer commonly credited without acting abilities. The assumption is that he is just there, and just by being there a statement is made. In so far as any other meaning can be attributed to him in a particular film, it has to come from montage, *mise*

38 *John Wayne and Henry Fonda in* Fort Apache, *1948.*

en scène, what is said, etc. – or so runs the argument. This in fact was my view of him. However, an analysis of his performance in the scene in *Fort Apache* where he, as Captain York, and Colonel Thursday (Henry Fonda) go with a cavalry troop to meet Cochise, proved me wrong. Let it be stressed that this has nothing to do with evaluation (I am not remotely interested in vindicating Wayne as a 'good' actor) nor with (Wayne's) 'authorship'. Performance is defined as what the performer does, and whether s/he, the director or some other person is authorially responsible for this is a different question altogether. What is of interest here is whether performance – what Wayne does – contributes to the construction of Wayne/York or whether that construction is achieved purely by other means. (The latter include Wayne as an already-signifying star image, but not Wayne as performing.)

Near the beginning of this scene, there is a single take in which Wayne/York (hereinafter, W/Y), having been summoned from the rear of the cavalry column by Fonda/Thursday (hereinafter F/T), comes up to discuss with the latter where they are to meet Cochise. F/T is placed right (as we look at it); he is rigidly upright against the sky. W/Y is placed left, lower on the screen than F/T, only partially against the sky; he moves in the saddle. In the course of the conversation, F/T announces his plans to deploy his men. W/Y tells him these are inappropriate to the actual position of the Indians, which he (W/Y) knows because he has been following the dust swirls. He points offscreen. The shot ends here, and there is a cut to a shot of Indians riding up *en masse* over the brow of a hill through 'creative geography' (where W/Y has pointed) with threatening music over.

Clearly *mise en scène* and montage are important *vis-à-vis* W/Y here. The placing of him in relation to F/T not only expresses their relative positions in the military hierarchy but also contrasts F/T's self-styled epic aspirations with W/Y's more down-to-earth/natural (but still in fact 'epic') qualities. (This reading depends of course on knowledge of the elaboration of this contrast throughout the film.) The cut to the Indians confirms the 'truth' of what W/Y has said, and hence stamps him with the mark of authenticity (allied to the fact that he knows this truth through his understanding of 'nature' – the dust swirls).

However, performance *also* signifies. The contrast between F/T's rigidity and W/Y's movement suggests the greater 'relaxedness' of the latter, thus picking up on another aspect of the film's opposition between them, namely, his immediate, intuitive, at-home-ness with military life as compared to F/T's bookish approach. (This has class connotations that are explicitly presented in the film in a displaced aristocratic/populist opposition.) When F/T announces that he will be deploying two troops to the North, the placing means that he has only to make a slight turn of his head to the left (of the screen), whereas W/Y has to turn the whole of his body round in the saddle. This he does very swiftly and easily. The placing demands the larger movement, but this performance of the movement both suggests a sense of urgency (F/T is making a disastrous decision) and, because it is so easily done, signifies again W/Y's total at-home-ness in the saddle.

Later in this scene, the Spanish interpreter repeats Cochise's extremely derogatory descriptions of the gun-runner Meecham. There is a reaction shot, showing Meecham and F/T seated and the other men standing behind, W/Y to the rear and slightly to the right of F/T. W/Y expresses 'amusement' at Cochise's words by the following performance: his eyes look slightly left, slightly heavenward, there is a faint smile on his face, he moves his right leg and upper body just a little, keeping his arms behind his back. (This performance ends with him casting a contemptuous look at Meecham.) Three points are of interest for our purposes about this: (i) nothing in *mise en scène* or montage constructs for the character the response 'amusement'; it resides in performance alone; (ii) it fits with what we know of the character – we can read it in terms of relaxedness, etc.; (iii) its more specific signification, beyond 'amusement', is not clear. On the one hand, its subtlety and relative unusualness (i.e. it's not just a grin) suggest 'meaningfulness', yet what that meaning is one would have to select from 'translations' such as 'This proves me right', 'Cochise is cute', 'This puts Thursday on the spot', etc. (Arguably, it expresses all these fleeting thoughts.)

This sort of exercise is useful not only as part of the business of putting performance signs in their determinate context but also to distinguish between different modes of articulation of character in film (e.g. to test Braudy's distinction between 'closed' and 'open' films); to distinguish between films in which performance fits with other signs of character (the case, as far as I have gone with it, with Wayne in *Fort Apache*) and those in which the fit is more contradictory; and following from that, to test the possibility of stars resisting their material not only by what they inescapably signify (i.e. miscasting) but also through performance (e.g. the Haskell thesis invoked throughout this book).

The film as a whole

As has already emerged in the discussion of *Fort Apache,* performance signs in a given scene may gain much of their meaning from what is indicated about character and situation elsewhere in the film. In an article on acting in film ('Acting Up'), Robin Wood argues that this is the key context for reading (and, for him, evaluating) performance. This is basically divided into two different emphases: the film as belonging to a given set of films (within a genre, by a particular director), and the film as a discrete whole, built up (*à la S/Z*) from various codes, but crucially signifying in its particular combination of them and their subordination to the authorial code. It is with an example of the second, Bogart in *The Big Sleep,* that Wood's article ends:

> What I have tried to suggest is that the context needs to be defined in terms of the most intricate network of specific codes. Without at all wishing to denigrate the actor, one can question whether it is valid to claim that he gives a great performance in *The Big Sleep,* or even to discuss his performance except in the context the film gives it. (p. 25)

Barthes is here being used in support of a holistic view of individual films. While this may be true of *The Big Sleep,* and while the individual film is certainly a determinate context of performance signs, the possibility of performance signs signifying according to the other contextual codes discussed and not in accord with other aspects of the film needs to be borne in mind.

Bette Davis in The Little Foxes

I'd like to end this chapter with an analysis of Bette Davis in two moments from the scene in *The Little Foxes* in which she/Regina refuses to fetch Horace (Herbert Marshall) his medicine, thereby obliging him to crawl upstairs for it himself, an action that leads to his death.

When Horace asks for the bottle of medicine, he is front of screen, she further back, sitting on a wing-backed sofa. She remains motionless and her expression does not alter. There are in this shot only two performance signs of Davis to discuss, facial expression and posture. The former is in many respects indecipherable; partly it is not near enough, partly it is set as it has been throughout the film, mouth closed, eyes looking straight ahead. The make-up makes the face look particularly white (an accurate period note) and the mouth particularly small and pursed. The posture is rigid, but set back in the sofa (against its right (to us) and taller wing), her right hand placed on the curve of the other wing and her left on her knee.

What do this face and posture mean? It is first a very formal pose, and such attention to formality suggests aristocratic manners of a particularly stiff kind. We are already drawing on our cultural knowledge that *this* formalisation is aristocratic, unlike, for example, the formal poses adopted by ballet dancers when not dancing. In the context of the film such rigidity is compared both to Regina's brothers (more naked capitalistic with more free-and-easy manners) and to the northern businessman whose easy fine manners betoken him a true gentleman rather than, as Regina and her brothers, an *arriviste.* Thus a general cultural determinant of this sign's meaning is made more complex by the way it and

39 The Little Foxes, *1941.*

related performance signs (of rigid social formality) have been used elsewhere in the film. The total stillness of Davis is also striking. Characteristically, Davis never sits still. Even when playing as formal a role as Elizabeth I of England, her still bearing is enlivened by the Davis trademarks of moodily moving eyes and hands that rapidly clench and unclench at her side, thus signalling the anxiety and emotion beneath the monarch's icy demeanour. Throughout *The Little Foxes*, Davis's mannerisms are much less in evidence, and here, at so crucial a moment, they are absent altogether. In the context of Davis, it is hard not to read this as repression, the deliberate suppression of all expression of emotion and perhaps, in terms of character, the suppression thereby of emotion itself.

There is a cut from this to a medium close-up of Horace's face, and as the realisation that she does not intend to fetch the bottle (and is therefore prepared to kill him) spreads visibly across his face (a performance sign it would be interesting to try and determine!), so sinister music seeps in on the soundtrack. The cut tells us we are to read the face and posture we have just seen as 'evil'; but the face and posture have already told us much more complicated things about class and repression. The cut can be read as indicating that evil which *arrivisme* and repression lead to or else as contradicting the interesting preceding shot (which may have an element of 'tout comprendre, c'est tout pardonner' working for it).

The next shot is an extremely long-held view of Regina/Davis's face as Horace brushes past her. We see her in large close-up centre right of frame and him (out of focus) clambering up the stairs back left. At first Regina/Davis is sitting back in the same rigid position as before – but now her eye pupils are to (her) extreme left, and twice her eyes very slightly widen as Horace passes. Gradually, in tiny movements, she sits up and turns her face to her left, her shoulders following. In other words, as we see Horace back right of the screen, Regina/Davis turns ever more to the left, as if to see him over the shoulder that is furthest from where he is. When finally he collapses on the stairs, she leaps up and rushes to him, calling out for the maid.

Regina/Davis's performance here is much less easily placed in general cultural terms, but clearly placed in terms of performance traditions within melodrama. However muted compared with the full gamut of melodramatic histrionics (often more subdued than they are given credit for), the very artifice of the pose (looking at something on one's right over one's left shoulder) makes it necessary to read it in terms of emotion and nothing else; and the almost distorted movement of the eyes to the left means this is to be intense emotion to boot. Such use of the eyes is also characteristic of Davis's performances, and usually signifies duplicity, doing or thinking something other than she appears to be. In this context, this at any rate cuts across the simple reading of Regina as evil. What she is doing is evil, clearly; but the eyes also signal that some other kind of emotion is to be read as going on inside her. The problem with both the melodrama and the Davis context is that they point to contrary and intense emotion, without having any more specific emotional signification. Regina is feeling something contrary and intense – but what? This lack of clarity (forcing us into that troubling relationship with a character discussed above in relation to Maurice/Clift in *The Heiress*) is reinforced by the sudden rise from the chair when Horace collapses, which cannot be read as calculated (on the part of the character) and retrospectively confers on Davis's performance signs before Horace collapses further ambiguity as to what is going on inside her head.

Our understanding of these very minimal performance signs depends on situating them in their different determining contexts. What we learn is that the character of Regina is not pure evil, but ambiguously motivated. What we do with this information partly depends on our critical perspective. We could see the lack of clarity about Regina arising from the documented disagreements Davis and director William Wyler had about the role. (This has its own fascination, not at the anecdotal level, but in the questions it raises about the relationship between actual production personnel and what gets on the screen. For it was Davis, the performer, who wanted Regina to be pure evil (as Tallulah Bankhead had successfully played her on the stage), and the 'liberal' Wyler who wanted to humanise Regina. Yet in this scene it is the imponderables of performance that mitigate Regina's evil, while what one might think of as directorial decisions – e.g. the reaction shot of Horace – tend to simplify Regina's character. Thus Davis seems in the film, perhaps because she was not able to develop the characterisation herself, to carry, through the melodramatic references of the performance style and its association with her, ambiguities that she did not 'intend'.) This confusion may be read as symptomatic of the kinds of contradiction liberalism leads to when attempting to deal with capitalists and aristocrats. Equally, one could read the ambiguity as fitting, but in one of two ways: as 'humanising' Regina, but leaving the audience 'free' to interpret that humanity in its (the audience's) own terms (given Bazin's admiration for the film, it might be possible to relate this to his view of its use of deep-focus); as working on that stereotype of female evil that film noir was later to elaborate so anxiously, namely that the evil of woman resides precisely in her unknowability. Finally, one could insist on the overriding power of the Davis image in the interpretation of her performance and this might lead us to read the ambiguity relatively sympathetically along the lines of the 'super-bitch' syndrome outlined by Molly Haskell (see Part Two; cf. also Christian Viviani on Davis in this film in 'Sans Metro ni Mayer'). (I realise that I have made the case particularly tricky by suggesting that in these scenes the characteristic Davis performance signs signify in part by their absence or 'repression'. In fact, this would help the Haskell thesis, since it reinforces the notion of 'frustration' so important to the development of the 'superbitch'. The strong sense of Regina having to operate within the house while her brothers move about the public world also supports this reading.)

9   A Note on Authorship

Authorship has long been an issue in film studies, in terms of who is to be considered the author of a film. Film poses this question with peculiar insistence because of its industrial production, involving hundreds of personnel and a very high degree of division of labour. (See Ivan Butler's *The Making of a Feature Film* for a breakdown of this.) In the process of examining this, however, the very notion of authorship has been radically revised.

In order to cope with the corporate or collaborative nature of film-making, various models of authorship have been proposed.

Individual authorship
It is this model that has so far had most success in film studies under the title of the 'auteur theory'. This proposes a single person – usually but not invariably the director – as the author of a film. This is argued for in one of two ways. First, that everything in the film text can be attributed to the decisions of the director (or other auteur); this view generally recognises that the director may have to take over ready-made narratives, star images, etc., but argues that s/he submits them to her/his creative will. Generally speaking, this view has an evaluative emphasis, that is, it is only the 'good' directors who can be seen in this way. Second, that the work of the director or other auteur can be discerned on investigation (usually by looking at a run of films on which s/he worked), but that this may not account for everything in a film; in this view, the auteur is one element among many composing the film text, and her/his work can run counter to the rest of the text; this view does not need to be evaluative – by looking at a body of work directed by the same person one can discern continuities that may be attributable to him/her and so establish him/her as an auteur, but these continuities may be of no other interest.

Multiple authorship
This model extends the latter version of individual authorship by arguing that a film text is composed of many different authorial 'voices' (director, producer, scriptwriter, star, cameraperson, etc.) that may or may not be in harmony.

Collective authorship
Here it is argued that a group of people working closely together constitute a team who are properly thought of as the author of the film. The only examples one can point to are all identified by the name of the director around whom the group is formed – John Ford, Ingmar Bergman, Satyajit Ray – and thus the relationship between collective and individual authorship remains problematic. This model

has not to my knowledge been theoretically elaborated or defended outside of alternative film-making practices (e.g. the London Women's Film Group).

Corporate authorship
Here it is argued that the organisations or social structures that produce films are the authors of them. These may be the individual studios, Hollywood as a whole, or even American capitalism and/or patriarchy. This implies that the personnel working on a film essentially 'carry' the meanings and values of the larger structures within which they work without significantly inflecting or altering them.

The major problem that all concepts of authorship present us with – in, be it said, all the arts – is the relationship between the semiotic or aesthetic text and the author. Traditionally this has been thought of as 'expression': the text expresses the ideas, feelings and/or 'personality' of the author. It has long been recognised, however, that such a formulation is inadequate, if only on the simple empirical grounds that authors are often not much like their texts. Various solutions to this have been posed, including the notions of the text as an expression of the author's unconscious and of her/his 'artistic personality' (as something distinct from her/his personality in the rest of life). In film studies, this led to the habit of writing not of the films of Howard Hawks but of those of 'Howard Hawks' (first suggested by Peter Wollen in the revised edition of his *Signs and Meaning in the Cinema*).

The problem, however, with any version of the expression theory is that it supposes a transparency between an author and her/his text. Yet it is a feature of all human expression that it 'escapes' those who use it, precisely because expression is only possible through languages and codes that are more general, because shared, than an individual person or even group. This does not mean, though, that one can jettison individual persons from consideration of authorship altogether. Rather, we have to think of it in terms of people working on and in those languages and codes, and in so far as questions of personality are still in order, it is in the characteristic way of working with the codes that we can identify a film as 'Hawks' or 'Dietrich'. Films then cannot be assumed to carry or embody authorial personality, but none the less people do work on films and make determinant decisions about them, and this is a legitimate area of enquiry.

Stars as authors
The study of stars as themselves authors belongs essentially to the study of the Hollywood production situation. It is certainly possible to establish, as 'auteur theory' enjoins us, continuities, contradictions and transformations either in the totality of a star's image or in discrete elements such as dress or performance style, roles, publicity, iconography. However, the relationship between these and the star always has to be established by examination of what sources there are concerning the actual making of the image and films. That is to say, a star, in films, publicity and promotion, is a semiotic construction and the fact that that construction exhibits continuities does not prove that the star as person is responsible for them. S/he may be, but also may not be.

In his study of James Cagney, *Cagney: The Actor as Auteur*, Patrick McGilligan makes this point very clearly:

> The auteur theory can be revised and reproposed with actors in mind: under certain circumstances, an actor may influence a film as much as a writer, director or producer; some actors are more influential than others; and there are certain rare few performers whose acting capabilities and screen personas are so powerful that they embody and define the very essence of their films. If an actor is responsible only for acting but is not involved in any of the artistic decisions of film-making, then it is accurate surely to refer to the actor as a semi-passive icon, a symbol that is manipulated by writers and directors. But actors who not only influence artistic decisions (casting, writing, directing etc.) but demand certain limitations on the basis of their screen personas, may justly be regarded as 'auteurs'. When the performer becomes so important to a production that he or she changes lines, adlibs, shifts meaning, influences the narrative and style of a film and altogether signifies something clear-cut to audiences despite the intent of writers and directors, then the acting of that person assumes the force, style and integrity of an auteur. (p. 199)

He then proceeds to argue that Cagney does fit the category of actor-auteur, drawing on interviews with him and those he worked with, as well as observing how, for instance, Cagney's films made with directors such as Lloyd Bacon, William Keighley and Roy Del Ruth are all very similar to each other, and more like Cagney's other films than films by those directors with different stars. (Unfortunately this last point lacks the precision of most of McGilligan's study; one needs the specific aspects of performance, characterisation, narrative structure, etc. pinpointed in the way that one would expect from auteurist analyses of directors and not the vague references to 'spontaneity' (Bacon), 'a polished emphasis on action and dialogue' (Keighley) and 'urbanity' (Del Ruth).)

McGilligan's aim is to demonstrate that Cagney is the author of his films, the classic auteurist position. However, any of the models of authorship outlined above might apply to given stars. In considering this, we must first distinguish between on the one hand authorship of the star image and/or performance, and on the other hand authorship of films.

In the case of images and/or performance, there may be stars who totally controlled this (Fred Astaire, Joan Crawford), or only contributed to it (Marlene Dietrich, Robert Mitchum), as part of a collective team (John Wayne) or just one disparate voice among many (Marilyn Monroe, Marlon Brando); alternatively there will be others who were almost totally the product of the studio/Hollywood machine (Lana Turner). (The names in brackets are guesses only and require further research to confirm or disprove.) The fact that the person of the star coincides with a text (the star image, the character, the performance) in the construction of which s/he was only a collaborator or even a mere vehicle should warn us not to elide the star-as-person with the star-as-text and assume that the former is the author of the latter. Although I find it hard to conceive of a star having no power in the decisions made about her/his image or performance, just how much power s/he had and how s/he exercised it has to be determined by looking at specific cases.

In the case of stars as authors of the films they starred in, we must begin by excepting those cases where stars directed (or scripted) themselves in films: for instance, Charlie Chaplin, Buster Keaton, Mae West (scripts), Ida Lupino, Jerry Lewis, John Wayne, Clint Eastwood. In these cases, we have to make a theoretical distinction between their role as star and their other role in the production. The number of cases in which the totality of a film can be laid at the door of the star must be very few indeed. (Candidates include Greta Garbo and *Queen Christina*, Ellen Burstyn and *Alice Doesn't Live Here Any More*, and most persuasively Barbra Streisand and *A Star Is Born*.) However, the star as one of the 'voices' in a film (always remembering any voice can only be returned to its author as the point of decision-making in production, not that of unmediated expressivity) is surely very common. This 'voice' is not necessarily confined to matters of performance, dress, etc., but may affect almost any aspect of the film, depending upon how the star exercised her/his power.

Within the theoretical issues sketched above, each example has to be argued on the basis of the evidence. Although working in a strictly untheoretical manner, Alexander Walker's chapter on Greta Garbo in *Sex in the Movies* illustrates some of the empirical complexities of the issue. In examining the various people and pressures involved in the production of Greta Garbo, Walker is essentially arguing for the 'voices' model, of which Greta Gustafsson's is only one. Thus he suggests that Gustafsson had, first of all, certain given features, including her appearance (the fine 'feminine', 'spiritual' face and strong 'masculine', 'earthy' body, p. 102) and her 'pessimistic' temperament (p. 103). Gustafsson was the 'possessor' of these, if not exactly their 'author'. However, Walker also stresses 'the ways in which she employed her talent to gain her effects' (p. 99), definitely an authorial perspective (and we'll leave aside that problematic word 'talent'). He notes that 'Almost every eye-witness report of her at work stresses the same point: the amazing suddenness with which her nature changed the instant she started acting' (p. 110). The evidence suggests that an enormous amount of what she did in front of the cameras she determined through, Walker, suggests, a technique close to that of Stanislavsky. Yet there were collaborators in the total effect. Walker does not discuss how her many directors worked with her, but points to two men, Mauritz Stiller and William Daniels, as key figures. The former discovered her in Sweden and seems to have moulded her performance style in line with his own idea of her. Gustafsson was to him 'malleable feminine material' which he could make into 'an image that [fed] his emotional needs' (p. 107). It was he who gave her the name Garbo, meaning 'wood nymph' in Swedish. Daniels was Garbo's lighting cameraperson on all but two of her sound films. In Walker's account this relationship was more collaborative in achieving the various emotional effects that were required (by whom?) for the parts she was playing (p. 117).

All this, however, takes place within the elaborate structures of MGM. Here Walker argues both that MGM's scriptwriters 'got to be very cunning about how they conscripted . . . characteristics of [Garbo] into their stories' (p. 103) and that Garbo had huge battles over scripts with MGM (p. 104), battles that she generally won. Yet if this is true, it is also clear that she allowed herself to be fitted into certain MGM notions. It was the studio that made her say 'I want to be alone' in *Grand Hotel* in 1933, feeding on an image that was based on misquoting what she said to the press;[8] it was the studio that bought up various 'classic' or 'historical' vehicles for her and later tried to change her image with *Ninotchka* and *Two-Faced*

Woman. Moreover, the studio was itself seeking to respond to certain shifts at a more general ideological level in the representation of women. Walker sees Garbo as MGM's attempt at reconciling the 'vivid' sexuality of the flapper and 'the Lillian Gish girl's continual battle for her honour' (p. 113). At this level, the author of Garbo is ideology (in its complex articulation with capitalism and patriarchy). Although Walker does not present as much detailed evidence as one might like, and does not question terms like 'talent' and 'nature', this chapter and others in *Sex in the Movies* and *Stardom* (especially on Mae West and Elizabeth Taylor in the first, and Bette Davis, Joan Crawford and Clark Gable in the second) do suggest the kind of work that is needed in this area. (So may some (auto-) biographies – this is not a field I have researched in any detail.)

Stars and authors

Star images and performance are also used by other authors. Here I will restrict the discussion to directors, although examples such as Louis B. Mayer and Judy Garland, David O. Selznick and Jennifer Jones, Howard Hughes and Jane Russell would undoubtedly repay examination. As V. F. Perkins puts it in *Film as Film*, 'With actors, as with scripts, the director is given material which can be used and organised but not transformed at will' (p. 182). What interests Perkins is the way that a director can make 'the familiar personality of the actor' fit with her/his (the director's) concerns and characteristic 'patterns'. S/he may do this by judicious casting – Perkins cites Hitchcock's use of Cary Grant and James Stewart – but directors rarely have much control over casting, and it is usually a case of having to 'exploit and organise imaginatively' pre-given material, the star image and performance capacities. Here Perkins notes that a star image can suggest certain possibilities to directors – Stewart in relation to Hitchcock, Anthony Mann, John Ford and Otto Preminger – and equally that a director use stars to express her/his 'authorial pattern' in different ways – Nicholas Ray and Humphrey Bogart, Robert Mitchum, James Cagney and Charlton Heston.

This notion of the star and the director mutually bringing something out in each other informs much auteurist criticism. This approach does usually privilege the director over the star in their collaborative interaction, and examples are typically confined to a few paragraphs within broader considerations of a director's work. In *Horizons West*, Jim Kitses notes the Mann/Stewart, Budd Boetticher/Randolph Scott collaborations, while John Baxter in *The Cinema of John Ford* writes of Ford's different views of the hero according to whether he is using John Wayne, James Stewart or Henry Fonda. Other less satisfactory examples of this approach include Stanley Solomon's discussion in *The Film Idea* of the use made of Cary Grant by Stanley Donen and Alfred Hitchcock and Gary Carey's article 'The Lady and the Director' dealing with Bette Davis and William Wyler.

One need not, as Perkins, Kitses and Baxter are, be concerned to find a perfect fit between star image and directorial pattern. Disjunctions between them may be just as interesting, especially from an ideological point of view, since they may correspond to, or at any rate suggest, ideological contradictions. I would cite here Monroe v. Hawks in *Gentlemen Prefer Blondes*. Lorelei, as Anita Loos wrote her, is the hero[9] of the film, and she is the hero by her deliberate use of her (socially constructed) femininity. In Hawks's films such a character (e.g. Rita Hayworth in

155

Only Angels Have Wings) is not so sympathetic, or central. Thus he submits her here to humiliation (trapped in a porthole up to her hips, themselves part of her sexual armoury) and send-up (Jane Russell's impersonation of her in the court scene), while constructing the Russell character as a warm, practical buddy-woman comparable to other 'Hawksian' women (cf. Jean Arthur in *Only Angels Have Wings*). In this context. Monroe's construction of Lorelei as innocently, utterly but not manipulatively, sexual, a construction stemming from the basic pattern of Monroe's image and at variance with Loos's Lorelei, confuses Hawks's division of the female world into manipulative feminine women and likeable masculine (or non-feminine) ones. There is reason for Hawks to deride Loos's Lorelei, but not Monroe's – but this then throws us back to the problem of just what place the 'feminine' has in Hawks's films, and, more importantly, in Holly-wood and in patriarchy generally. 'Femininity' is primarily a social construction and, moreover, a construction made by men. Yet it is a construction men often find it hard to cope with – it is the category onto which they project more funda-mental fears about gender, which one can conceive psychoanalytically in terms of castration or socio-historically in terms of men's power over women and simul-taneous dependence on them. Hawks's films, like most films, legitimate this fear. They say, in effect, that women, especially 'feminine' women, really should be feared by men; in other words, they take what is a projection from men and claim that it really emanates from women. Monroe as Lorelei, however, disturbs this pattern, because Lorelei, as Monroe's image has already constructed her and as she plays her, is both extremely feminine and not evil or castrating. Monroe as Lorelei refuses to corroborate this male construction of the female.

Most star/director studies are concerned with the star as a signifying complex in terms of its appropriateness to the director's concerns or approach. The group of films made by Marlene Dietrich and Josef von Sternberg are often read in this way, but also raise other possibilities. The standard view of the Dietrich/Sternberg films is that the former is a pure vehicle for the latter's fantasies and formalist con-cerns. Thus Marjorie Rosen in *Popcorn Venus* sees the films as the 'canonization' of Dietrich 'as the von Sternberg ideal' (p. 174). Claire Johnston goes further and argues that far from promoting a male ideal of the feminine, the films actually deny the presence of the female:

> in order that the man remain within the centre of the universe in a text which focuses on the image of woman, the auteur is forced to repress the idea of woman as a social and sexual being (her otherness) and to deny the opposition man/woman altogether. The woman as sign, then, becomes the pseudo-centre of the filmic discourse. The real opposition posed by the sign is male/non-male, which Sternberg establishes by his use of masculine clothing enveloping the image of Dietrich. This masquerade indicates the absence of man, an absence which is simultaneously negated and recuperated by man. The image of the woman becomes merely the trace of the exclusion and repression of woman. (Notes on Women's Cinema, p. 26)

Whether thought of as absent as Dietrich or absent as woman, both these views also correspond to Sternberg's own statement, quoted by Tom Flinn in his article 'Joe, Where Are You?': ' "In my films Marlene is not herself. Remember that, Mar-lene is Marlene. I am Marlene, she knows that better than anyone" ' (p. 9). However, as Laura Mulvey points out in her article 'Visual Pleasure and Narrative Cinema':

It is well known that Sternberg once said he would welcome his films being projected upside down so that story and character involvement would not interfere with the spectator's undiluted appreciation of the screen image. This statement is revealing but ingenuous. Ingenuous in that his films do demand that the figure of the woman (Dietrich, in the cycle of films with her, as the ultimate example) should be identifiable. (p. 14)

This suggests that while the tendency of Sternberg is to use Dietrich as part of his erotic-formalist ('fetishistic') concerns, the fact is that Dietrich as an already-signifying element is also present. It is this that enables Molly Haskell to put Dietrich into the category of women stars who resist the stereotype to which they were assigned. Thus she discusses Dietrich in relation to Jean Harlow and Mae West and argues:

In the resplendence of her beauty, Dietrich comes closest to being a goddess, but she refuses to be one, refuses to take on the generalized aspects of love and suffering with which a mass audience could identify, and refuses to pretend for the sake of a man's ego that love will not die or that she will love only him. (*From Reverence to Rape*, p. 109)

Similarly Tom Flinn in the article mentioned above notes:

Of primary importance in the creation of 'Dietrich' was Dietrich herself, her air of detachment, her independence even from society's taboos – demonstrated by her occasional appropriation of male attire, usually to parody the 'stronger' sex, which she invariably bested in one way or another. (p. 14)

These views – Dietrich as an empty vehicle for Sternberg's erotic formalism, Dietrich as resisting the construction of her as a goddess for male dreams – conceptualise the Dietrich/Sternberg films in terms of the conjunction or disjunction of two 'voices'. Several writers have suggested, however, that one can read the films in terms of the actual erotic-emotional relationship between star and director. As Jack Babuscio puts it, one can 'sense something of an "affaire" between Dietrich and her director' ('Camp and the Gay Sensibility', p. 51). Laura Mulvey suggests a formal characteristic of the films that supports this – the absence or subordination, in blatantly voyeuristic films, of a male protagonist who stands in for the director or audience. The relationship between Sternberg and Dietrich as star and as character is one of direct voyeurism – him of her – and the audience is placed in the same position as the director. Robin Wood further suggests that through the films one can see

a process ... which may correspond to von Sternberg's feelings about their relationship. From *Shanghai Express* through *The Scarlet Empress* to *The Devil is a Woman* there is a growing insistence on the impotence of the male and the ruthlessness of the woman. (*Personal Views*, p. 113)

Mulvey and Wood imply that the films express *Sternberg's* view of the relationship. However, if we accept the 'resistance' arguments of Haskell and Flinn, we might argue that the deterioration noted by Wood is related to Dietrich's unwillingness to become everything Sternberg wanted her to become, and it is precisely her 'insolence' – the key word in Alexander Walker's account of her in *Sex in the Movies* – that prevents her being subsumed into Sternberg's *mise en scène* and leads to his finding her, in Wood's terms, 'ruthless'. In this way, the films can be seen as the traces of the complexities of their relationship rather than just the combination of two voices.

I have tried in discussing authorship to avoid the trap of thinking of authors in terms of self-expression. The theoretical problems of the concept of self-expression, as I noted above, are, firstly, that it cannot acknowledge that all language of whatever kind 'escapes' its individual users to a greater or lesser extent and, secondly, that it assumes a self that exists outside of and prior to language rather than one that is formed in and through language (though not only language). Yet the notion of self-expression persists as part of our habits of thought. In his chapter on stars in *The Spoken Seen* (which is in the main a polemic for taking stars seriously), Frank McConnell argues that stars – because they seem to be really there on the screen but are not, and because *they* are what we experience though much else constructs them – dramatise the crisis of the notion of self-expression. This he sees as inherited from the Romantic movement, especially Byron: 'central to the Byronic line of romantic writing is the assumption of its own impossibility. Self-expression may be the goal of the art, as of the life; but it is a goal militated against and undercut by the art itself' (p. 180). He goes on to compare Humphrey Bogart and James Cagney, seeing the former expressing the 'incertitude' of the person caught within 'the part fate and the film [have] assigned him' (p. 185), and Cagney as expressing a 'newfound ability to survive *within* fiction' (p. 186). McConnell's account reworks (in a somewhat literary, existentialist vein) a point that has recurred throughout this book, namely, that in addition to the way they articulate and deal with contradictions within and between ideologies, stars also dramatise the problem of self and role. If one contemplates them as authors, then one is brought up against this problem in a slightly different form – the relationship, often problematic, between self and expression.

Notes

1. I should like to thank Phil Dring for this account of Eisenstein's theory of typage.
2. See Claude Brémond, 'Le Message narratif' and 'La Logique des possibles narratifs'.
3. Peter Wollen, *Signs and Meaning in the Cinema*; Jim Kitses, *Horizons West*.
4. Fred Camper argues in his article on *Dishonored* that 'The mystique that has grown up around Dietrich … is not really corroborated by an examination of von Sternberg's films' (p. 16).
5. It seems likely that Costa-Gavras chose to cast Yves Montand as the reactionary character in *State of Siege*, perhaps precisely to complicate too easy a taking of sides.
6. Charles Affron's *Star Acting* came to my notice too late for inclusion in the main body of the text. This is a detailed study of the film performances of Lillian Gish, Greta Garbo and Bette Davis. Subsidiary interests in the book include the relationship between the star's performance and the director (particularly Gish and D. W. Griffith and Davis and William Wyler) and the vehicle aspects of a star's career. (He notes, for instance, that Garbo's films include a deliberate delaying and dramatising of her first instance, an emphasis on motifs of seeing and being seen in connection with her and the establishment

of mood and emotion through touching and handling objects and surfaces.) However, the issue of authorship and of the vehicle are not extensively examined, and the main emphasis of the book is an analysis of performances in particular films (the most extended instances being *Broken Blossoms*, *Camille* and *All About Eve*), using stills and frame enlargements to illustrate points. This means that the book is very useful as a resource, but needs careful handling. The interpretations Affron makes of the illustrations often involve doubtful inferences and the aim is essentially to celebrate the detail of the performances in terms of the performers' genius.

7. See Georg Lukács, 'The Intellectual Physiognomy of Literary Characters'.
8. Walker points out that Garbo only asked to be left alone by the press, but that the press and later the studio chose to interpret this as the expression of a fundamental and 'metaphysical' desire.
9. I use the term 'hero' here, not 'heroine', partly to stress that for Loos Lorelei is 'heroic', admirable, a winner, and partly because the term 'heroine' implies a structural position in narratives in relation to a male protagonist – as the object of his quest or his love.

Conclusion

A conclusion is difficult. As stated in the introduction, this book is a survey of what has been done in the study of stars and what needs to be done. I'd like to make four concluding remarks, which should be taken not as a summing up, much less as drawing things to a point of closure, but rather as suggestions of priorities or emphases for future work. First of all, there is the question of the audience. Throughout this book – as throughout most film studies – the audience has been conspicuous by its absence. In talking of manipulation consumption, ideological work, subversion, identification, reading and placing, a concept of the audience is clearly crucial, and yet in every case I have had to gesture towards this gap in our knowledge and then proceed as if this were *merely* a gap. But how one conceptualises the audience – and the empirical adequacy of one's conceptualisations – is fundamental to every assumption one can make about how stars, and films, work. It's not as if we aren't ignorant enough in other areas. We do not know enough about the production of media texts, and little empirical work has been done in the light of recent, more sophisticated theories of cultural production.[1] Equally, the status as knowledge of the various formal or interpretative approaches to media texts has to remain problematic.[2] Yet these weaknesses are as nothing compared to our ignorance, theoretical and empirical, of how films work for, on, with audiences – and which preposition you plump for is crucial. There are signs, however, that this absence is beginning to be made up by new theoretical developments[3] and research projects.[4] In addition, there is still quite a lot of data in much of the old empirical audience research work of which to make new sense.[5]

One of the ways in which the question of the audience has been approached in recent years is through the notion of people as 'subjects'.[6] Briefly, at its broadest, this approach is concerned with the way that ideology works not just as a set of ideas and representations that people use but as a process which also constructs people (as 'subjects'). What is decisive about this approach is that it refuses once and for all any notion of people as 'essences' existing outside of, over against ideology. What this approach puts in crisis consequently – as has an important tradition in literature and drama, discussed by Elizabeth Burns in *Theatricality* as 'depersonalisation' (pp. 174f.) – is the sense of freedom, creativity, continuity, optimism and enterprise that founded the concept of the person in bourgeois society, and has informed much Marxist thought as well. This sense of crisis as to what a person is seems to me to be central also to the star phenomenon. It can be seen to lie behind star charisma as a generalised phenomenon, in that stars speak centrally to this crisis and seem to embody it or to condense it within themselves. How they speak to, embody or condense it may be predominantly in terms of reaffirming the reality of people as individuals or subjects over against ideology and history, or else in terms of exposing precisely the uncertainty and anxiety concerning the definition of what a person is. Whether affirming or exposing, or moving between the two, stars articulate this crisis always through the cultural and historical specificities of class, gender, race, sexuality, religion, subcultural formations, etc. Yet all stars seem to me to work also at the more general level – itself culturally and historically specific – of defining what a person is. I have suggested at various points in this book how the stars can be seen variously to handle opposed, or uneasily related, notions such as:

star-as-person : star-as-image
star-as-image : star-as-character
star-as-auteur : star-as-text
star-as-self : star-as-role
and now star-as-essence : star-as-subject.

A fruitful way of studying the stars then would seem to be charting the ways that this crisis is articulated in, through and by them.

The approach just outlined remains concerned to understand, and demystify, how the stars in practice work. However, reference to exposure of crisis suggests that stars can be not only of ideology but also about it – a position close to that taken by Marx and Engels in relation to literature.[7] This leads me to my third concluding point, the question of the radical potential of the stars. I start from the assumption that the moment of radical work within the mass media is as indispensable to cultural struggle as work within the avant-garde.[8] The question then is, what work is possible in relation to the mass media?

I have indicated certain possibilities of work at the level of the text at various points above. Among these, one needs a little elaboration and defence. In the discussion of 'the rebel' (pp. 52f.) and the 'independent woman' (pp. 54f.), as well as in my reference throughout to Molly Haskell's thesis of women stars who 'resist' their demeaning roles, I have been assuming that, in so far as these stars and star types could work progressively, they would do so through audience *identification* with them. This identification would work *either* by providing an affirmation of an alternative or oppositional attitude/response by audience members to their life situations that is not otherwise recognised by the dominant media, *or* by providing an image of a way out of those situations through role models that suggested alternative ways of inhabiting or transforming them. I am aware that some recent theorisation sees all forms of identification as reactionary, for two related reasons. First, it is argued that identification confirms us in the illusion that we are whole and unified subjects. However, as the theory from which this position emerges itself makes clear, this illusion is necessary to living in human culture at all, and while it is important to be aware of all aspects of human culture as culture (rather than thinking of them as natural), the more urgent task is to distinguish between modes of representation and identification in political terms. The second argument stresses that we can only identify through recognition, and that since we can only recognise that which is, all recognition/identification can only serve to confirm the *status quo*. While this view does have a certain logic to it, it operates with the assumption that the *status quo* is uniform and homogeneous, rather than riven by contradictions within and between ideologies, and hence within and between modes of representation and identification. Thus while it is true to say that one can only recognise that which is, it is also true that that which is is more than simply the dominant ideology and that the latter is anyway far from simple. To these objections to blanket anti-representation/identification positions, I would add a more immediate political one, and this is that for groups – the working class, women, blacks, gays – who have been excluded from the culture's system of representations in all but marginal or demeaning forms, the call for an end to identification figures is, if nothing else, premature. As Paul Hallam and Ronald L. Peck observe in an article on 'Images of Homosexuality' in films (*Gay Left*, no. 5, Winter 1977), 'Narrative identification is being rejected by the avant-garde ... at a point in time when gays can claim they still have not had it. An initial period of identification is important to a repressed group that has *never* had adequate self-images' (p. 25).

Whatever radical/progressive/subversive form some stars may take – articulating contradictions, foregrounding stereotypes, Brechtian representation through 'leaps and jumps', alternative or oppositional identification figures, etc. – it needs to be stressed that one is talking about what readings texts make possible. While the above implies a programme of radical film production, it also requires a programme of radical film reading. This latter programme can in addition be concerned with exposing the reactionary ideological work of stars as media texts as well as pointing to arguable instances of progressive texts. (I would expect most stars to be both, in tension.)

Fourthly, and finally, I feel I should mention beauty, pleasure, delight . . . The emphasis in this book has been on analysis and demystification, and I would defend this emphasis to the last. However, we should not forget that what we are analysing gains its force and intensity from the way it is experienced, and that ideology shapes the experiential and effective as much as the cognitive. When I see Marilyn Monroe I catch my breath; when I see Montgomery Clift I sigh over how beautiful he is; when I see Barbara Stanwyck, I know that women are strong. I don't want to privilege these responses over analysis, but equally I don't want, in the rush to analysis, to forget what it is that I am analysing. And I must add that, while I accept utterly that beauty and pleasure are culturally and historically specific, and in no way escape ideology, none the less they are beauty and pleasure and I want to hang on to them in some form or another.

Notes

1. See for instance Pierre Macherey, *Pour une théorie de la production littéraire*; Julia Kristeva, 'Signifying Practice and Mode of Production'; Steve Burniston and Chris Weedon, 'Ideology, Subjectivity and the Artistic Text'; Rachel Harrison, '*Shirley*: Relations of Reproduction and the Ideology of Romance'.
2. See Janet Wolff, *Hermeneutic Philosophy and the Sociology of Art*.
3. For instance, Stuart Hall, 'Encoding and Decoding in the Television Discourse'; Dave Morley, 'Reconceptualising the Media Audience'; Colin MacCabe, 'Theory and Film: Principles of Realism and Pleasure'.
4. For instance, the work of Dave Morley and Dorothy Hobson at the Centre for Contemporary Cultural Studies, University of Birmingham.

5. For example, Leo Handel, *Hollywood Looks at Its Audience*; J. P. Mayer, *British Cinemas and their Audiences;* Margaret Thorpe, *America at the Movies.*
6. See the journal *Ideology and Consciousness,* in particular Diana Adlam et al., 'Psychology, Ideology and the Human Subject'; Luce Irigaray, 'Women's Exile'; Brian Roberts, 'G. H. Mead: The Theory and Practice of His Social Philosophy'; Stuart Hall, 'Some Problems with the Ideology/Subject Couplet'.
7. Cf. Karl Marx and Friedrich Engels, *On Literature and Art,* especially Engels's letter to Margaret Harkness, pp. 116–17.
8. For discussion of the politics of cultural struggle, see Sylvia Harvey, *May '68 and Film Culture.*

Bibliography

This bibliography is divided into five parts. Section One includes articles and books that deal in general terms with the stars. Although not definitive, I have aimed to be comprehensive. This section includes books which have chapters on the stars in them, and books and articles which deal with the phenomenon of stardom in areas other than film. Section Two includes works dealing with individual stars. This section is more selective. It includes reference back to the previous section in the case of books and articles which, while having a general interest in the stars, also deal substantially with specific stars. Section Three lists source material for the study of star images. Titles included here are restricted to those cited in the text and to collections of source material. Section Four lists works dealing with the cinema in general, but not – or only marginally – with the stars. Section Five includes all other works cited in the text.

1 Stars: General

Affron, Charles, *Star Acting*, E. P. Dutton, New York, 1977.

Agel, Henri, 'Le Dandy à l'écran', *Revue d'esthétique*, vol. 20, nos. 2 and 3, 1967, pp. 153–68.

Alberoni, Francesco, 'L'Elite irresponsable: théorie et recherche sociologique sur '*le divismo*', *Ikon*, vol. 12, 40/1, 1962, pp. 45–62; reprinted (trans. Denis McQuail) in McQuail, Denis (ed.), *Sociology of Mass Communications*, Penguin, London, 1972, pp. 75–98 (title, 'The Powerless Elite: Theory and Sociological Research on the Phenomenon of the Stars').

Alloway, Lawrence, 'Iconography of the Movies', *Movie*, no. 7; reprinted in Cameron, Ian (ed.), *Movie Reader*, November Books, London, 1972.
   Violent America, Museum of Modern Art, New York, 1971.

Alpert, Hollis, *The Dreams and the Dreamers*, Macmillan, New York, 1962.

Anderson, Joseph I. and Richie, Donald, *The Japanese Film: Art and Industry*, Charles E. Tuttle, Rutland VT and Tokyo, 1959.

Babuscio, Jack, 'Screen Gays', *Gay News*, nos. 73 ('Camp Women'), 75 ('Images of Masculinity'), 92 ('Sissies'), 93 ('Tomboys').
   'Camp and the Gay Sensibility', in Dyer, Richard (ed.), *Gays and Film*, British Film Institute, London, 1977.

Barthes, Roland, 'La Vedette, enquêtes d'audience?', *Communications* 2.
   Mythologies, Seuil, Paris, 1970; reprinted (trans. Annette Lavers), Cape, London, 1972.

Becker, Raymond de, *De Tom Mix à James Dean*, Arthème Fayard, Paris, 1959.

Bobker, Lee R., *Elements of Film*, Harcourt, Brace and World, New York, 1969.

Boorstin, Daniel, *The Image*, Weidenfeld and Nicolson, London, 1962; Penguin, 1963.

Braudy, Leo, *The World in a Frame*, Anchor Press/Doubleday, Garden City, New York, 1976.

Burns, Elizabeth, *Theatricality*, Longman, London, 1972.

Cavell, Stanley, *The World Viewed*, Viking Press, New York, 1971.

Durgnat, Raymond, 'Getting Cinema on the Right Wavelength', *Films and Filming*, vol. 11, no. 5, February 1965, pp. 46–50.

Films and Feelings, Faber and Faber, London, 1967.

Dyer, Richard, 'It's Being So Camp As Keeps Us Going', *Body Politic* (Toronto), no. 36, September 1977, pp. 11–13.

Eisenstadt, S. N. (ed. and introduction), *Max Weber on Charisma and Institution Building*, University of Chicago Press, Chicago and London, 1968.

Elkin, Fred, 'Popular Hero Symbols and Audience Gratifications', *Journal of Educational Psychology*, 29, 1955, pp. 97–107.

Gough-Yates, Kevin, 'The Hero', *Films and Filming*, December 1965–March 1966. 'The Heroine', *Films and Filming*, May–August 1966.

Griffith, Richard, *The Movie Stars*, Doubleday, New York, 1970.

Handel, Leo, 'La Bourse des vedettes', *Communications* 2, 1963, pp. 86–104.

Harris, Thomas B., 'The Building of Popular Images: Grace Kelly and Marilyn Monroe', *Studies in Public Communications* 1, 1957, pp. 45–8.

Haskell, Molly, *From Reverence to Rape*, Holt, Rinehart and Winston, New York, 1974; Penguin, London, 1974.

Hess, Thomas B., 'Pinup and Icon', in Hess, Thomas, B. and Nochlin, Linda (eds.), *Woman as Sex Object*, Newsweek, New York, 1972, pp. 223–37.

Hollywood and the Great Stars Monthly, nos. 1–9, 1974–5.

Jarvie, I. C., *Towards a Sociology of the Cinema*, Routledge, London, 1970.

Johnston, Claire (ed.), *Notes on Women's Cinema*, Society for Education in Film and Television, London, 1973. 'Feminist Politics and Film History', *Screen*, vol. 16, no. 3, Autumn 1975, pp. 115–124.

King, Barry, 'The Social Significance of Stardom', unpublished manuscript, 1974.

Klapp, Orrin E., *Heroes, Villains and Fools*, Prentice-Hall, Englewood Cliffs, NJ, 1962. *Collective Search for Identity*, Holt, Rinehart and Winston, New York, 1969.

Lowenthal, Leo, 'The Triumph of Mass Idols', in *Literature, Popular Culture and Society*, Prentice-Hall, Englewood Cliffs, NJ, 1961, pp. 109–40.

Manvell, Roger, *Love Goddesses of the Movies*, Hamlyn, London, 1975.

McArthur, Colin, 'The Real Presence', *Sight and Sound*, vol. 36, no. 3, Summer 1967, pp. 141–3.

McConnell, Frank, *The Spoken Seen*, John Hopkins University Press, Baltimore, and London, 1975.

McCreadie, Marsha, *The American Movie Goddess*, Wiley, New York, 1973.

McVay, Douglas, 'The Art of the Actor, Part Five: The Actor and the Star', *Films and Filming*, November, 1966, pp. 26–33.

Mellen, Joan, *Big Bad Wolves: Masculinity in the American Film*, Elm Tree Books, London, 1978.

Mercer, Jane, *Great Lovers of the Movies*, Hamlyn, London, 1975.

Merton, Robert K., *Mass Persuasion*, Harper, New York and London, 1946.

Meyers, Janet, 'Dyke Goes to the Movies', *Dyke* (New York), Spring 1976.

Mills, C. Wright, *The Power Elite*, Oxford University Press, New York, 1956.

Morella, Joe and Epstein, Edward Z., *Rebels – the Rebel Hero in Films*, Citadel Press, New York, 1971.

Morin, Edgar, *Les Stars*, Seuil, Paris, 1957; reprinted (trans. Richard Howard), Grove Press, New York, 1960.

Morin, Violette, 'Les Olympiens', *Communications* 2, pp. 105–21.

Mulvey, Laura, 'Visual Pleasure and Narrative Cinema', *Screen*, vol. 16, no. 3, Autumn 1975, pp. 6–18.

Myrdal, Gunnar, *An American Dilemma*, Harper, New York, 1944 ('glamour personalities', pp. 734–5).

Pascall, Jeremy (ed.), *Hollywood and the Great Stars*, Phoebus, London, 1976.

Patalas, Enno, *Sozialgeschichte der Stars*, Marion von Schröeder, Hamburg, 1963; reprinted as *Stars, Geschichte der Filmidole*, Fischer-Bücherei, Hamburg and Frankfurt, 1967.

Pate, Michael, *The Film Actor*, Yoseloff, London, 1970.

Perkins, V. F., *Film as Film*, Penguin, London, 1972.

Powdermaker, Hortense, *Hollywood, the Dream Factory*, Little, Brown and Co., Boston, 1950.

Pudovkin, V. I., *Film Technique and Film Acting* (trans. and ed. Ivor Montagu), Mayflower, London, 1958.

Rosen, Marjorie, *Popcorn Venus*, Coward, McCann and Geoghegan, New York, 1973.

Schickel, Richard, *His Picture in the Papers*, Charterhouse, New York, 1974.

Scott, James F., *Film – the Medium and the Maker*, Holt, Rinehart and Winston, New York, 1975.

Shaffer, Lawrence, 'Some Notes on Film Acting', *Sight and Sound*, vol. 42, no. 2, Spring 1973.
'Reflections on the Face in Film', *Film Quarterly*, vol. xxxi, no. 2, Winter 1977–8.

Sheldon, Caroline, 'Lesbians and Film: Some Thoughts', in Dyer, Richard (ed.), *Gays and Film*, British Film Institute, London, 1977, pp. 5–26.

Shils, E. A., 'Charisma, Order and Status', *American Sociological Review*, 30, 1965, pp. 199–213.

Shipman, David, *The Great Stars – the Golden Years*, Hamlyn, London, 1970.
The Great Stars – the International Years, Hamlyn, London, 1972.

Siclier, Jacques, *Le Mythe de la femme dans le cinéma américain*, Cerf, Paris, 1956.
La Femme dans le cinéma français, Cerf, Paris, 1957.

Solomon, Stanley, *The Film Idea*, Harcourt Brace Jovanovich, New York, 1972.

Thomson, David, 'The Look on the Actor's Face', *Sight and Sound*, vol. 46, no. 4, Autumn 1977, pp. 240–4.

Tudor, Andrew, *Image and Influence*, Allen and Unwin, London, 1974.

Walker, Alexander, *The Celluloid Sacrifice*, Michael Joseph, London, 1966; reprinted (new title, *Sex in the Movies*), Penguin, London, 1968.
Stardom, the Hollywood Phenomenon, Michael Joseph, London, 1970; Penguin, London, 1974.

Weber, Max, *On Charisma and Institution Building* (ed. S. N. Eisenstadt), University of Chicago Press, Chicago and London, 1968.

Whitaker, Sheila, 'The Rebel Hero', *Hollywood and the Great Stars Monthly*, no. 8, pp. 10–13.

Wolfenstein, Martha and Leites, Nathan, *Movies: A Psychological Study*, Free Press, Glencoe, 1950.

Wood, Michael, *America in the Movies*, Secker and Warburg, London, 1975.

Wood, Robin, 'Acting Up', *Film Comment*, vol. 12, no. 2, March–April 1976, pp. 20–5.

2 Stars: Individual Studies

Affron, Charles, *Star Acting* (Lillian Gish, Garbo, Davis).

Alpert, Hollis, 'Marlon Brando and the Ghost of Stanley Kowalski', *The Dreams and the Dreamers*, pp. 40–61.

Babuscio, Jack, 'Screen Gays', *Gay News*, nos. 79 (James Dean), 85 (Marilyn Monroe), 102 (Dirk Bogarde), 104 (Montgomery Clift), 111 (Carmen Miranda).

Barr, Charles, *Laurel and Hardy*, Studio Vista, London, 1967.

Barthes, Roland, 'Le Visage de Garbo', *Mythologies*, pp. 77–9; reprinted in Mast, Gerald and Cohen, Marshall (eds.), *Film Theory and Criticism*, Oxford University Press, New York, 1974, pp. 567–9.

Bazin, André, 'Le Destin de Jean Gabin', *Radio-Cinéma-Télévision*, 1 October, 1950; reprinted in *Qu'est-ce que le cinéma?*, Cerf, Paris, 1961, pp. 79–82; reprinted (trans. Hugh Gray), 'The Destiny of Jean Gabin', in *What Is Cinema?*, vol. 2, University of California Press, Berkeley, Los Angeles and London, 1971, 1972, pp. 176–9.

Beauvoir, Simone de, *Brigitte Bardot and the Lolita Syndrome* (trans. Bernard Frechtman), Deutsch, Weidenfeld and Nicolson, London, 1960.

Brown, Geoffrey, 'The Marx Brothers', *Cinema* (Cambridge), no. 8, pp. 29–31.

Brown, William R., *Imagemaker: Will Rogers and the American Dream*, University of Missouri Press, 1970.

Camper, Fred, 'Jerry Lewis, *The Nutty Professor*', *Cinema* (Cambridge), no. 8, pp. 32–4.

Carey, Gary, 'The Lady and the Director' (Davis and William Wyler), *Film Comment*, vol. 6, no. 3, Autumn 1970, pp. 18–24.

Cooke, Alistair, *Douglas Fairbanks: The Making of a Screen Character*, Museum of Modern Art, New York, 1940.

Croce, Arlene, *The Fred Astaire and Ginger Rogers Book*, Outerbridge and Lazard, New York, 1972.

Durgnat, Raymond, *Greta Garbo*, Studio Vista, London, 1965.

Dyer, Richard, 'Four Films of Lana Turner', *Movie*, no. 25, pp. 30–52.
  'Resistance Through Charisma: Rita Hayworth and *Gilda*', in Kaplan, E. Ann (ed.), *Women and Film Noir*, British Film Institute, London, 1978, pp. 91–9.

Eckert, Charles, 'Shirley Temple and the House of Rockefeller', *Jump Cut*, no. 2, July–August 1974, pp. 1, 17–20.

Finn, Tom, 'Joe, Where Are You?' (Marlene Dietrich), *The Velvet Light Trap*, no. 6, Autumn 1972, pp. 9–14.

Godard, Jean-Luc and Gorin, Jean-Pierre, *Letter to Jane*, transcript prepared by Nicky North, British Film Institute, 1974.

Haskell, Molly, 'Partners in Crime and Conversion' (James Cagney, Joan Blondell, Ann Sheridan), *The Village Voice*, 7 December 1972.

Hembus, Joe, *Marilyn Monroe, die Frau des Jahrhunderts*, Wilhelm Heyne Verlag, Munich, 1973; reprinted (trans. Rosalind Parr), *Marilyn, the Destruction of an American Dream*, Tandem, London, 1973.

Hill, G., 'John Wayne', *Kinema*, no. 3, Autumn 1971, pp. 5–12.

Kaplan, E. Ann, 'The Importance and Ultimate Failure of *Last Tango in Paris*' (Marlon Brando), *Jump Cut*, no. 4, November–December 1974, pp. 1, 9–11.

Kobal, John, *Marlene Dietrich*, Studio Vista, London; E. P. Dutton, New York, 1968.

'The Time, the Place and the Girl: Rita Hayworth', *Focus on Film*, no. 10, Summer 1972, pp. 15–29.

McCreadie, Marsha, *The American Movie Goddess* (Garbo, Rita Hayworth, Monroe).

McGilligan, Patrick, *Cagney: The Actor as Auteur*, A. S. Barnes, South Brunswick; Tantivy, London, 1975.

Mellen, Joan, 'The Mae West No-body Knows', in *Women and their Sexuality in the New Film*, Horizon Press, New York, 1973; Davis-Poynter, London, 1974, pp. 229–43.

Merton, Robert K., *Mass Persuasion* (Kate Smith).

Morin, Violette, 'James Bond Connery: Le Mobile', *Communications*, 6, 1965, pp. 88–102.

Morris, Gary, 'Sex, Love and Joan Crawford', *Bright Lights*, vol. 1, no. 1, Autumn 1974, pp. 4–12.

Posadas, J., 'The Contribution of the Films of Chaplin to the Class Struggle of the Proletariat', *The Necessity of the Revolutionary Role of Cinema in the Capitalist Countries, in the Construction of the Workers' States and Socialism*, European Marxist Review, 1977, pp. 105–17.

Schickel, Richard, *His Picture in the Papers* (Douglas Fairbanks).

Young, Tracy, 'Fonda Jane', *Film Comment*, vol. 14, no. 2, March–April 1978, pp. 54–7.

NOTE: There are two series of books devoted to studies of individual stars, of varying usefulness and quality. These are *The Films of . . .* series, Citadel Press, New York, and *Pyramid Illustrated History of the Movies* (general ed. Ted Sennett), Pyramid, New York, some titles reprinted by W. H. Allen, London.

3 Source Material

Anger, Kenneth, *Hollywood Babylone*, Editions J-J. Pauvert, Paris, 1959; reprinted (expurgated) Straight Arrow Books, San Francisco, 1975.

Brough, James, *The Fabulous Fondas*, W. H. Allen, London, 1973.

Gelman, Barbara, (ed.), *Photoplay Treasury*, Crown Publishers, New York, 1972.

Graham, Sheilah, *Scratch an Actor*, W. H. Allen, London, 1969; Mayflower paperback, 1970.

Griffith, Richard, *The Talkies*, Dover, New York, 1971.

Guiles, Fred Lawrence, *Norma Jean*, W. H. Allen, London, 1969.

Kobal, John, *Fifty Years of Movie Posters*, Hamlyn, London, 1973.

Hollywood Glamour Portraits, Dover, New York, 1976.

Levin, Martin, *Hollywood and the Great Fan Magazines*, Arbour House, New York, 1970.

Lucas, Bob, *Naked in Hollywood*, Lancer Books, New York, 1962.

Mayer, J. P., *Sociology of Film*, Faber and Faber, London, 1946.

British Cinemas and their Audiences, Dobson, London, 1948.

Mayersberg, Paul, *Hollywood the Haunted House*, Allen Lane, London, 1967.

Morella, Joe and Epstein, Edward Z., *Lana – The Public and Private Lives of Miss Turner*, W. H. Allen, London, 1972.

Newquist, Roy, *Showcase*, William Morrow, New York, 1966.

Springer, John, *The Fondas*, Citadel, Secaucus NJ, 1970.

Thorpe, Margaret Farrand, *America at the Movies*, Yale University Press, New Haven, 1939.

Trent, Paul, *The Image Makers*, Octopus, London, 1973.

Zolotow, Maurice, *Marilyn Monroe*, W. H. Allen, London, 1961.

4 Films: General

Balazs, Bela, *Theory of the Film*, Dobson, London, 1952; reprinted Dover, New York, 1970

'The Close-Up' and 'The Face of Man' reprinted in Mast, Gerald and Cohen, Marshall (eds.), *Film Theory and Criticism*.

Basinger, Jeanine, 'Ten That Got Away', in Kay, Karyn and Peary, Gerald (eds.), *Women and the Cinema*, E. P. Dutton, New York, 1977, pp. 61–72.

Baxter, John, *Hollywood in the Thirties*, Zwemmer, London, A. S. Barnes, New York, 1968.

The Cinema of John Ford, Zwemmer, London; A. S. Barnes, New York, 1971.

Hollywood in the Sixties, Tantivy, London; A. S. Barnes, New York, 1972.

Bettetini, Gianfranco, *The Language and Technique of Film* (trans. David Osmond-Smith), Mouton, The Hague, 1973.

Brady, Robert, A., 'The Problem of Monopoly', in Watkins, Gordon S. (ed.), *The Motion Picture Industry, Annals of the American Academy of Political and Social Science*, vol. 254, November 1947, pp. 125–36.

Branigan, Edward, 'Formal Permutations of the Point-of-View Shot', *Screen*, vol. 16, no. 3, Autumn 1975, pp. 54–64.

Brewster, Ben, '*Justine* by the Marquis de Sade', Edinburgh International Film Festival News, 1976.

Buscombe, Edward, 'The Idea of Genre in the American Cinema', *Screen*, vol. 11, no. 2, pp. 33–45.

Butler, Ivan, *The Making of a Feature Film*, Penguin, London, 1971.

Camper, Fred, '*Dishonored* by Josef von Sternberg', *Cinema* (Cambridge), no. 8, pp. 16–18.

Caughie, John (ed.), *Theories of Authorship*, Routledge/British Film Institute, London, 1981.

Cowie, Elizabeth, 'Woman as Sign', *m/f*, no. 1, pp. 49–63.

Dyer, Richard, '*The Way We Were*', *Movie*, no. 22, pp. 30–3.

'Entertainment and Utopia', *Movie*, no. 24, pp. 2–13.

'Stereotyping', in Dyer, Richard (ed.), *Gays and Film*, British Film Institute, London, 1977, pp. 27–39.

Elsaesser, Thomas, 'Why Hollywood', *Monogram*, no. 1, April 1971, pp. 4–10.

'Tales of Sound and Fury', *Monogram*, no. 4, pp. 2–15.

Fell, John L., *Film and the Narrative Tradition*, University of Oklahoma Press, Norman, 1974.

Field, Alice Evans, *Hollywood USA, from Script to Screen*, Vantage Press, New York, 1952.

Geraghty, Christine, '*Alice Doesn't Live Here Anymore*', *Movie*, no. 22, pp. 39–42.

Gledhill, Christine, 'Whose Choice?: Teaching Films about Abortion', *Screen Education*, no. 24, Autumn 1977, pp. 35–45.

Gow, Gordon, *Hollywood in the Fifties*, Zwemmer, London; A. S. Barnes, New York, 1971.

Harrild, Tony, '*Killer Elite*: Emotion Expression', *Film Form*, vol. 1, no. 2, 1977, pp. 51–66.

Harvey, Sylvia, *May '68 and Film Culture*, British Film Institute, London, 1978.

Higham, Charles and Greenberg, Joel, *Hollywood in the Forties*, Zwemmer, London; A. S. Barnes, New York, 1968.

Kay, Karyn and Peary, Gerald (eds.), *Women and the Cinema*, E. P. Dutton, New York, 1977.

Kitses, Jim, *Horizon West*, Thames and Hudson, London, 1969.

Knight, Arthur, *The Liveliest Art*, Macmillan, New York, 1957; Muller, London, 1959.

Kracauer, Siegfried, 'National Types as Hollywood Presents Them', *Public Opinion Quarterly*, 13, 1949, pp. 53–72.

Theory of Film. Oxford University Press, New York, 1965.

Kuleshov, Lev, *Kuleshov on Film* (ed. Ronald Levaco), University of California Press, Berkeley, Los Angeles, and London, 1974.

Mast, Gerald and Cohen, Marshall (eds.), *Film Theory and Criticism*, Oxford University Press, New York, 1974.

McArthur, Colin, *Underworld USA*, Secker and Warburg, London, 1972.

MacCabe, Colin, 'Realism and the Cinema: Notes on Some Brechtian Theses', *Screen*, vol. 15, no. 2, Summer 1974, pp. 7–27.

'Theory and Film: Principles of Realism and Pleasure', *Screen*, vol. 17, no. 3, Autumn 1976, pp. 7–27.

Mellors, Bob, *Clint Eastwood Loves Jeff Bridges True*, Quantum Jump Publications, London, 1978.

Morse, David, 'The American Cinema: A Critical Statement', *Monogram*, no. 1, April 1971, pp. 2–4.

Neale, Steve, 'New Hollywood Cinema', *Screen*, vol. 17, no. 2, Summer 1976, pp. 117–22.

Genre, British Film Institute, London, 1980.

Nichols, Bill (ed.), *Movies and Methods*, University of California Press, Berkeley, Los Angeles, and London, 1976.

Nowell-Smith, Geoffrey, *Visconti*, Secker and Warburg, London, 1967; revised 1973.

O'Dell, Paul, *Griffith and the Rise of Hollywood*, Zwemmer, London; A. S. Barnes, New York, 1970.

Panofsky, Erwin, 'Style and Medium in the Motion Picture', *Bulletin of the Department of Art and Archaeology* (Princeton), 1934; reprinted in Mast, Gerald and Cohen, Marshall (eds.), *Film Theory and Criticism*.

Pines, Jim, *Blacks in Films*, Studio Vista, London, 1975.

Place, J. A. and Peterson, L. S., 'Some Visual Motifs of *Film Noir*', *Film Comment*, vol. 10, no. 1, January–February 1974, pp. 30–5; reprinted in Nichols, Bill (ed.), *Movies and Methods*, University of California Press, Berkeley, Los Angeles, and London, 1976, pp. 325–38.

Pollock, Griselda, 'What's Wrong with Images of Women?', *Screen Education*, no. 24, Autumn 1977, pp. 25–33.

Robinson, David, *Hollywood in the Twenties*, Zwemmer, London; A. S. Barnes, New York, 1968.

Slide, Anthony, *Early American Cinema*, Zwemmer, London; A. S. Barnes, New York, 1970.

Thompson, John O., 'Screen Acting and the Commutation Test', *Screen*, vol. 19, no. 2, Summer 1978, pp. 55–69.

Vardac, A. Nicholas, *From Stage to Screen: Theatrical Method from Garrick to Griffith*, Harvard University Press, Cambridge MA, 1949.

Viviani, Christian, 'Sans Metro ni Mayer: les productions Samuel Goldwyn entre 1929 et 1959', *Positif*, no. 178, February 1976, pp. 41–8.

Wollen, Peter, *Signs and Meaning in the Cinema*, Secker and Warburg, London, 1969; reprinted with new conclusion, 1973.
　　'*North by Northwest*: A Morphological Analysis', *Film Form*, vol. 1, no. 1, 1976, pp. 19–34.

Wood, Robin, *Personal Views*, Gordon Fraser, London, 1976.

5 Miscellaneous

Adlam, Diana et al., 'Psychology, Ideology and the Human Subject', *Ideology and Consciousness*, no. 1, May 1977, pp. 5–56.

Baran, Paul A. and Sweezy, Paul M., *Monopoly Capital*, Monthly Review Press, New York, 1966; Penguin, London, 1968.

Barthes, Roland, *S/Z*, Seuil, Paris, 1970; (trans. Richard Miller), Hill and Wang, New York, 1974.

Beauvoir, Simone de, *Le Deuxième Sexe*, Gallimard, Paris, 1949; (trans. H. M. Parshley), Cape, London, 1953; Penguin, London, 1971.

Birdwhistell, Ray L., *Kinesics and Context*, Allen Lane, London, 1971.

Brecht, Bertolt, *Brecht on Theatre* (ed. John Willett), Methuen, London, 1964.

Brémond, Claude, 'Le Message narratif', *Communications* 4, 1964, pp. 4–32.
　　'La Logique des possibles narratifs', *Communications* 8, 1966.

Brooks, Cleanth and Warren, Robert Penn, *Understanding Fiction*, Appleton-Century-Crofts, New York, 1959.

Brown, John Russell, *Effective Theatre*, Hutchinson, London, 1968.

Brownmiller, Susan, *Against Our Will*, Secker and Warburg, London, 1975.

Burke, Kenneth, *A Grammar of Motives*, Prentice-Hall, New York, 1945.

Burniston, Steve and Weedon, Chris, 'Ideology, Subjectivity and the Artistic Text', *Working Papers in Cultural Studies* (Birmingham), no. 10, 1977, pp. 203– 33.

Centre for Contemporary Cultural Studies, *On Ideology*, Hutchinson, London, 1978 (reprint of *Working Papers in Cultural Studies*, 10).

Chatman, Seymour, 'The Structure of Fiction', *University Review* (Kansas City), Spring 1971, pp. 199–214.
'On the Formalist-Structuralist Theory of Character', *Journal of Literary Semantics*, no. 1, 1972, pp. 57–79.

Cole, Toby and Chinoy, Helen Krich (eds.), *Actors on Acting*, Crown, New York, 1970.

Coquelin, Benoît Constant, *L'Art du comédien*, Paris, 1894; reprinted (trans. Elsie Fogerty), George Allen and Unwin, London, 1972.
'The Dual Personality of the Actor', in Cole, Toby and Chinoy, Helen Krich (eds.), *Actors on Acting*.

Culler, Jonathan, *Structuralist Poetics*, Routledge and Kegan Paul, London, 1975.

Dawson, S. W., *Drama and the Dramatic*, Methuen, London, 1970.

Delsarte, François, see Stebbins, Geneviève.

Diderot, Denis, *Le Paradoxe sur le comédien*, Santelet, Paris, 1830; reprinted (trans. W. H. Pollock), Chatto, London, 1883; in Green, F. C. (ed.), *Diderot's Writings on the Theatre*, Cambridge University Press, 1936.

Ellman, Mary, *Thinking About Women*, Harcourt Brace Jovanovich, New York, 1970; reprinted Virago, London.

Fast, Julius, *Body Language*, M. Evans, New York, 1970; Pocket Books, 1971.

Forster, E. M., *Aspects of the Novel*, Edward Arnold, London, 1927; Penguin, London, 1962.

Frye, Northrop, *An Anatomy of Criticism*, Princeton University Press, 1957.

Galbraith, J. K., *The Affluent Society*, Hamish Hamilton, London, 1958.

Goffman, Erving, *The Presentation of Self in Everyday Life*, Social Sciences Research Centre (Edinburgh), Monograph no. 2, 1956; Doubleday, New York, 1959; Allen Lane the Penguin Press, London, 1969; Penguin, 1971.

Hall, Stuart, 'Encoding and Decoding in the Television Discourse', Occasional Paper no. 7, Centre for Contemporary Cultural Studies, University of Birmingham, reprinted (revised) in Hall, Stuart, *Reproducing Ideologies*, Macmillan, London.
'Culture, the Media and the "Ideological Effect" ', in Curran, James, Gurevitch, Michael and Wollacott, Janet (eds.), *Mass Communication and Society*, Edward Arnold, London 1977, pp. 315–48.
'Some Problems with the Ideology/Subject Couplet', *Ideology and Consciousness*, no. 3, Spring 1978, pp. 113–21; with response, pp. 122–7.

Hall, Stuart, Lumley, Bob and McLennan, Gregor, 'Politics and Ideology', Gramsci', *Working Paper in Cultural Studies* (Birmingham), no. 10, pp. 77–105.
'Politics and Ideology, *Working Papers in Cultural Studies*, no. 11, pp. 176–97.

Harvey, W. J., *Character and the Novel*, Chatto and Windus, London, 1965.

Hawthorn, Jeremy, *Identity and Relationship*, Lawrence and Wishart, London, 1973.

Holland, Norman N., *The Dynamics of Literary Response*, Oxford University Press, 1968; W. W. Norton, New York, 1975.

Ideology and Consciousness, nos. 1, 2, 3, continuing.

Irigary, Luce, 'Women's Exile', *Ideology and Consciousness*, no. 1, May 1977, pp. 62–76; introduction by Diana Adlam and Couze Venn, pp. 57–61.

Kirby, E. T., 'The Delsarte Method: Three Frontiers of Actor Training', *TDR: The Drama Review*, vol. 16, no. 1 (T-53), March 1972, pp. 55–69.

Kristeva, Julia, 'Signifying Practice and Mode of Production', *Edinburgh 76 Magazine*, no. 1, 1976, pp. 64–76.

Lovell, Terry, 'The Social Relations of Cultural Production: The Absent Centre of a New Discourse', unpublished.

Lowenthal, Leo, *Literature and the Image of Man*, Beacon Press, Boston, 1957.

Lukács, Georg, 'The Intellectual Physiognomy of Literary Characters', in Baxandall, Lee (ed.), *Radical Perspectives in the Arts*, Penguin, London, 1972, pp. 89–141.
Der Historische Roman, Aufbau-Verlag, Berlin, 1955; (trans. Hannah and Stanley Mitchell), Merlin Press, London, 1962.

Macherey, Pierre, *Pour une théorie de la production littéraire*, Maspero, Paris, 1966; (trans.) *A Theory of Literary Production*, Routledge and Kegan Paul, London, 1978.

Marcuse, Herbert, *One-Dimensional Man*, Beacon Press, Boston, 1964.

Marx, Karl and Engels, Friedrich, *On Literature and Art* (eds. Lee Baxandall and Stefan Morawski), International General, New York, 1973.

Maslow, Abraham H., *Motivation and Personality*, Harper Row, New York, 1970.

Mattick, Paul, *Critique of Marcuse: One-Dimensional Man in Class Society*, Merlin Press, London, 1972.

McArthur, Colin, *Television and History*, British Film Institute, London, 1978.

McCarthy, Mary, 'Characters in Fiction', in *On the Contrary*, Noonday Press, New York, 1962.

McLean, Albert F. Jnr, *American Vaudeville as Ritual*, University of Kentucky Press, 1965.

Morin, Edgar, *New Trends in the Study of Mass Communications*, Centre for Contemporary Cultural Studies, University of Birmingham, 1969.

Morley, Dave, 'Reconceptualising the Media Audience', Occasional Paper no. 9, Centre for Contemporary Cultural Studies, University of Birmingham.

Munk, Erika (ed.), *Stanislavsky and America*, Hill and Wang, New York, 1966.

Paris, Bernard J., *A Psychological Approach to Fiction*, Indiana University Press, 1974.

Perkins, Tessa, 'Rethinking Stereotypes', in Barrett, Michele, Corrigan, Phil, Kuhn, Annette and Wolff, Janet (eds.), *Ideology and Cultural Production*, Croom Helm, New York, 1979.

Polhemus, Ted. (ed.), *Social Aspects of the Human Body*, Penguin, London, 1978.

Price, Martin, 'The Other Self: Thoughts about Character in the Novel', in Mack, Maynard and Gregor, Ian (eds.), *Imagined Worlds*, Methuen, London, 1968; reprinted in Burns, Elizabeth and Tom (eds.), *Sociology of Literature and Drama*, Penguin, London, 1973.

Propp, Vladimir, *Morfologiya skazki*, Academia, Leningrad, 1928; reprinted (trans. L. Scott), *Morphology of the Folk Tale*, Indiana University Publications in Anthropology, Folklore and Linguistics, no. 10, Bloomington; Austin, New York, 1968.

Roach, Mary Ellen and Eicher, Joanne Bubolz (eds.), *Dress, Adornment and the Social Order*, Wiley, New York, 1965; Chichester, 1970.

Roberts, Brian, 'G. H. Mead: The Theory and Practice of his Social Philosophy', *Ideology and Consciousness*, no. 2, Autumn 1977, pp. 81–106.

Rockwell, Joan, *Fact in Fiction*, Routledge and Kegan Paul, London, 1974.

Ruesch, Jurgen and Kees, Weldon, *Non-Verbal Communication: Notes on the Visual Perception of Human Relations*, University of California Press, Berkeley and Los Angeles, 1956.

Sartre, Jean-Paul, *Questions de méthode*, Gallimard, Paris, 1960; reprinted as *Search for a Method* (trans. Hazel E. Barnes), Alfred A. Knopf, New York, 1963.

Schechner, Richard with Mintz, Cynthia, 'Kinesics and Performance', *TDR: The Drama Review*, vol. 17, no. 3 (T-59), September 1973, pp. 102–8.

Scholes, Robert and Kellogg, Robert, *The Nature of Narrative*, Oxford University Press, New York, 1966.

Stanislavsky, Konstantin, *An Actor Prepares* (trans. Elizabeth Reynolds Hapgood), Geoffrey Bles, London, 1936.

Stebbins, Geneviève, *The Delsarte System of Expression*, Edgar S. Werner, New York, 1902; reprinted, Dance Horizons, 1977.

Styan, J. L., *The Elements of Drama*, Cambridge University Press, 1960.
Drama, Stage and Audience. Cambridge University Press, 1975.

Todorov, Tzvetan, 'Categories of the Literary Narrative', *Film Reader*, no. 2, pp. 19–37.

Van Laan, Thomas, F., *The Idiom of Drama*, Cornell University Press, Ithaca, NY, 1970.

Veblen, Thorstein, *Theory of the Leisure Class*, Macmillan, New York, 1899; Mentor, 1953; George Allen and Unwin, London, 1925; 1970 (paperback).

Walcutt, Charles C., *Man's Changing Mask*, University of Minnesota Press, Minneapolis, 1966.

Walters, Margaret, *The Nude Male*, Paddington Press, New York and London, 1978.

Watt, Ian, *The Rise of the Novel*, Chatto and Windus, London, 1957; Penguin, London, 1963.

White, Llewellyn, *The American Radio*, University of Chicago Press, 1947.

Willett, John, *The Theatre of Bertolt Brecht*, Methuen, London, 1959.

Williams, Raymond, *The Long Revolution*, Chatto and Windus, London, 1961; Penguin, London, 1965.
Television Technology and Cultural Form, Fontana, London, 1974.
Keywords, Fontana, London, 1976.

Wolff, Janet, *Hermeneutic Philosophy and the Sociology of Art*, Routledge and Kegan Paul, London, 1975.

Women's Studies Group, Centre for Contemporary Cultural Studies, *Women Take Issue* (*Working Papers in Cultural Studies*, no. 11), Heinemann, London, 1978.

Working Papers in Cultural Studies, nos. 1–10.

SUPPLEMENTARY CHAPTER

Reconceptualising Stardom

By Paul McDonald

In *Stars*, Richard Dyer proposed a perspective for studying the social meaning of film stars in what he called the 'star image'. This approach involves an investigation of how cinema circulates the images of individual film performers and how those images may influence the ways in which we think about the identity of ourselves and others. In the decades since the original publication of *Stars* (1979), the star image approach has continued to feature in critical studies of cinema, but other critical perspectives have also been advanced. This chapter reviews some of the key developments in the ways of looking at film stars, and proposes some of its own recommendations for the analysis of stardom.

Stars and History

Stars appeared in a period when academic studies of cinema saw a concerted effort to address critical questions around the social significance of film representations. In more recent years – in response to what was regarded as the ahistoricism of much of that work – film studies has seen a return to questions of cinema history. This movement has had two effects on the studies of stars. As part of a general interest in early cinema, historians have begun to re-examine the origins of the star system in American cinema. Other work has historicised stardom by exploring the ways in which social circumstances act as a context for the production of a star's significance.

The origins of the star system in America

Although most readily associated with film, the star system in America originated in the theatre. Benjamin McArthur discusses how the star system grew out of the shift from 'stock' to 'combination' theatre companies in America during the 19th century. Stock companies hired thirty to forty actors for a forty-week season, producing a wide repertory of short-run plays, performed at a permanent theatrical venue (*Actors and American Culture, 1880–1920*, pp. 5–6). The star system began to emerge during the 1820s when well-known performers did tours in which they would play the same role in different cities, with a local stock cast taking supporting roles. McArthur argues that these star tours transformed American theatre, for by the end of the century, the stock companies were gradually replaced by combination companies which toured regional venues with a single play fronted by a star name (pp. 9–10). In this system, it was common to classify actors according to 'lines of business', a form of typecasting which divided actors into such categories as 'stars', 'leading men/ladies', 'heavies', 'juveniles' or 'eccentric comedians/comediennes' (pp. 11–16).

A star can only be a star if s/he is recognised and known as a star. In *Picture Personalities* Richard deCordova has traced how the star system emerged in American cinema with the circulation of different types of knowledge about the people who performed in early film. These types of knowledge regulated what was known about film performers, producing the configurations which deCordova calls the 'discourse on acting', the 'picture personality', the 'star' and the 'star scandal'. Early commentaries on cinema concentrated on the illusory effects of film technology without mention of the figures seen performing on screen. DeCordova places at around 1907 the first examples of a discourse on film acting which makes known the behind-the-scenes labour of film performance (pp. 30–3). The infamous Florence Lawrence trolley-car incident of 1910 is usually taken as the first case where the name of an individual film performer is made publicly available, but deCordova also cites the Kalem and Edison companies naming their stock of film performers in 1909 (pp. 52–3). By naming a performer, a link was formed across separate films, producing the identity which deCordova calls the 'picture personality'. The picture personality was named as someone who worked in film and was only known for that work. A 'star' discourse emerged as commentary extended to the off-screen life of film performers. If the discourse on acting and the picture personality constructed knowledge about the professional life of screen actors, from 1913 the star discourse made known the private lives of film actors. As a general point about star studies, overuse of the term 'star' to describe any well-known film actor obscures how with most popular film performers, knowledge is limited to the on-screen 'personality'.

Producer control of the star discourse saw the mutual reinforcement of the professional and private identities of performers, constructing the star as a coherent and non-contradictory image: the professional image of the star seemed simply to reflect the private life of the star. In 1921, allegations of murder were brought against the popular comedy actor Roscoe 'Fatty' Arbuckle, after the suspicious death of Virginia Rappe in his hotel bedroom. Although Arbuckle was acquitted, his career was wrecked. With further unseemly revelations about the star community, deCordova sees the 'star scandal' emerge as a type of discourse which exposed contradiction and problematised the moral closure of the professional and private images of stars. Scandal discourse had a special status, for it appeared to tell the ultimate truth which the fabrications of film narratives and promotional campaigns could not hide. In particular, where the scandal discourse made known the sexual appetites of stars, then a most intimate truth was believed to be found in knowledge of the star as a desiring being.

DeCordova's history traces the emergence of the public/private dialectic which Dyer finds in the images of stars. The discourses of acting, personality, star and scandal indicate the types of knowledge about performers which circulated in the early film star system. These categories also provide levels of analysis for tracing a broader history of film stardom, considering changing patterns in the distribution of knowledge, along with the shifting contents of discourses on acting, star lives and scandalous incident. Differences between popular performers and phases in the history of the star system are not only produced through what is known about stars but also in what types of knowledge are available to make film performers knowable.

Locating stars

In 'Dyer Straits' Marian Keane criticises Dyer's star-image approach for reading stars as representing beliefs about identity without considering how such representations relate to the ways in which identity is more generally conceptualised in society. Keane argues that any understanding of the images of film stars always involves a wider set of beliefs about personal identity which exist for the culture in which the star image circulates. This is an important criticism, for it raises questions of the cultural conditions which make stars and stardom significant. However, Keane's suggestion that these questions can be addressed through reference to works of philosophy which reflect on personal identity is problematic, for such an approach would use a highbrow currency of ideas to understand film stardom which was removed from the forms of popular thought which moviegoers bring to their reading of stars. Additionally, philosophy has tended to provide universalistic accounts of human identity which do not acknowledge the ways in which concepts of identity change historically or the contradictions experienced by any society between competing concepts of identity. Locating stars historically in their cultural context is an attempt to ascertain what forms of belief and knowledge co-exist with a star's image to make that image intelligible and representative of a period's key social concerns.

One possible answer to Keane's criticisms of Dyer's work can be found in Dyer's own analysis of Marilyn Monroe in *Heavenly Bodies*. Looking at Monroe's popularity in the 50s, Dyer uses the launch of *Playboy* magazine and the publication of Alfred Kinsey's report on sexual behaviour to interrogate how star, magazine and popular science represented beliefs about femininity and sexuality in the period (pp. 27–42). This extends the intertextuality of the star image into an inter-discursive context of other sources and knowledges, which exist outside film stardom but which are potentially significant for understanding what a star signifies in a particular period.

Contextualising the meaning of stars is always open to the charge of presenting a simple 'reflectionist' history of stardom: societies change historically and stars reflect those changes. A balance needs to be struck between the signs and discourses which are particular to film stardom at any moment and a sense of the context of social beliefs and conditions in which the star circulates. This raises questions of what defines and delimits a 'context', and what forms of context are to be judged as of most relevance to the study of stardom. Such questions do not make historical studies of stars impossible, only provisional.

Star Bodies and Performance

Beliefs or concepts of identity are intangible things. Stars are significant for how they make such elusive and metaphysical notions into a visible show. It is this visualising of identity which makes the bodies of stars and the actions performed by those bodies into such a key element of a star's meaning.

The embodiment of culture

One obvious development in the Hollywood cinema of the 80s and 90s has been the appearance of muscular male action stars such as Arnold Schwarzenegger, Sylvester Stallone, Bruce Willis and the leaner Jean-Claude Van Damme. In *Spectacular Bodies*, Yvonne Tasker suggests two possible readings of this phenomenon. On the one hand, a familiar criticism is that the body of the male action hero represents an assertive and confident declaration of masculinity, which naturalises male physical power (p. 9). On the other, writers like Barbara Creed have taken the view that by exaggerating the signs of maleness the built body shows male power as something 'made up', insubstantial and unnatural (see 'From Here to Moder-

40 Kickboxer *(Mark DiSalle, David Worth, 1989).*

nity', p. 65). Indeed, audiences do appear to adopt contrasting responses to the heroic body, for where some moviegoers seriously admire the hero's strength, for others the incredibility of his power becomes a source of disdain or laughter. Tasker also sees major female performers like Sigourney Weaver in the first three *Alien* movies (Ridley Scott, 1979, US; James Cameron, 1986, US; David Fincher, 1992, US) and Linda Hamilton in *Terminator 2: Judgment Day* (James Cameron, 1991, US) as occupying narrative roles comparable to those of the male action hero, with their heroic status also signified through physical strength (*Spectacular Bodies*, p. 149). For Tasker, these muscular action heroines disrupt the traditional binary oppositions which have differentiated masculine and feminine bodies.

These new hard-body stars show by their obvious physicality how bodies act as key signifiers of cultural beliefs. Emerging during the 80s, the muscular heroes of

41 Aliens.

American cinema belonged to a culture for which the disciplinary regime of physical development worked as a metaphor for the striving and enterprise which motivated the Reagan years and the 'yuppie' revolution. In *Perfect* (James Bridges, 1985, US), Jamie Lee Curtis, who acquired the nickname 'the body', is an ex-Olympic-class swimmer turned aerobics instructor, and her body acts as not only a mechanism for narrative causation but also the aggressive fitness culture which emerged during the decade. Recent developments in the sociology of the body have set out to examine the changing forms of the body as a social fact (see for example Featherstone, Hepworth and Turner, *The Body*; and Shilling, *The Body and Social Theory*). To understand the presence of the body in society, Bryan S. Turner has referred to what he calls 'somatic society', 'a society within which major political problems are both problematised in the body and expressed through it' (*The Body and Society*, p. 1). It is from such a perspective that the significance of star bodies can be read for the ways in which they *embody* culture.

Action films could be described as a genre of the body. In action cinema, the body is foregrounded and its significance made obvious. What should not be lost in the appeal of wanting to study the idealised bodies of some stars is that film presents a far wider currency of bodily types than the physical perfections of the male and female action heroes. For example, what is the significance of say John Candy's weight in relation to comedy: what is it that makes fat funny and what kinds of funniness can fat legitimately convey? Eddie Murphy's remake of *The Nutty Professor* (Tom Shadyac, 1996, US) replaces the transformation from academic nerd to smooth lounge lizard which Jerry Lewis enacted in the original with a change from overweight professor to playboy stud. Both films play on the different physicalities of the two stars, and contrasting the two performances highlights how their differences also play on racial presumptions about the sexuality of the black or white male body. Stars offer examples for a wider conceptualising of the ways in which films have presented embodiments of culture.

Action, acting, stars and actors

A limitation of Tasker's work is that she identifies muscles as a sign but does not examine in any detail what those muscles do. This has the effect of taking the action out of Action cinema. The muscular body is not only a body with the potential for action but is continually shown to be a body in action. Approaching the body as a sign of meaning may obscure the reading of the body as a source of doing, neglecting how the body produces meaning precisely through doing. For example, the fight sequences in *Enter the Dragon* (Robert Clouse, 1973, US/Hong Kong) show not only that Bruce Lee's body is toned and strong but, by its speed and motion, that the body is also flexible, fluent and accurate. With each action, Lee's body represents a sense of being in the world by its movement through space and time.

Studying stars as moving bodies involves analysis of acting and performance. In acting, stars represent characters by the uses of the body and voice, and the significance of these minute actions may be described in terms of what Valentin Nikolaevic Volosinov saw in the potential of the body to produce what he called 'ideological scraps' (*Marxism and the Philosophy of Language*, p. 92). For example,

42 Silence of the Lambs.

in the opening scene of *Silence of the Lambs* (Jonathan Demme, 1991, US), Jodie Foster as Clarice Starling is seen jogging. Her breathlessness, sweat-matted hair, regular running rhythm and gritted teeth immediately establish the perseverance and resilience of the character, qualities which the rest of the investigative narrative will only further confirm. Ideologically, these small actions of the body already serve to indicate the 'temperament' which federal law must necessarily take if it is to contain the visceral, psychological and sexual threats posed by the narrative.

James Naremore sees cinema as producing a 'performance frame', which is not only the boundary of the individual shot but also the separation of the ordinary world of moviegoers from the extraordinary world onscreen (*Acting in the Cinema*, p. 14). One effect of the frame is that any figure who appears onscreen is immediately removed from the everyday and 'framed' as meaningful. Frequently this can lead to the overuse of the term 'star', as the frame in itself is seen to be the sufficient condition for conferring star status. What is lost by such overuse is how ways of performing and acting in film differentiates between performers. Richard Maltby proposes a distinction between modes of film acting where the actor is either integrated into the dramatic fiction or appears to stand apart as independent and autonomous from the surrounding players and circumstances (*Hollywood Cinema*, p. 256). Autonomous performance supports the exceptional status of the star. In the two Rodeo Drive sequences of *Pretty Woman* (Garry Marshall, 1990, US), editing, lighting and the looks of other characters combine to position Julia Roberts playing Vivian as the centre of attention. When Roberts/Vivian walks down the street at the end of the second sequence, she is closely framed, with the camera tracking backwards to keep her pace. The non-diegetic soundtrack is a song 'for' Vivian (Roy Orbison's 'Pretty Woman'), and extras in the scene turn to

43 Out of Africa.

44 Predator.

admire her. Everything comes together to confirm that Vivian is a 'pretty woman' and Roberts is the autonomous star.

Star autonomy can also be achieved by masking or de-emphasising the actor. In *Apocalypse Now* (Francis Ford Coppola, 1979, US), the narrative builds towards the final meeting between Martin Sheen as Willard and Marlon Brando as Kurtz. As the scene is so heavily predetermined, Brando/Kurtz can be almost entirely obscured in darkness during the meeting but still retain his star significance. Where with Roberts, star autonomy was produced by foregrounding her as glamorous spectacle, Brando's autonomy is signified by the 'anti-spectacle' he occupies. However, it is not only visual elements which produce Brando's autonomy. His ponderous delivery of the speech about inoculating the Vietnamese villagers shows the star's voice controlling the overall tempo of the film. When combined with stories of indulgent improvisations (Peter Manso, *Brando*, p. 843), the scene becomes an example of how the power of star autonomy is partly achieved through control of the voice or body.

Barry King draws another distinction between what he calls 'impersonation' and 'personification' in acting ('Articulating Stardom', p. 42). Impersonation is produced by the actor transforming the body and voice in ways which signify differences between the characters s/he plays. For example, Meryl Streep is well known for the various accents she has adopted for her roles in *The French Lieutenant's Woman* (Karel Reisz, 1981, US), *Sophie's Choice* (Alan J. Pakula, 1982, US), *Silkwood* (Mike Nichols, 1983, US) and *Out of Africa* (Sydney Pollack, 1985, US). In contrast, Arnold Schwarzenegger's performances in *Predator* (John McTiernan, 1987, US), *Twins* (Ivan Reitman, 1988, US) and *Terminator 2: Judgment Day*, display many similarities in the uses of the body and voice. Schwarzenegger's 'personification' foregrounds the continuities of the star's image over and above differences of character.

While all film performers can be said to act onscreen, how they act will determine if they are respected as an 'actor'. Streep's accents signify her commitment to the representational skills of dramatic acting. Each change of accent in the above roles was justified by the realist objective of plausibly integrating the actor into the narrative circumstances. Respectful recognition of Streep's impersonatory skills came when each of the aforementioned performances received an Oscar nomination in the Best Actress category, with the portrayal of Sophie Zawistowska winning the 1982 award. With Schwarzenegger, although each of his films is located in a fictional narrative situation – and so he is undoubtedly acting – the lack of difference in his performances has resulted in the familiar criticism that he is not acting because he 'always plays himself'. While the personal earnings and box-office receipts from Schwarzenegger's performances are considerably higher than those of Streep, he has still to receive a single Oscar nomination for acting. Schwarzenegger's lack of critical recognition may be based simply on the judgment that he can't act, but at a further level, the snubbing of Schwarzenegger can be read as the effect of a common opposition in cultural production in which profit is believed to be the antithesis of art (see Pierre Bourdieu 'The Field of Cultural Production'). The personification effect in Schwarzenegger's acting commodifies his star image and his wealthy stardom places him apart from the artistry of acting which Streep represents. Additionally, the muscularity of the male action hero associates stars such as Schwarzenegger with a physical culture of manual work, where in the field of cultural production the highest esteem for artistic achievements, including those of acting, have produced an image of 'genius' as a roughly intellectual property. Streep's vocal transformations have a cultural status denied to Schwarzenegger's bodily continuities. While Schwarzenegger acts, he does not have the image of being an 'actor'. Streep's impersonatory skills integrate her into the narrative, yet she retains some self-conscious personal mannerisms across her roles, positioning her somewhere between integrated impersonation and autonomous personification as a 'star-actor'. Ways of performing in film represent and embody not only a culture's beliefs about personal identity but also the ways in which any culture will conceptualise the legitimate professional identities of stars and other film performers.

Stars and Audiences

By reading the images of stars as meaningful or significant, it is implied that there is a someone for whom the star is meaningful or significant. Pam Cook criticised *Stars* for studying the star as text without attention to how the images of stars construct the fantasies and pleasures of moviegoers ('Star Signs'). Where questions of the audience have been raised in critical studies of cinema, the audience has been conceptualised as a 'spectator' (see Judith Mayne's *Cinema and Spectatorship*). Spectatorship theory sees the moviegoer as an identity produced exclusively in how the organisation of looks construct a particular position which addresses members of the audience. There are many difficulties with this view. Most simply, 'spectator' suggests that cinema is only a visual pleasure, ignoring the aural effects of film. Of greater difficulty is the way in which spectatorship theory would cast the moviegoer as the passive product of meanings which are already determined onscreen. While films do construct positions which limit how they may be understood and interpreted, moviegoers also respond actively as individuals producing a diversity of responses.

Where spectatorship theory has dominated studies of cinema, research into television audiences has provided quite different ways of understanding viewers (see Shaun Moores's *Interpreting Audiences*). This research has shown how a broader context of social relationships – for example those at work, or in the family – are influential in how people view television. In her study of a London family viewing a video of *Rocky III* (Sylvester Stallone, 1982, US) in the home, Valerie Walkerdine linked the father's identification with Sylvester Stallone to his role as a union representative at work, and how he sees himself 'fighting' for his family ('Video Replay'). Identification is therefore seen to be the result of multiple social positions, not just the preferred position(s) constructed by the film text. In this chapter, the term 'moviegoer' is preferred to 'spectator' because it suggests that going to the cinema is only one of many social activities which influence the complex ways people respond and relate to films and stars. At this time, spectatorship theory has continued to dominate readings of the relationship of audiences to stars, although studies are beginning to emerge which look at the significance of film stars in the everyday life of moviegoers.

Stars and spectators

Fundamental to spectatorship theory was Laura Mulvey's 1975 essay 'Visual Pleasure and Narrative Film', in which she argues, using a psychoanalytic framework, that classic narrative cinema continually organises looks which centre on the woman as spectacle. For Mulvey, the effect of this way of looking is that the

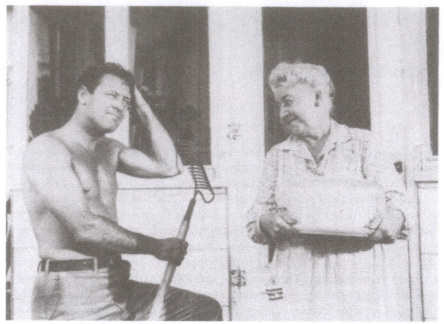

45 Picnic.

moviegoer is positioned according to the pleasures of male heterosexual desire. Difficulties with the empirical evidence, theoretical foundations and universalising claims of Mulvey's argument have produced various critiques. Narrative film continually includes looks directed at the male body and also looks between male characters. Steve Neale argues that looks between male characters on film are made obviously threatening and aggressive in order to divert their erotic potential ('Masculinity and Spectacle', p. 14). Richard Dyer explores a similar disavowal of the look by highlighting how male pin-ups appear in the image to be looking in ways which suggest they are not an erotic object. This can involve looking off as if disinterested in the viewer, glancing upwards to appear lost in a higher spiritual form of thinking, or staring to confront the fact of being looked at ('Don't Look Now', pp. 63–6).

In his discussion of *Picnic* (Joshua Logan, 1955, US), Steven Cohan considers how the film constructs a look that eroticises William Holden's body but which is contradicted by elements of the star's image ('Masquerading as the American Male in the Fifties'). In certain scenes, Holden as Hal Carter continually removes his shirt to reveal an athletic physique. The female cast of Kim Novak as Madge Owens, Betty Field as Flo Owens and Rosalind Russell as Rosemary Sidney each register their erotic recognition of the objectified male body. In these scenes, Holden/Hal is placed in a position conventionally coded as feminine. However, Holden's star image as 'a red-blooded American boy', his ambivalent attitude to acting and anecdotes about his reckless stunts when showing off to acquaintances are read by Cohan as constructing a star profile which attempts to counteract Holden's objectification and authenticate the 'reality' of his masculinity (pp. 63–4).

46 *Emil Jannings as Professor Rath in* Der blaue Engel.

Laura Mulvey's use of Freudian/Lacanian thinking leads her to conclude that the male gaze produces a sadistically voyeuristic pleasure. Gaylyn Studlar argues that the fetishisation of the female body has the potential for producing the alternative pleasure of a masochistic relationship between male moviegoer and female star. Sadistic voyeurism results from an Oedipal identification with the father and the repression of the mother. Using the work of Gilles Deleuze, Studlar suggests that masochism is a pre-Oedipal formation, where the original bond with the mother results in the masochist retaining that bond ('Masochism, Masquerade, and the Erotic Metamorphoses of Marlene Dietrich', p. 233). As this bond refuses the symbolic power of the father, Studlar argues that masochism challenges the gendered and sexual difference of the male Oedipus.

Studlar sees masochism as central to the allure and power of Marlene Dietrich. In some of the films which the star made with Josef von Sternberg, a narrative is enacted in which the characters played by Dietrich present an inescapable attraction for male characters. For example, in *Der blaue Engel* (1930, Germany), Emil

Jannings as Professor Rath is a willing victim, destroyed by his own desire rather than by Dietrich as Lola-Lola (p. 236). To the masochistic narrative, Dietrich added her idiosyncratically cool sensuality which represented her indifference to male desire (p. 237). Narrative and star image combine to eroticise Dietrich, while also indicating the impossibility of ever 'having' her. Sadistic voyeurism would cast the looker as entirely powerful, with the woman passively objectified. With masochism, ultimately the victim retains control of the masochistic contract, requiring the dominator to submit to the desire of the dominated. However, that relationship cannot work if the figure of the woman is not admired and revered as much as she is desired and feared. Studlar's account of masochism suggests how the image of the female star can represent a power found in performance which transforms the pleasure and control of the male gaze.

Since Mulvey's polemical article, various commentators have dealt with trying to conceptualise the female spectator and the pleasures of women looking at stars. Studlar argues that by excluding a strong male protagonist as the mediator for the moviegoer's look, the Dietrich/Sternberg films provide a position for the female moviegoer directly to contemplate and desire the female star (p. 248). Miriam Hansen has suggested that Rudolph Valentino's star image destabilised conventional forms of looking in the cinema because he was continually placed as someone who not only looks but also as someone who is looked at ('Pleasure, Ambivalence, Identification: Valentino and Female Spectatorship'). Valentino assumed shifting roles in which he was both sadistic punisher and masochistic victim, constructing what Hansen describes as an 'ambivalent' quality. Hansen sees this ambivalence as a feminisation of the Valentino, destabilising conventional masculine constructions of dominance. This ambivalence, argues Hansen, encouraged women spectators to identify with and desire Valentino.

A severe limitation of all spectatorship theory is that it hypothesises the positioning of moviegoers without researching if moviegoers occupy those positions. It has been argued that the 'spectator' is not intended to account for the actual responses or readings of moviegoers, only the spectating position which the film seems to prefer. In an untitled entry for *Camera Obscura*, Mary Ann Doane remarks that the 'female spectator is a concept, not a person' (p. 142). However, work in this area does seem to consistently read the spectator as a person, and if these studies are to have any critical value, it is important that they should not reduce the moviegoer to a position.'

Stardom in everyday life

Spectatorship theory assembles readings of films and stars without reference to the terms in which moviegoers actually articulate their pleasures. By publishing advertisements in popular women's magazines, Jackie Stacey gathered correspondence and questionnaires from British women about their memories of film stars in the 40s and 50s (*Star Gazing*). Stacey's analysis of these replies shows how respondents recall stars by patterns of escapism, identification and consumption. In rationed wartime and post-war Britain, American films of the period were seen as representing images of abundance and affluence which offered an escapist spectacle. While the British film studio Rank had stars such as James Mason and Margaret Lockwood, American films offered a greater degree of 'glamour', and American film stars acted as the special representatives of that glamour.

Stacey's respondents described their identifications with stars in many different ways. Inside the cinema, some respondents described how they admired and worshipped the star as someone whose life was different and unattainable (pp. 138–45). Others, while recognising the difference of stars, determined to overcome it, either by aspiring to the ideals of feminine 'attractiveness' which the star represented or taking inspiration from the confident way in which stars appeared to handle situations (pp. 151–8). Stacey calls these relationships 'cinematic identificatory fantasies', as they are formed by the moviegoer in the cinema imagining the star as an ideal other.

Some of Stacey's respondents discussed how their identifications with stars motivated practical actions outside the cinema. Respondents described the various actions they took to transform the self and construct similarity between moviegoer and performer. In childhood, respondents had played games in which they pretended to be like their favourite stars (pp. 160–1). For others, similarity was constructed by selectively emphasising an actual physical resemblance to a star. Respondents remembered imitating part of a star's behaviour or performance style, or copying clothing and hairstyles (pp. 161–70). As these actions carried the influences of stardom into everyday life, Stacey refers to these ways of becoming like stars as 'extra-cinematic identificatory practices'.

Hollywood film became integrated with the consumer economy in America through the means of product displays and tie-ins (Charles Eckert, 'The Carole Lombard in Macy's Window'). In ' "Powder Puff" Promotion' Charlotte Herzog studied how that integration addressed women in particular as consumers. Fashion-show sequences were integrated into the narratives of films like *Roberta* (William A. Seiter, 1935, US) and *Mannequin* (Frank Borzage, 1938, US) in the 30s, and *Designing Woman* (Vincente Minnelli, 1957, US), *Lovely to Look At* (Mervyn LeRoy, 1952, US) and *Funny Face* (Stanley Donen, 1957, US) in the 50s. These films displayed fashions on the screen and there was a movement to transfer screen fashions to the highstreet. Joan Crawford's gowns in *Letty Lynton* (Clarence Brown, 1932, US), designed by Gilbert Adrian, were made available to highstreet consumers as ready-to-wear copies (Herzog and Gaines ' "Puffed Sleeves before Tea-Time" ').

Jackie Stacey argues that the consumption of star styles placed British female moviegoers in a contradictory discourse. While the styles were designed as spectacle for male desire, they also provided glamorous examples of resistance and escape from the material difficulties experienced by British women of the period.

Stacey's respondents described how straitened material circumstances meant they bypassed the consumer market and made their own versions of star styles. These kinds of creative cultural economies have become objects of interest in the field of fan studies (see Fiske, 'The Cultural Economy of Fandom'). To use a term developed by Henry Jenkins (*Textual Poachers*), Stacey's respondents 'poached' star styles. In poaching, Jenkins argues that fans 'construct their cultural and social identity through borrowing and inflecting mass-culture images, articulating concerns which often go unvoiced within the dominant media' (p. 23).

Stars and subcultures

The possibilities for resisting dominant cultures provided by star identifications have made stars of key significance to subcultural groups. Through shared sets of beliefs, signs, meanings, values and practices, subcultures produce a sense of collective belonging that negotiates an alternative or oppositional relationship to cultural dominant groups (see Dick Hebdige's *Subculture*). Andrea Weiss and Richard Dyer, among others have examined the significance of certain stars for lesbians and gay men. Weiss and Dyer identify the images of Marlene Dietrich, Greta Garbo and Judy Garland as part of the subcultural capital by which lesbians and gay men have negotiated their identities in relation to heterosexual culture. Weiss describes how Dietrich and Garbo became significant stars for lesbians in America during the 30s, a period when a middle-class white lesbian subculture was first emerging in metropolitan centres (*Vampires and Violets*, pp. 35–6). Weiss argues that the significance of Dietrich and Garbo for lesbians came from subcultural gossip about the sexual lives of the two stars, together with readings of how the performances of both stars consistently made ironic references to the institution of marriage and played with dress codes to disrupt conventional definitions of female heterosexuality (pp. 32–9). Both stars became important for the emerging subculture because they were not only desirable but also functioned as public representations of a 'truth' which was only fully comprehended by subcultural knowledge.

In *Heavenly Bodies*, Richard Dyer considers the significance of Judy Garland's image in relation to gay culture. Garland's image celebrated the happy family values of a dominant heterosexual culture, a sense of 'ordinariness' and 'normality' contradicted by stories of the star's unhappy private life. Garland's 'normality'

47 Ziegfeld Follies.

was therefore only an act (p. 159). Like Dietrich and Garbo, Garland's performances also frequently mixed dress codes to cultivate an androgynous appearance (pp. 169–77). Garland's androgyny suggested that differentiation between femininity and masculinity was not something deep and natural, but something constructed only in appearances. Her roles in films such as *Ziegfeld Follies* (Vincente Minnelli, 1945, US) and *The Pirate* (Vincente Minnelli, 1948, US) made theatricality and the revelation of artifice a central narrative theme. It is from this play of appearances, Dyer argues, that the Garland image can be read as camp (p. 178). Garland did not directly represent a gay lifestyle but her contradictory ordinariness and androgyny played on surface appearances and problematised dominant definitions of gender and sexuality in ways which were amenable to a gay reading.

Stardom as Labour

Stars perform representational work, and any examination of the place of stars in film production cannot be disconnected from the issues of representation raised by the image and the audience. Whatever the status of stars in film production, their value is bargained through their representational power. As the analysis of star images has considered issues of power in the struggles and negotiations of the moviegoer's making of meanings, so explorations of performers in film production will be concerned with how stars negotiate power relationships in their work of making meaning.

Images of star work

In many ways, the separation of consumption from production in star studies replicates a similar division in the institution of stardom, for while stars do have to work, star discourses constantly focus on stars as people who already appear onscreen, or as leading relatively fantastic offscreen lives. Stars will continue to appear as 'idols of consumption' while their lifestyles are seen to involve basking on yachts at Cannes each year, being beautiful, meeting and marrying other beautiful people, paying huge divorce bills and having the free time and money to devote to worthy causes. To a large extent, stardom still seems to be a life of what

48 & 49 *Al Pacino and Robert De Niro in* Heat.

194

Leo Lowenthal described as 'organised leisure time' ('The Triumph of Mass Idols', p. 121). The image of star work is that it is all play and no work.

The emergence of a discourse on acting which Richard deCordova pinpoints in 1907 continues today in articles which produce images of the work of stars. Differences in the ways work is represented will produce professional inequalities between performers: generally, the work of stars enters discourse and becomes known, while the work of 'unknown' performers goes unrecognised. This discourse on acting has an effect of legitimating or de-legitimating the work of stars. For example, publicity for *Heat* (Michael Mann, 1996, US) made much of the film's inclusion of Al Pacino and Robert De Niro, with words to the effect that these performers were 'the finest actors of their generation'. The major scene between the two star-actors is a duologue in a coffee shop. Following the release of the film in March 1996, the British Film Institute's magazine *Sight and Sound* carried an article on this one scene, reproducing director Michael Mann's copy of the script and accompanying notes on the subtexts of both characters. Mann made the following note about Pacino's character:

> Came off of: rejecting the chaos of domestic dysfunction for the attraction of the more complex out-at-the-edge-of-overload arena because simmering in the subconscious was what to do about the absurd situation; you are surveilling him; he is aware he is being surveilled. Off the dysfunctional moment with Justine, an idea just jams into your head: the audacious move. Go meet him. Go talk to him. ('Bob and Al in the Coffee Shop', p. 18)

No commentary is included in the article, and so *Sight and Sound's* reverence for the notes leave them to speak for themselves. The incoherence of the remarks says nothing more than that film acting is very complex and psychological, and that people like Pacino and De Niro work in complex and psychological ways.

In June 1996, *Empire* (published by EMAP consumer magazines), claiming to be 'Britain's biggest-selling movie magazine', carried an article on Sharon Stone and the Clouzot remake *Diabolique* (Jeremiah Chechik, 1996, US). Reporting from the set of the film, Jeff Dawson's article opens with an account of Stone on the set wailing 'Penis, penis, penis'. This is explained as the star 'making a point (all about Jungian philosophy and how the unconscious mind reacts to certain promptings and other such stuff)' (' "The Best Thing About It Is the Boobs . . . " ', p. 94). After reflecting on some pretentious comments by the director, the reporter remarks that 'with the aforementioned rantings of Stone . . . there's clearly a lot of bollocks being talked here' (p. 96). Earlier in 1996, some surprise had greeted Stone's nomination for the Best Actress Oscar for her role in *Casino* (Martin Scorsese, 1996, US). Dawson's *Empire* article ironically describes Stone as a 'serious' actress and recognises the cultural respectability of *Casino*'s director Martin Scorsese and lead star actor Robert De Niro as Stone has 'important new friends like "Marty" and "Bobby" to play with' (p. 96). The article makes further fun of the star's possession of Plato's collected works on set, commenting that this is 'the very thing to set off your dinky little retro-chic outfit, darling. And quite the *object d'art* to have resting on your high canvas chair' (p. 97). Stone is associated with the trappings of stardom as the reporter wonders if 'she gets a chance to read [the book] in her limo' (p. 97). As the limo ride takes only 300 yards to Stone's trailer, Dawson remarks that this is simply 'one of the perks of the job of Film Star' (p. 97). The 'seriousness' of Stone's acting work is completely undermined by focusing on the work of being a star. As a star, Stone is represented in the midst of leisure even when she is at work.

Discourses of star labour do not simply report the work of film performance but also regulate hierarchies and power relationships between performers determined by judgments of artistic legitimacy. As with any discourse, images of star labour are open to the differentiated readings of socially situated moviegoers, and beliefs about the work of stars are never separate from beliefs about other types of work and experiences of working.

Stardom as a system

Speaking of stardom as a 'system' involves understanding the ways in which the work of stars is influenced by the market of performance labour and the organisation of film production. As Barry King points out, one of the factors limiting the economic power of stars is the continual condition of oversupply in the labour market of actors ('Articulating Stardom', p. 46). The star system is therefore influenced by a wider market of performers who do not enjoy the status of stars. All film actors face difficulties in determining their careers. Compared to occupations in other industries, the routes to screen-acting work remain informal. Film performers are freelance labour and this has the effect of making actors highly dependent on agents, casting officers and unions to mediate between performer and industry. Contacts become a vital means for hearing about work and gaining competitive advantage. Anne K. Peters and Muriel G. Cantor point out that for many film performers, a great deal of their working time involves the unwaged labour of 'studying acting, seeking agents, going to casting interviews ... keeping the body in shape, socialising with other actors, and making [influential] contacts' ('Screen Acting as Work', p. 60). When it is considered that many actors do not earn a living from acting but spend long periods employed in other types of work, then the star system can be seen to extend into telesales, secretarial work, being a 'hostess', delivering pizzas, couriering, and so on. With so many actors looking for work, there is always the sense that a star is replaceable. However, a star can assert their individual values by using 'personification' to cultivate an individual image which acts as what King calls their 'personal monopoly', the bid by the star to represent a set of meanings which are uniquely marketable (p. 46).

Emanuel Levy argues that stardom rests on a central paradox: 'A discrepancy exists between acting's egalitarian orientation – anybody can become a movie star – and its highly stratified structure – only a few players actually become stars' ('The Democratic Elite', p. 49). A sample of American stars from the 30s to the 80s shows them emerging from diverse ethnic backgrounds, although African-Americans are under-represented (p. 39). Class privilege also did not appear to determine stardom and most stars were successful without receiving formal higher education (pp. 41–5). The social identities of the stars in the sample would suggest that while stars are the aristocrats of film performers, stardom seems open to anyone. When combined with beliefs that a star can only be a star if they win public popularity – which problematically implies that consumers determine film production – stardom achieves the image of being a 'democratic elite'. Representing values of 'upward mobility, monetary success, competitiveness, and individual attainment', Levy argues that the star elite symbolises the American Dream (p. 52). This 'rags to riches' image is very important, for it obscures the conditions of exploitation in the star system, while at the same time promising the optimistic possibility of success which reproduces that system.

In Hollywood cinema, the 'studio system' of the 30s and 40s emerged from the concentration of power by five major studios (Warner Bros., Loew's/MGM, Paramount, RKO and 20th Century-Fox) and three minor studios (Universal, Columbia and United Artists). The five majors consolidated power by their 'vertically integrated' ownership of the means of not only producing but also distributing and exhibiting films. Standard in this period was the seven-year term-contract, making a star the property of the studio for a definite time. Jane M. Gaines reads star contracts as a negotiation between the film star and the film industry which documents the legal ownership and control of the star's image (*Contested Culture*, pp. 143–74). The term contract allowed the studios to benefit from various abuses of the star's employment. In the studio period, executives decided on the casting of stars and the lending of contracted stars to other studios. Written into the term-contract were the conditions for suspending stars. Jack Warner in particular was known to use suspension to discipline stars by casting expensive performers in unsuitable roles which they would inevitably refuse, allowing the producer to suspend the star. As stars were not paid when suspended, savings on salaries could be made, and as the period of suspension did not count towards the length of the contract, such actions effectively extended the duration of the contract (p. 152).

When the studio system underwent reorganisation in the 50s, term-contracts did not entirely disappear, but long-term contracting ceased to be cost effective for the studios. Instead, stars came to be hired on a single-film basis. This brought advantages and disadvantages for stars. Gorham Kindem describes how, freed from the exploitative conditions of term-contracts, stars could more flexibly determine their own careers ('Hollywood's Movie Star System', p. 88). Additionally, organising production around single film projects meant that the studios required each individual film to be a success in its own right. This increased the potential value of stars as a guarantee against loss, placing them in a position where they could demand higher salaries (p. 88). Several stars also set up their own production companies, which allowed for greater control over production and provided a means for saving on high income-tax rates (see also Barry King 'Stardom as an Occupation'). At the same time, film production declined and the marketing of single films gave new importance to the use of expensive spectacle to differentiate films. This decline in the quantity of films produced, together with rising costs, therefore saw fewer actors finding work in films. With the arrival of television, many chose to pursue their careers outside of cinema (Kindem, p. 89).

Thomas Schatz has argued that since the mid-70s, American cinema has seen significant changes in its corporate structure, methods of marketing and stylistic conventions. In this 'New Hollywood', Schatz argues that three categories of film are mainly produced ('The New Hollywood', p. 35). Each of these categories can be associated with particular groups of stars. From the expensive spectacle of the single-film deal has emerged the big-budget 'blockbuster'. Justin Wyatt refers to

50 Batman.

this same sector of production by the more contemporary industry vernacular of 'high-concept'. High concept film-making does not necessarily mean big budget or large box-office returns but is defined by Wyatt as 'a form of narrative which is highly marketable' (*High Concept*, p. 12). In high-concept, marketing possibilities are already influential in pre-production planning. Effective marketing requires a film project to have an image which can be simply and directly communicated to the public. Wyatt sees the images of stars as instrumental in this strategy, with marketing seeking to fit a star's image to the premise of the film narrative. In other words, the star personifies the concept of the film. With high-concept, style over-rides narrative content, foregrounding and possibly exaggerating of the qualities that stars are best known for. Wyatt's example of this is Jack Nicholson's perform-ance as the Joker in *Batman* (Tim Burton, 1989, US), where Nicholson's demonic, maniacal quality witnessed in *The Shining* (Stanley Kubrick, 1980, US) and *The Witches of Eastwick* (George Miller, 1987, US) is turned into comic hysteria to per-form an excessive display of Jack Nicholson-ness. This performance exaggerates the qualities of the star over the character which Barry King sees in star perform-ance ('Articulating Stardom', p. 42), and the excessiveness of Nicholson in *Batman* could be described as exemplifying how acting can lead to the 'hyper-personifica-tion' of the star's image in high-concept cinema. In this single performance, the quality of sinister wackiness which characterises the whole film is entirely conceptualised. Nicholson's grin says it all.

Schatz argues that the commercial success of a director such as Steven Spielberg in the blockbuster or high concept sector has seen stardom extend to include other leading production personnel, not just the performers ('The New Holly-wood', p. 35). Putting aside the argument that in *Jurassic Park* (Steven Spielberg, 1993, US) the dinosaurs were the real stars (an argument that would raise the possibility of technology as 'star' in the new Hollywood), the director's star status was greater than that of any member of the cast. The phenomenon of the director as star should not be overestimated, however. To what extent are the directors John McTiernan (*Die Hard*, 1988, US; *Die Hard with a Vengeance*, 1995, US) or Richard Donner (*Lethal Weapon 3*, 1992, US, *Maverick*, 1994, US) household names? Male stars such as Arnold Schwarzenegger, Bruce Willis and Tom Cruise are most readily associated with blockbuster production. Despite the high earning power of a female star like Demi Moore, who in 1996 was reputed to have received $12.5 million to appear in *Striptease* (Andrew Bergman, 1996, US), the Hollywood industry still remains largely unconvinced that women deserve the stellar salaries that come with the ability to 'open' big budget films.

Schatz's second category is the mainstream A-class star vehicle, which showcases the specific image of a performer. Here the list could be endless, but as examples, *Dead Poets Society* (Peter Weir, 1989, US) and *Mrs Doubtfire* (Chris Columbus, 1993, US) enabled Robin Williams to show off his comic skills.

A direct consequence of the breakdown of the vertically integrated studio system was the growth of independent film production in America. Schatz identifies the low-cost independent feature as the third type of film produced in the New Hollywood. Certainly this sector has produced its 'name' directors, such as David Lynch (*Eraserhead* (AFI Centre for Advanced Film Studies, 1976, US)) and Quentin Tarantino (*Reservoir Dogs* (Dog Eat Dog Productions/Live America, 1992, US)). Also, independent production has its regular performers, for example Steve Buscemi (*Parting Glances* (Bill Sherwood, Rondo Productions, 1985, US); *Somebody to Love* (Alexandre Rockwell, Lumiere Films, 1994, US)), or Tim Roth (*Rosencrantz and Guildenstern Are Dead* (Tom Stoppard, Brandenberg International/Odyssey, 1990, US); *Jumpin' at the Boneyard* (Jeff Stanzler, Boneyard, 1991, US)). If these names are not as widely known as those of blockbuster stars, then distinctions need to be drawn between 'popular' stars and 'cult' stars.

Danae Clark criticises histories of the star system which only see stars as controlled by the corporate power of the studios or the industry, as these histories exclude the possibility of stars resisting such control by either individual or collective bargaining (*Negotiating Hollywood*, p. 5). Clark also argues that the study of star images focuses on significant individuals, neglecting the hierarchies which exist in film production between the relatively powerful stars and the other supporting actors. For Clark, the power of stars can only be judged in the context of the entire star system, requiring analysis of the labour relations between stars and other actors (p. xi). In a study of the foundation of the Screen Actors' Guild as the organised representative of film actors in Hollywood, Clark looks at stardom as a system of labour power differences, in which the interests of stars compete with those of the producers and other performers. Clark's criticisms suggest a more complex reading of the star system, one which encompasses collective or individual resistance as well as corporate power.

Conclusion

These developments in the study of stars throw up various points worthy of further work. First, the star image approach, reading the meaning of a single star in isolation, has tended to lose sight of the ways in which the meaning or professional power of one star are conditional upon a system of differences and distinctions between stars and other performers. That system can be seen to operate in the distribution of discourses about stars, the performance strategies of stars, audience identifications and tastes, and the positioning of stars in different sectors of production.

Second, analysis of stars in context shows how these differences change historically and culturally: what is different about 'Monroe' in the 90s to Monroe in the 50s? Are film stars still significant in how moviegoers negotiate their social positions? Or have other figures such as pop stars, models or sports men and women become more significant? What is the status of performance labour in the New Hollywood, and how does it relate to or contrast with the working conditions of performers in other national cinemas?

A further consideration is how critical analysis of the images of stars and positionings of spectatorship theory have concentrated on stardom as the effect of texts and discourse, but not practice. The privileging of discourse has led to studies of stardom becoming trapped in a realm of textuality which leaves out the many practical actions which stardom motivates in society. The studies by Clark or Stacey show how in the production and consumption of stardom, stars and moviegoers do things. To appreciate the social activity of stardom, a pragmatics of star practices is needed to accompany a semiotics of star meanings. Instead of asking 'what does stardom mean?', a new question would be 'what does stardom do?'

Finally, the shift from text to practice necessitates a rethinking of identity. Theoretically, film studies is dominated by notions of the 'subject'. Subjectivity is an important concept, for it draws attention to how identity is formed by structures of representation and power. Such a view counteracts beliefs in identity as a freely determined individuality. While both Stacey and Clark prefer to use the term 'subject' in their work, both indicate possibilities by which stars and moviegoers may be better thought of as social 'agents'. Agency does not presume that stars and moviegoers can freely determine structures of representation or power, only that they can negotiate movements within those structures. Such a reconceptualising of identity may be necessary for examining effectively the practical complexities of difference, distinction, context and identity in the institution of stardom.

Supplementary Bibliography

1 Stars: General

Adler, Moshe, 'Stardom and Talent', *American Economic Review*, vol. 71, no. 5, 1981, pp. 208-212.

Archer, Robyn and Simmonds, Diana, *A Star Is Torn*, Virago, London, 1986.

Base, Ron, *Starring Roles: How Movie Stardom in Hollywood Is Won and Lost*, Little, Brown and Co., London, 1994.

Basinger, Jeanine, *A Woman's View: How Hollywood Spoke to Women 1930–1960*, Alfred A. Knopf, New York, 1993.

Bell-Metereau, Rebecca, *Hollywood Androgyny*, Columbia University Press, New York, 1985.

Berlin, Gloria and Bruce, Bryan, 'The Superstar Story', *CineAction!*, no. 7, December 1986, pp. 52–63.

Blum, Richard, *American Film Acting: The Stanislavski Heritage*, UMI Research Press, Ann Arbor MI, 1984.

Bourne, Stephen, 'Star Equality Part 1', *Films and Filming*, no. 351, December 1983, pp. 31–4.

'Star Equality Part 2', *Films and Filming*, no. 352, January 1984, pp. 24–5.

Butler, Jeremy G. (ed.), *Star Texts: Image and Performance in Film and Television*, Wayne State University Press, Detroit, 1990.

' "I'm not a Doctor, but I Play One on TV": Characters, Actors and Acting in Television Soap Opera', *Cinema Journal*, vol. 30, no. 4, 1991, pp. 75–91, reprinted in Allen, Robert C. (ed.), *To Be Continued . . .: Soap Operas Around the World*, Routledge, London, 1995, pp. 145–63.

Clark, Danae, *Negotiating Hollywood: The Cultural Politics of Actors' Labour*, University of Minnesota Press, Minneapolis, 1995.

Cook, Bruce, 'Why TV Stars Don't Become Movie Stars', *American Film*, vol. 1, no. 8, June 1976, pp. 58–61.

Cook, Pam, 'Star Signs', *Screen*, vol. 20, no. 3–4, Winter 1979–80, pp. 80–8.

Das Gupta, Chidananda and Hoberman, J., 'Pols of India', *Film Comment*, vol. 23, no. 3, May–June 1987, pp. 20–4.

Davis, Ronald L., *The Glamour Factory: Inside Hollywood's Big Studio System*, Southern Methodist University Press, Dallas, 1993.

DeCordova, Richard, 'The Emergence of the Star System in America', *Wide Angle*, vol. 6, no. 4, 1985, pp. 4–13.

Picture Personalities: The Emergence of the Star System in America, University of Illinois Press, Urbana, 1990.

Donald, James, 'Stars', in Cook, Pam (ed.), *The Cinema Book*, British Film Institute, London, 1985, pp. 50–6.

Dyer, Richard, *The Dumb Blonde Stereotype*, British Film Institute, London, 1979.

Teacher's Study Guide 1: The Stars, British Film Institute Education, London, 1979.

Heavenly Bodies: Film Stars and Society, Macmillan, London, 1987.

Ellis, John, *Visible Fictions: Cinema, Television, Video*, Routledge and Kegan Paul, London, 1982.

Erens, Patricia, 'In Defence of Stars: A Response', in Steven, Peter (ed.), *Jump Cut:_Hollywood, Politics and Counter Cinema*, Praeger, New York, 1985, pp. 240–6.

Fernandez, Rick, 'Designing for the Stars: Interview with Walter Plunkett', *The Velvet Light Trap*, no. 18, 1978, pp. 27–9.

Finney, Angus, 'Falling Stars', *Sight and Sound*, vol. 4, no. 5, May 1994, pp. 22–4, 26.

Fowles, Jib, *Starstruck: Celebrity Performers and the American Public*, Smithsonian Institute Press, Washington, 1992.

Friedberg, Anne, 'Identification and the Star: A Refusal of Difference', in Gledhill, Christine (ed.), *Star Signs: Papers from a Weekend Workshop*, British Film Institute Education, London, 1982, pp. 47–53.

Gaines, Jane M., *Contested Culture: The Image, the Voice, and the Law*, British Film Institute, London, 1992.

Gaines, Jane M. and Herzog, Charlotte (eds.), *Fabrications: Costume and the Female Body*, Routledge, New York, 1990.

Gledhill, Christine (ed.), *Star Signs: Papers from a Weekend Workshop*, British Film Institute Education, London, 1982.

(ed.), *Stardom: Industry of Desire*, Routledge, London, 1991.

Goldman, William, 'Everything You Ever Wanted to Know About Stars ...', *American Film*, vol. 8, no. 5, March 1983, pp. 57–64.

Goodwin, Andrew, *Dancing in the Distraction Factory: Music Television and Popular Culture*, Routledge, London, 1993.

Hanson, Steve, King Hanson, Patricia and Broeske, Pat H., 'Ruling Stars', *Stills*, no. 20, June–July 1985, pp. 20–23.

Hayward, Susan, 'Stars/Star System/Star as Capital Value/Star as Construct/Star as Deviant/Star as Cultural Value: Sign and Fetish/Star-Gazing and Performance', *Key Concepts in Cinema Studies*, Routledge, London, 1996, pp. 337–48.

Hilmes, Michelle, 'The "Ban" That Never Was: Hollywood and the Broadcasting Industry in 1932', *The Velvet Light Trap*, no. 23, Spring 1989, pp. 39–48.

Hirsch, Foster, *Acting Hollywood Style*, Harry N. Abrams Inc. and AFI Press, New York, 1991.

Jarvie, Ian C., 'Stars and Ethnicity: Hollywood and the United States, 1932–51', in Friedman, Lester D. (ed.), *Unspoken Images: Ethnicity and the American Cinema*, University of Illinois Press, Champaign, 1990, pp. 82–111.

Jeffords, Susan, *Hard Bodies: Hollywood Masculinity in the Reagan Era*, Rutgers University Press, New Brunswick NJ, 1994.

Keane, Marian, 'Dyer Straits: Theoretical Issues in Studies of Film Acting', *Postscript*, vol. 12, no. 2, 1993, pp. 29–39.

Kent, Nicholas, *Naked Hollywood: Money, Power and the Movies*, BBC Books, London, 1991.

Kindem, Gorham, 'Hollywood's Movie Star System: A Historical Overview', in Kindem, Gorham (ed.), *The American Movie Industry: The Business of Motion Pictures*, Southern Illinois University Press, Carbondale and Edwardsville, 1982, pp. 79–93.

King, Barry, 'Articulating Stardom', *Screen*, vol. 26, no. 5, September–October 1985, pp. 27–50.

'Stardom as an Occupation', in Kerr, Paul (ed.), *The Hollywood Film Industry*, Routledge and Kegan Paul, London, 1986, pp. 154–84.

'The Star and the Commodity: Notes Towards a Performance Theory of Stardom', *Cultural Studies*, vol. 1, no. 2, 1987, pp. 145–61.

Krutnik, Frank, 'A Spanner in the Works? Genre, Narrative and the Hollywood Comedian', in Karnick, Kristine Brunovska and Jenkins, Henry (eds.), *Classical Hollywood Comedy*, Routledge, New York, 1995, pp. 17–38.

Langer, John, 'Television's "Personality System" ', *Media, Culture and Society*, vol. 3, no. 4, 1981, pp. 351–65.

Levy, Emanuel, 'The Democratic Elite: America's Movie Stars', *Qualitative Sociology*, vol. 12, no. 1, Spring 1989, pp. 29–54.

'Social Attributes of American Movie Stars', *Media, Culture and Society*, vol. 12, no. 2, 1990, pp. 247–67.

Lewis, George, 'Positive Deviance: A Labelling Approach to the Star Syndrome in Popular Music', *Popular Music and Society*, vol. 8, no. 2, 1982, pp. 73–83.

Lusted, David, 'The Glut of Personality', in Masterman, Len (ed.), *Television Mythologies: Stars, Shows and Signs*, Comedia/Routledge, London, 1984, pp. 73–81.

McArthur, Benjamin, *Actors and American Culture, 1880–1920*, Temple University Press, Philadelphia, 1984.

MacCann, Richard Dyer, *The Stars Appear*, Scarecrow Press, Metuchen NJ, 1992.

MacDonald, Glenn M., 'The Economics of Rising Stars', *American Economic Review*, vol. 78, no. 1, 1988, pp. 155–66.

McDonald, Paul, 'I'm Winning on a Star: the Extraordinary Ordinary World of Stars in Their Eyes', *Critical Survey*, vol. 7, no. 1, 1995, pp. 59–66.

'Star Studies', in Hollows, Joanne and Jancovich, Mark (eds.), *Approaches to Popular Film*, Manchester University Press, Manchester, 1995, pp. 79–97.

Maltby, Richard, *Hollywood Cinema: An Introduction*, Blackwell, Oxford, 1996.

Mann, Denise, 'The Spectacularization of Everyday Life: Recycling Hollywood Stars and Fans in Early Television Variety Shows', *Camera Obscura*, no. 16, 1988, pp. 48–77; reprinted in Butler, Jeremy G. (ed.), *Star Texts: Image and Performance in Film and Television*, Wayne State University Press, Detroit, 1990, pp. 335–60.

May, Lary, 'Movie Star Politics: The Screen Actors' Guild, Cultural Conversion and the Hollywood Red Scare', in May, Lary (ed.), *Recasting America: Culture and Politics in the Age of the Cold War*, University of Chicago Press, 1989, pp. 125–53.

Munn, Michael, *Stars at War*, Robson Books, London, 1995.

Naremore, James, *Acting in the Cinema*, University of California Press, Los Angeles, 1988.

Natale, Richard, 'The Price Club', *American Film*, vol. 14, no. 8, June 1989, pp. 42–5.

Pearson, Roberta, *Eloquent Gestures: The Transformation of Performance Style in the Griffith Biograph Films*, University of California Press, Berkeley, 1992.

Peters, Anne K. and Cantor, Muriel G, 'Screen Acting as Work', in Ettema, James S. and Whitney, D. Charles (eds.), *Individuals in Mass Media Organisations*, Sage, Beverly Hills CA, 1982, pp. 53–68.

Phillips, Patrick, 'Genre, Star and Auteur: An Approach to Hollywood Cinema', in Nelmes, Jill (ed.), *An Introduction to Film Studies*, Routledge, London, pp. 121–63.

Roberts, Jenny, 'Unbilled Stars', *Films in Review*, vol. 42, no. 7–8, pp. 228–30.

Rodman, Howard A., 'Talent Brokers', *Film Comment*, vol. 26, no. 1, January–February 1990, pp. 35–7.

Rosen, Sherwin, 'The Economics of Superstars', *American Economic Review*, vol. 71, no. 5, pp. 845–58.

Rosenkrantz, Linda, 'The Role That Got Away', *Film Comment*, vol. 14, no. 1, January–February 1978, pp. 42–8.

Schickel, Richard, *Common Fame: The Culture of Celebrity*, Pavilion Books and Michael Joseph, London, 1985.

Slide, Anthony, 'The Evolution of the Film Star', *Films in Review*, no. 25, 1974, pp. 591–4.

Stacey, Jackie, *Star Gazing: Hollywood Cinema and Female Spectatorship*, Routledge, London, 1994.

Staiger, Janet, 'Seeing Stars', *The Velvet Light Trap*, no. 20, Summer 1983, pp. 10–14.

Stine, Whitney, *Stars and Star Handlers: The Business of Show*, Roundtable, Santa Monica, 1985.

Tasker, Yvonne, *Spectacular Bodies: Gender, Genre, and the Action Cinema*, Comedia/Routledge, London, 1993.

Thompson, Grahame F., 'Approaches to "Performance"', *Screen*, vol. 26, no. 5, September–October 1985, pp. 78–90.
    'Screen Acting and the Commutation Test', *Screen*, vol. 19, no. 2, Summer 1978, pp. 55–69.

Thompson, John O., 'Beyond Commutation – a Reconsideration of Screen Acting', *Screen*, vol. 26, no. 5, September–October 1985, pp. 64–76.

Turow, Joseph, 'Casting for TV Parts: The Anatomy of Social Typing', *Journal of Communication*, vol. 28, no. 4, Autumn 1978, pp. 19–24.

Vineberg, Steve, *Method Actors: Three Generations of an American Acting Style*, Schirmer Books, New York, 1991.

Watney, Simon, 'Stellar Studies', *Screen*, vol. 28, no. 3, Summer 1987, pp. 110–14.

Yacowar, Maurice, 'An Aesthetic Defence of the Star System', *Quarterly Review of Film Studies*, vol. 4, no. 1, Winter 1979, pp. 39–52.
    'Actors as Conventions in the Films of Robert Altman', *Cinema Journal*, vol. 20, no. 1, Fall 1980, pp. 14–28.

Zucker, Carole, (ed.), *Making Visible the Invisible: An Anthology of Original Essays on Film Acting*, Scarecrow Press, Metuchen, NJ, 1990.

2 Stars: Individual Stars

Balio, Tino, 'Stars in Business: The Founding of United Artists', in Balio, Tino (ed.), *The American Film Industry*, rev. edn., University of Wisconsin Press, Madison, 1985, pp. 153–72.

Baxter, Peter, 'On the Naked Thighs of Miss Dietrich', *Wide Angle*, vol. 2, no. 2, pp. 18–25.

Belton, John, 'John Wayne: As Sure as the Turning O' the Earth', *The Velvet Light Trap*, no. 7, Winter 1972–3, pp. 25–8.

Bingham, Dennis, *Acting Male: Masculinities in the Films of James Stewart, Jack Nicholson and Clint Eastwood*, Rutgers University Press, New Brunswick, 1994.

'Bob and Al in the Coffee Shop', *Sight and Sound*, vol. 6, no. 3, March 1996, pp. 14–19.

Bourget, Jean-Loup, 'Faces of the American Melodrama: Joan Crawford', *Film Reader*, no. 3, pp. 24–34.

Britton, Andrew, *Cary Grant: Comedy and Male Desire*, Tyneside Cinema, Newcastle Upon Tyne, 1983, reproduced in *CineAction!*, no. 7, December 1986, pp. 36–51.

Katharine Hepburn: The Thirties and After, Tyneside Cinema, Newcastle upon Tyne, 1984.

Brown, Jeffrey A., ' "Putting on the Ritz": Masculinity and the Young Gary Cooper', *Screen*, vol. 36, no. 3, Autumn 1995, pp. 193–213.

Budd, William, 'Genre, Director and Stars in John Ford's Westerns: Fonda, Wayne, Stewart and Widmark', *Wide Angle*, vol. 2, no. 4, 1978, pp. 52–61.

Budge, Belinda, 'Joan Collins and the Wilder Side of Women – Exploring Pleasure and Representation', in Gamman, Lorraine and Marshment, Margaret (eds.), *The Female Gaze: Women as Viewers of Popular Culture*, The Women's Press, London, pp. 102–11.

Clark, Jane and Simmonds, Diana, *Move Over Misconceptions: Doris Day Reappraised*, BFI Dossier 5, British Film Institute, London, 1981.

Cohan, Steven, 'Masquerading as the American Male in the Fifties: *Picnic*. William Holden and the Spectacle of Masculinity in Hollywood Film', *Camera Obscura*, 25–6, 1991, pp. 43–72.

'Cary Grant in the Fifties: Indiscretions of the Bachelor's Masquerade', *Screen*, vol. 33, no. 4, Winter 1992, pp. 394–412.

' "Feminising" the Song-and-Dance Man: Fred Astaire and the Spectacle of Masculinity in the Hollywood Musical', in Cohen, Steven and Hark, Ina Rae (eds.), *Screening the Male: Exploring Masculinities in Hollywood Cinema*, London, Routledge, 1993, pp. 46–69.

Curry, Ramona, *Too Much of a Good Thing: Mae West as Cultural Icon*, University of Minnesota Press, Minneapolis, 1996.

Dargis, Manohla, 'Method and Madness', *Sight and Sound*, vol. 5, no. 6, June 1995, pp. 6–8.

'A Man for All Seasons', *Sight and Sound*, vol. 6, no. 12, December 1996, pp. 6–8.

Davis, D. William, 'A Tale of Two Movies: Charlie Chaplin, United Artists, and the Red Scare', *Cinema Journal*, vol. 27, no. 1, Fall 1987, pp. 47–62.

Dawson, Jeff, ' "The Best Thing About It Is the Boobs ..." ', *Empire*, no. 84, June 1996, pp. 94–8.

Dobbs, Lem, 'Dad's the Word', *Sight and Sound*, vol. 6, no. 2, February 1996, pp. 12–15.

Doty, Alexander, 'The Cabinet of Lucy Ricardo: Lucille Ball's Star Image', *Cinema Journal*, vol. 29, no. 4, Summer 1990, pp. 3–22.

Dyer, Richard, *Star Dossier 1: Marilyn Monroe*, British Film Institute Education, London, 1980.

'*A Star Is Born* and the Construction of Authenticity', reprinted in Gledhill, Christine (ed.), *Stardom: Industry of Desire*, Routledge, London, 1991, pp. 132–40.

'Rock – The Last Guy You'd Have Figured?', in Kirkham, Pat and Thumin, Janet (eds.), *You Tarzan: Masculinity, Movies and Men*, Lawrence and Wishart, London, 1993, pp. 27–34.

'A White Star', *Sight and Sound*, vol. 3, no. 8, August 1993, pp. 22–4.

Fisher, Joe, 'Clark Gable's Balls: Real Men Never Lose Their Teeth', in Kirkham, Pat and Thumin, Janet (eds.), *You Tarzan: Masculinity, Movies and Men*, Lawrence and Wishart, London, 1993, pp. 35–51.

Francke, Lizzie, 'All About Leigh', *Sight and Sound*, vol. 5, no. 2, February 1995, pp. 8–9.

'Being Robin', *Sight and Sound*, vol. 4, no. 4, April 1994, pp. 28–9.

'Ready to Explode', *Sight and Sound*, vol. 6, no. 10, October 1996, pp. 6–8.

'Someone to Look At', *Sight and Sound*, vol. 6, no. 3, March 1993, pp. 26–7.

Francke, Lizzie and Wilson, Elizabeth, 'Gamine Against the Grain', *Sight and Sound*, vol. 3, no. 3, March 1993, pp. 30–2.

Fuentes, Annette and Schrage, Margaret, 'Deep Inside Porn Stars: Interview with Veronica Hart, Gloria Leonard, Kelly Nichols, Candida Royalle, Annie Sprinkle and Veronica Vera', *Jump Cut*, no. 32, 1987, pp. 41–3.

Gaines, Jane, 'In the Service of Ideology: How Betty Grable's Legs Won the War', *Film Reader*, no. 5, 1982, pp. 47–59.

Gandhy, Behroze and Thomas, Rosie, 'Three Indian Film Stars', in Gledhill, Christine (ed.), *Stardom: Industry of Desire*, Routledge, London, 1991, pp. 107–31.

Gelman, Howard, 'John Garfield: Hollywood Was the Dead End', *The Velvet Light Trap*, no. 7, Winter 1972–3, pp. 3–15.

Geraghty, Christine, 'Diana Dors', in Barr, Charles (ed.), *All Our Yesterdays: 90 Years of British Cinema*, British Film Institute, London, 1986, pp. 341–5.

'Albert Finney: Working-Class Hero', in Kirkham, Pat and Thumin, Janet (eds.), *Me Jane: Masculinity, Movies and Women*, Lawrence and Wishart, London, 1995, pp. 203–22.

Gunning, Tom, 'Buster Keaton, or the Work of Comedy in the Age of Mechanical Reproduction', *Cineaste*, vol. 21, no. 3, 1995, pp. 14–16.

Hagopian, Kevin, 'Declarations of Independence: A History of Cagney Productions', *The Velvet Light Trap*, no. 22, 1986, pp. 16–32.

Hansen, Miriam, 'Pleasure, Ambivalence, Identification: Valentino and Female Spectatorship', *Cinema Journal*, vol. 25, no. 4, Summer 1986, pp. 6–32.

Hoberman, J., 'Nietzsche's Boy', *Sight and Sound*, vol. 1, no. 5, September 1991, pp. 22–5.

Holmlund, Chris, 'Sexuality and Power in Male Doppelgänger Cinema: The Case of Clint Eastwood's *Tightrope*', *Cinema Journal*, vol. 26, no. 1, Autumn 1986, pp. 31–42.

'Masculinity as Multiple Masquerade: The "Mature" Stallone and the Stallone Clone', in Cohen, Steven and Hark, Ina Rae (eds.), *Screening the Male: Exploring Masculinities in Hollywood Cinema*, London, Routledge, 1993, pp. 213–29.

Hunt, Albert, ' "She Laughed at Me with My Own Teeth": Tommy Cooper – Television Anti-Hero', in Masterman, Len (ed.), *Television Mythologies: Stars, Shows and Signs*, Comedia/Routledge, London, 1984, pp. 67–72.

Jacobowitz, Florence, 'Joan Bennett: Images of Femininity in Conflict', *CineAction!*, no. 7, December 1986, pp. 22–34.

Jenkins, Henry, ' "Shall We Make It for New York or Distribution?": Eddie Cantor, *Whoopie*, and Regional Resistance to the Talkies', *Cinema Journal*, vol. 29, no. 3, Spring 1990, pp. 32–52.

Jennings, Wade, 'Nova: Garland in *A Star Is Born*', *Quarterly Review of Film Studies*, vol. 4, no. 3, Summer 1979, pp. 321–37.

Klaprat, Cathy, 'The Star as Market Strategy: Bette Davis in Another Light', in Balio, Tino (ed.), *The American Film Industry*, rev. edn., University of Wisconsin Press, Madison, 1985, pp. 351–76.

Koch, Gertrud, 'Dietrich's Destiny', *Sight and Sound*, vol. 2, no. 5, September 1992, pp. 22–4.

Kramer, Margia, 'Jean Seberg, the FBI and the Media', *Jump Cut*, no. 28, April 1983, pp. 68–9.

Kramer, Peter, 'Derailing the Honeymoon Express: Comicality and Narrative Closure in Buster Keaton's *The Blacksmith*', *The Velvet Light Trap*, no. 23, Spring 1989, pp. 101–16.

'The Making of a Comic Star: Buster Keaton and *The Saphead*', in Karnick, Kristine Brunovska and Jenkins, Henry (eds.), *Classical Hollywood Comedy*, Routledge, New York, pp. 190–210.

LaPlace, Maria, 'Bette Davis and the Ideal of Consumption: A Look at *Now Voyager*', *Wide Angle*, vol. 6, no. 4, 1985, pp. 34–43.

Lepper, Richard, *Star Dossier 2: John Wayne*, British Film Institute Education, London, 1980.

Lippe, Richard, 'Kim Novak: A Resistance to Definition', *CineAction!*, no. 7, December 1986, pp. 4–21.

MacCann, Graham, *Marilyn Monroe*, Polity Press, Cambridge, 1988.

Woody Allen: New Yorker, Polity Press, Cambridge, 1990.

Rebel Males: Clift, Brando and Dean, Hamish Hamilton, London, 1991.

Cary Grant: A Class Apart, Fourth Estate, London, 1996.

Macnab, Geoffrey, 'Valley Boys', *Sight and Sound*, vol. 4, no. 3, March 1994, pp. 20–3.

McKnight, Stephanie, *Star Dossier 3: Robert Redford*, British Film Institute Education, London, 1988.

McLean, Adrienne L. 'The Cinderella Princess and the Instrument of Evil: Surveying the Limits of Female Transgression in Two Postwar Hollywood Star Scandals', *Cinema Journal*, vol. 34, no. 3, Spring 1995, pp. 36–56.

Manso, Peter, *Brando*, Weidenfeld and Nicolson, London, 1994.

Matthews, Peter, 'Garbo and Phallic Motherhood – A "Homosexual" Visual Economy', *Screen*, vol. 29, no. 3, Summer 1988, pp. 14–39.

Medhurst, Andy, 'Dirk Bogarde', in Barr, Charles (ed.), *All Our Yesterdays: 90 Years of British Cinema*, British Film Institute, London, 1986, pp. 346–54.

Mellencamp, Patricia, 'Situation Comedy, Feminism and Freud: Discourses of Grace and Lucy', in Modleski, Tania (ed.), *Studies in Entertainment: Critical Approaches to Mass Culture*, Indiana University Press, Bloomington and Indianapolis, 1986, pp. 80–95, reprinted in Butler, Jeremy G. (ed.), *Star Texts: Image and Performance in Film and Television*, Wayne State University Press, Detroit, 1990.

Meyer, Richard, 'Rock Hudson's Body', in Fuss, Diana (ed.), *Inside/Out: Lesbian Theories, Gay Theories*, Routledge, New York, pp. 258–88.

Mueller, John, 'The Filmed Dances of Fred Astaire', *Quarterly Review of Film Studies*, vol. 6, no. 2, Spring 1981, pp. 135–54.

'Fred Astaire and the Integrated Musical', *Cinema Journal*, vol. 24, no. 1, Fall 1984, pp. 28–40.

Nadeau, Chantel, 'B B and the Beasts: Brigitte Bardot and the Canadian Seal Controversy', *Screen*, vol. 37, no. 3, Autumn 1996, pp. 240–50.

Penman, Ian, 'Sisyphus in Ray-Bans', *Sight and Sound*, vol. 4, no. 9, September 1994, pp. 6–9.

'The Dead', *Sight and Sound*, vol. 7, no. 1, January 1997, pp. 6–9.

Pepper, Linda, 'Sydney Greenstreet: Hollywood's Heaviest Heavy', *The Velvet Light Trap*, no. 7, Winter 1972–3, pp. 3–15.

Rai, Amit, 'An American Raj in Filmistan: Images of Elvis in Indian Films', *Screen*, vol. 35, no. 1, Spring 1994, pp. 51–77.

Reynaud, Bérénice, 'Gong Li and the Glamour of the Chinese Star', *Sight and Sound*, vol. 3, no. 8, August 1993, pp. 12–15.

Rich, B. Ruby, 'Nobody's Handmaid', *Sight and Sound*, vol. 1, no. 8, December 1991, pp. 6–10.

Richards, Jeffrey, 'Paul Robeson: The Black Man as Film Hero', in Barr, Charles (ed.), *All Our Yesterdays: 90 Years of British Cinema*, British Film Institute, London, 1986, pp. 334–40.

Roberts, Shari, ' "The Lady in the Tutti-Frutti Hat": Carmen Miranda, a Spectacle of Ethnicity', *Cinema Journal*, vol. 32, no. 3, Spring 1993, pp. 3–23.

Robertson, Pamela, ' "The Kinda Comedy That Imitates Me": Mae West's Identification with the Feminist Camp', *Cinema Journal*, vol. 32, no. 2, Winter 1993, pp. 57–72.

Romney, Jonathan, 'Arnold Through the Looking Glass', *Sight and Sound*, vol. 3, no. 8, August 1993, pp. 6–9.

Rosen, Miriam, 'Isabelle Adjani: The Actress as Political Activist', *Cineaste*, vol. 17, no. 4, 1990, pp. 22–4.

Schatz, Thomas, ' " Triumph of Bitchery": Warner Bros., Bette Davis and *Jezebel*', *Wide Angle*, vol. 10, no. 1, 1988, pp. 16–29.

Shingler, Martin, 'Masquerade or Drag? Bette Davis and the Ambiguities of Gender', *Screen*, vol. 36, no. 3, Autumn 1995, pp. 179–92.

Smith, Paul, *Clint Eastwood: A Cultural Production*, UCL Press, London, 1993.

Stuart, Andrea, 'Making Whoopi', *Sight and Sound*, vol. 3, no. 2, February 1993, pp. 12–13.

Studlar, Gaylyn, 'Discourses of Gender and Ethnicity: The Construction and De(con)struction of Rudolph Valentino', *Film Criticism*, vol. 13, no. 2, 1989, pp. 18–35.

'Masochism, Masquerade, and the Erotic Metamorphoses of Marlene Dietrich', in Gaines, Jane M. and Herzog, Charlotte (eds.), *Fabrications: Costume and the Female Body*, Routledge, New York, 1990, pp. 229–49.

'Valentino, "Optic Intoxication" and Dance Madness', in Cohen, Steven and Hark, Ina Rae (eds.), *Screening the Male: Exploring Masculinities in Hollywood Cinema*, Routledge, London, 1993, pp. 23–45.

Swanson, Gillian, 'Burt's Neck: Masculine Corporeality and Estrangement', in Kirkham, Pat and Thumin, Janet (eds.), *Me Jane: Masculinity, Movies and Women*, Lawrence and Wishart, London, 1995, pp. 203–22.

Taubin, Amy, 'An Upright Man', *Sight and Sound*, vol. 3, no. 9, September 1993, pp. 9–10.

Thomson, David, 'Waiting for Garbo', *American Film*, vol. 6, no. 1, October 1980, pp. 48–52.

'All Our Joan Crawfords', *Sight and Sound*, vol. 51, no. 1, Winter 1981–2, pp. 54–7.

'Charms and the Man', *Film Comment*, vol. 20, no. 1, February 1984, pp. 58–65.

Turim, Maureen, 'Jean-Pierre Léaud: Child of the French Cinema', *The Velvet Light Trap*, no. 7, pp. 41–8.

Vincendeau, Ginette, 'Community, Nostalgia and the Spectacle of Masculinity', *Screen*, vol. 26, no. 6, November–December 1985, pp. 18–38.

'Fire and Ice', *Sight and Sound*, vol. 3, no. 4, April 1993, pp. 20–2.

'Gérard Depardieu: The Axiom of Contemporary French Cinema', *Screen*, vol. 34, no. 4, Winter 1993, pp. 343–61.

'Juliette Binoche: From Gamine to Femme Fatale', *Sight and Sound*, vol. 3, no. 12, December 1993, pp. 22–4.

'From Proletarian Hero to Godfather: Jean Gabin and "Paradigmatic" French Masculinity', in Kirkham, Pat and Thumin, Janet (eds.), *Me Jane: Masculinity, Movies and Women*, Lawrence and Wishart, London, 1995, pp. 249–62.

Watney, Simon, 'Katharine Hepburn and the Cinema of Chastisement', *Screen*, vol. 26, no. 5, September–October 1985, pp. 52–76.

Weiss, Andrea, *Vampires and Violets: Lesbians in the Cinema*, Jonathan Cape, London, 1992.

White, Patricia, 'Supporting Character: the Queer Career of Agnes Moorehead', in Creekmur, Corey K. and Doty, Alexander (eds.), *Out in Culture: Gay, Lesbian and Queer Essays on Popular Culture*, Cassell, London, 1995, pp. 91–114.

Wilmington, Mike, 'Warren Beatty: The Sweet Smell of Success', *The Velvet Light Trap*, no. 17, Winter 1977, pp. 53–6.

Wolfe, Charles ,'The Return of Jimmy Stewart: The Publicity Photograph as Text', *Wide Angle*, vol. 6, no. 4, 1985, pp. 44-52, reprinted in Gledhill, Christine (ed.), *Stardom: Industry of Desire*, Routledge, London, 1991, pp. 92–106.

Zucker, Carole, 'Some Observations on Sternberg and Dietrich', *Cinema Journal*, vol. 19, no. 2, Spring 1980, pp. 17–24.

3 Films: General

Allen, Robert C. and Gomery, Douglas, *Film History Theory and Practice*, McGraw-Hill, New York, 1985.

Creed, Barbara, 'From Here to Modernity: Feminism and Postmodernism', *Screen*, vol. 28, no. 2, Spring 1987, pp. 47–67.

Doane, Mary Ann, untitled entry, *Camera Obscura*, 20–1, 1989, pp. 142–7.

Eckert, Charles, 'The Carole Lombard in Macy's Window', *Quarterly Review of Film Studies*, vol. 3, no. 1, Winter 1978, pp. 1–21.

Herzog, Charlotte, ' "Powder Puff" Promotion: The Fashion Show-in-the-Film', in Gaines, Jane M. and Herzog, Charlotte (eds.), *Fabrications: Costume and the Female Body*, Routledge, New York, 1990, pp. 134–59.

Herzog, Charlotte C. and Gaines, Jane M., ' "Puffed Sleeves Before Tea-Time": Joan Crawford, Adrian, and Women Audiences', *Wide Angle*, vol. 6, no. 4, 1985, pp. 24–33.

Mayne, Judith, *Cinema and Spectatorship*, Routledge, London, 1993.

Neale, Steve, 'Masculinity as Spectacle: Reflections on Men and Mainstream Cinema', *Screen*, vol. 24, no. 6, November–December 1983, pp. 2–16.

Pirie, David, 'The Deal', in Pirie, David (ed.), *The Anatomy of the Movies*, Windward, London, 1981, pp. 40–61.

Rajadhyaksha, Ashish and Willeman, Paul, *Encyclopaedia of Indian Cinema*, British Film Institute and Oxford University Press, London and New Delhi, 1994.

Schatz, Thomas, 'The New Hollywood', in Collins, James, Radner, Hilary and Preacher Collins, Ava (eds.), *Film Theory Goes to the Movies*, Routledge, New York, 1993, pp. 8–36.

Vincendeau, Ginette, 'Hijacked', *Sight and Sound*, vol. 3, no.7 , July 1993, pp. 22–5.

Wyatt, Justin, *High Concept: Movies and Marketing in Hollywood*, University of Texas Press, Austin, 1994.

4 Miscellaneous

Bourdieu, Pierre, 'The Field of Cultural Production, or: The Economic World Reversed', *Poetics*, vol. 12, no. 4–5, 1983, pp. 311–56.

Dyer, Richard, 'Don't Look Now: The Instabilities of the Male Pin-Up', *Screen*, vol. 23, no. 3–4, September–October 1982, pp. 61–73.

Featherstone, Mike, Hepworth, Mike and Turner, Bryan S. (eds.), *The Body: Social Process and Cultural Process*, Sage, London, 1991.

Fiske, John, 'The Cultural Economy of Fandom', in Lewis, Lisa A. (ed.), *The Adoring Audience: Fan Culture and Popular Media*, Routledge, London, 1992, pp. 30–49.

Gray, Ann, *Video Playtime: The Gendering of a Leisure Technology*, Routledge, London, 1992.

Hebdige, Dick, *Subculture: The Meaning of Style*, Methuen, London, 1979.

Jenkins, Henry, *Textual Poachers: Television Fans and Participatory Culture*, Routledge, New York, 1992.

Lewis, Lisa A. (ed.), *The Adoring Audience: Fan Culture and Popular Media*, Routledge, London, 1992.

Moores, Shaun, *Interpreting Audiences: The Ethnography of Media Consumption*, Sage, London, 1993.

Morley, David, *Family Television: Cultural Power and Domestic Leisure*, Comedia/Routledge, London, 1986.

Shilling, Chris, *The Body and Social Theory*, Sage, London, 1993.

Turner, Bryan S., *The Body and Society*, 2nd edn., Sage, London, 1996.

Volosinov, Valentin Nikolaevic, *Marxism and the Philosophy of Language*, Harvard University Press, Cambridge MA, 1986.

Walkerdine, Valerie, 'Video Replay: Families, Films and Fantasy', in Burgin, Victor, Donald, James and Kaplan, Cora (eds.), *Formations of Fantasy*, Routledge, London, 1989, pp. 167–99.

Index